COGNITIVE ANALYTIC ᴛʜᴇʀᴀᴘʏ
AND THE POLITICS OF
MENTAL HEALTH

Cognitive Analytic Therapy and the Politics of Mental Health provides an overview of the development of cognitive analytic therapy (CAT), and illuminates how the political context affects the way in which therapists consider their work and facilitates their practice.

This book examines how CAT contributes to wider debates over 'the politics of mental health'. With contributions from those working in services – including adult mental health, learning disabilities and child and adolescent therapists – the writers consider how contemporary politics devolves responsibility for mental illness on to those suffering distress. The evolving political and social attitudes clients bring to therapy are also addressed in several chapters, and there is a focus on groups in society who have been marginalised and neglected in mental and physical health services.

Cognitive Analytic Therapy and the Politics of Mental Health offers a fresh understanding of the contemporary politics of mental health that will be of interest to all therapists and mental health professionals.

Julie Lloyd is a clinical psychologist and cognitive analytic therapist and co-editor of *Cognitive Analytic Therapy for People with Intellectual Disabilities and their Carers* (2014).

Rachel Pollard is a cognitive analytic psychotherapist and the author of *Dialogue and Desire: Mikhail Bakhtin and the Linguistic Turn in Psychotherapy* (2008).

COGNITIVE ANALYTIC THERAPY AND THE POLITICS OF MENTAL HEALTH

Edited by Julie Lloyd and Rachel Pollard

Routledge
Taylor & Francis Group

LONDON AND NEW YORK

First published 2019
by Routledge
2 Park Square, Milton Park, Abingdon, Oxon OX14 4RN

and by Routledge
52 Vanderbilt Avenue, New York, NY 10017

Routledge is an imprint of the Taylor & Francis Group, an informa business

British Library Cataloguing in Publication Data
A catalogue record for this book is available from the British Library

Library of Congress Cataloging in Publication Data
Names: Pollard, Rachel (Psychotherapist), editor. | Lloyd, Julie,
    1952- editor.
Title: Cognitive analytic therapy and the politics of mental health /
    edited by Rachel Pollard and Julie Lloyd.
Description: Milton Park, Abingdon, Oxon ; New York, NY :
    Routledge, 2018. | Includes bibliographical references and index.
Identifiers: LCCN 2018028619| ISBN 9781138305137 (hardback) |
    ISBN 9781138305144 (pbk.) | ISBN 9781351395007 (epub) |
    ISBN 9781351394994 (mobipocket)
Subjects: LCSH: Cognitive-analytic therapy. | Mental health—
    Political aspects.
Classification: LCC RC489.C6 C63 2018 | DDC 616.89/14—dc23
LC record available at https://lccn.loc.gov/2018028619

ISBN: 9781138305137 (hbk)
ISBN: 9781138305144 (pbk)
ISBN: 9780203728857 (ebk)

Typeset in Bembo
by Swales & Willis Ltd, Exeter, Devon, UK

CONTENTS

CONTRIBUTORS

Nicola Armstrong works as a patient and carer involvement facilitator in Northumberland Tyne and Wear NHS Foundation Trust and has contributed to developing, evaluating and continuously improving services from a service user and carer perspective for over 23 years. She has a wealth of experience in delivering education and training, research, involvement, service improvement work, audit and evaluation. She recently presented at TEDx NHS to share her personal story, her experience of psychological therapy and her involvement in influencing and shaping mental health services.

Kieron Beard is a clinical psychologist, currently working full-time with people with learning disabilities within a specialist mental health in learning disabilities service in South London and Maudsley NHS Foundation Trust. The CAT model formed a core part of his doctoral training and he is currently completing the CAT Skills in Case Management Programme at the Munro Centre, London. Kieron has clinical and research interests in celebrating diversity in all its forms, human rights and social justice approaches to psychological care.

Anne Benson is a CAT psychotherapist now working in independent practice after many years in the NHS. She is a member of the ACAT Ethics Committee and the ACAT Equality and Diversity Committee. She also works as a principal consultant at the Tavistock Institute of Human Relations.

Jan Bostock has particular interests in community psychology, public health and cognitive analytic therapy informed practice. She works as a consultant clinical psychologist in adult community mental health services in Northumberland Tyne and Wear NHS Foundation Trust and is associate director for community and access services in the central locality.

Hilary Brown is a psychotherapist and former professor of social care, whose academic work focused on issues of abuse, social exclusion and adult safeguarding. She has conducted more than 20 serious case reviews into adult social care over the last 20 years, bringing together her interest in the personal and organisational dynamics that lead to less than optimal care. She coordinated a psychotherapeutic service to people with learning disabilities within the NHS and has contributed to the teaching, supervision and professional development of CAT therapists within the UK and in India. She currently runs a small private practice in the south-east.

Philip Clayton is a UKCP registered cognitive analytic psychotherapist who has predominantly worked in secure settings in the NHS over a period of 38 years. He has ten publications linked to working in secure settings and intellectual disabilities and is co-editor of and contributor to *Cognitive Analytic Therapy for People with Intellectual Disabilities and their Carers* (Jessica Kingsley Publishers, 2014). He also works in private practice and is currently in the process of applying to train as a CAT supervisor.

Bethan Davies is a clinical psychologist and CAT practitioner, working for Leeds and York Partnership NHS Foundation Trust.

Josephine F. Discepolo Ahmadi is a psychotherapist, dramatherapist, supervisor and a team consultant. She works in an NHS Psychology Department in Hampshire and in private practice. She is a tutor and a supervisor working with a number of ACAT training courses and a member of the ACAT Equality and Diversity Committee.

Cristina Fiorani is a psychologist and psychotherapist. She works in the Italian state-run health provision in the North of Italy in a child and adolescent service, mostly with adolescents with eating disorders. Together with Marisa Poggioli she became a founder member of ITACAT (Italian cognitive analytic therapy).

Lianne Franks is a highly specialist clinical psychologist working in a forensic setting with adults with intellectual disabilities for Mersey Care NHS Foundation Trust. She first became interested in CAT as an assistant psychologist and her interest grew throughout her doctoral training at the University of Liverpool, and she is now a CAT practitioner in training. Lianne's current role is to lead on reducing restrictive practices within the specialist learning disability division, which complements her interest in using CAT with staff teams and organisations.

Beth Greenhill is a socialist, community activist, CAT practitioner and clinical psychologist. In her clinical role, Beth works with and for people with learning disabilities in Halton Community Learning Disability Team as part of North-West Boroughs Healthcare NHS Foundation Trust. Beth is also joint clinical director of the University of Liverpool's Doctorate in Clinical Psychology Programme and lead for the programme's experts by experience group. Beth has clinical and research interests in applying human rights-based approaches in health care, sexuality and LGBT rights, co-production and in evaluating CAT.

Teresa Hagan works as a consultant clinical psychologist in the Sheffield Health and Social Care NHS Foundation Trust. She has a particular interest in CAT, community psychology approaches, research and theory development in psychotherapy and mental health.

Emily Handley is a clinical psychologist and CAT practitioner employed by the South London and Maudsley NHS Trust within a community mental health service for adults with learning disabilities. She is currently on a two-year secondment to NHS England, employed as the London Region Programme Manager for the Learning Disability Mortality Review (LeDeR) programme; this programme aims to drive service improvements across health and social care to reduce health inequalities and premature mortality among people with learning disabilities. Emily is interested in the application of psychologically informed approaches to understanding and overcoming relational and systemic barriers to the provision of holistic, person-centred and equitable health care in the NHS, particularly to patients with learning disabilities. Emily provides teaching on learning disabilities and cognitive analytic therapy for the Doctorate in Clinical Psychology courses at the Institute of Psychiatry, Psychology and Neuroscience (IOPPN) and the Salomons Centre for Applied Psychology at Canterbury Christchurch University.

Julie Lloyd is a clinical psychologist, CAT practitioner and supervisor. She works in a community team for people with learning disabilities for Surrey and Borders NHS and in a psychiatric intensive care unit for Southern Health, NHS. She co-edited *Cognitive Analytic Therapy for People with Intellectual Disabilities and their Carers* (Jessica Kingsley Publishers, 2014), chairs the CAT special interest group for people working in learning disability services and is a visiting lecturer teaching CAT on several clinical psychology training courses.

Marisa Poggioli was born and educated in the UK but also lived in Brazil and Italy during her childhood. She is a HCPC registered practitioner psychologist, CAT therapist and CAT supervisor. She has experience in primary care, complex care, forensic and learning disability services in the NHS in the UK and of student counselling, private practice and supervision in Italy where she is qualified as a psychologist and psychotherapist. She has collaborated for over 20 years with Cristina Fiorani and is a founder member ITACAT. Cristina and Marisa have jointly authored several articles in relation to CAT in British journals.

Rachel Pollard is a CAT psychotherapist in independent practice in London. She has previously worked as a social worker and as a therapist in NHS adult mental health. She has a particular interest in the ethical implications for psychotherapy of the work the Russian philosopher, Mikhail Bakhtin, and is the author of *Dialogue and Desire Mikhail Bakhtin and the Linguistic Turn in Psychotherapy* (Karnac Books, 2008).

Matthew Tinker is a registered mental health nurse (RMN) and CAT practitioner. He currently works for Berkshire NHS Foundation Trust as a psychological therapist, based within Bracknell community mental health team.

Jo Varela is a consultant clinical psychologist and CAT practitioner. She works with people with learning disabilities and their carers and is employed by Derbyshire Community Health Services NHS Foundation Trust.

William Wallace is a cognitive analytic psychotherapist, supervisor and referrals coordinator working in secondary mental health services in Somerset NHS Trust.

Lawrence Welch is a founder member of ACAT and of the ACAT North/ Catalyse training group. He completed his PhD on the reliability, validity and process of reformulation in 2010. He has worked as a psychotherapist in the NHS since 1996 with his last five years as a consultant psychotherapist in North Tyneside Psychological Therapies Services before being made redundant in December 2014. He has a special interest in the relationship between the macro-political issues and the micro-psychological experience.

ABBREVIATIONS

ACAT	Association for Cognitive Analytic Therapy
BDSM	bondage domination sadism and masochism
BPS	British Psychological Society
CAT	cognitive analytic therapy
CBT	cognitive behavioural therapy (or 'cognitive therapy')
CCG	Care Commissioning Group
CJS	criminal justice system
CMHT	community mental health team
CSA	child sexual abuse
DSA	dialogical sequence analysis
DSM	*Diagnostic and Statistical Manual* (American Psychiatric Association most recent edition DSM 5, 2013)
GDP	gross domestic product
GIRES	Gender Identification Research and Education Society
IAPT	increasing access to psychological therapies
ID	intellectual disability
LD	learning disability
MAPPA	multi-agency public protection arrangements
NCCL	National Council for Civil Liberties
NHS	National Health Service (UK)
PIE	Paedophile Information Exchange (UK: 1970–1980s)
PTSD	post-traumatic stress disorder
RR	reciprocal role
RRP	reciprocal role procedure
SDR	sequential diagrammatic reformulation (also referred to as a 'map')
SOC	standards of care

SRT   Social Reproduction Theory
TREC   Trans Resource Empowerment Centre
UKCP   United Kingdom Council for Psychotherapy
WPATH   World Professional Association for Transgender Health
ZPD   Zone of Proximal Development

ACKNOWLEDGEMENTS

We are indebted to the following people for their sound advice, encouragement and contribution to the ideas that led to this book being written: Barbara Williams, Rose Hughes, Dr Babak Fozooni, Deirdre Haslam, Dr Annie Nehmad, Professor Ian Parker and last but not least to our husbands, Tim Lloyd and Izzat Darwazeh.

RICHARD HANDLEY'S STORY

This book is dedicated to Richard Handley (1979–2012).

Richard was a much-loved son, uncle and friend who died too young at the age of 33; he was also my big brother. Growing up, I didn't notice his disabilities. Richard was just Richard in quite the same way that I am just me and you are just you. As I grew older though, I started to see Richard through the eyes of others and recognised that he had Down's syndrome and that he wasn't learning to drive, getting a job or moving out like other older brothers.

Richard developed mental health difficulties around the age of 18. He had always spoken highly of this milestone birthday and I suspect he noticed that 'coming of age' did not afford him the same freedoms that the rest of us take for granted. Richard was never offered psychological therapy despite being deeply distressed, sometimes very low in mood and sometimes hearing voices and lashing out in fear. Richard instead received a label of 'schizoaffective disorder' and was prescribed a concoction of psychotropic medications. Having a learning disability seemed to blind people to Richard's humanity. If I experienced such distress, there would be a committed quest by others to understand why. I started to recognise the differences and inequalities when comparing my life and Richard's. Richard's mental health and, indeed his humanity, was overshadowed by his learning disability.

After some relatively settled years, Richard withdrew again aged 33. He stopped attending his day centre and stayed in bed for the most part. My parents were not told of this by his support workers although they saw Richard every weekend. Richard's right to make choices was not being upheld and he was denied his right to the same relational supports and encouragement that most of us would need if we were going off track.

Richard was eventually admitted to a mental health assessment and treatment unit but the staff there took him immediately to A&E. Richard died within days after over 10kg of faeces was removed from his bowel. He aspirated stomach contents due to a massive bowel blockage owing to undiagnosed constipation; a painful, premature and entirely preventable death.

An inquest in 2018 found that Richard experienced 'gross failures' from both health and social care services. This time Richard's physical health and his humanity was overshadowed by his mental health, which is ironic given that his mental health and humanity were for so long overshadowed by his learning disability.

So many labels, so many arbitrary distinctions in the systems providing (or not providing) the supports that Richard relied upon. Health or 'social care'? 'Mental' health or physical pain? Patient or person? Arbitrary distinctions leaving vulnerable people at risk of facing layer upon layer of inequality in accessing appropriate health and social care and sustaining the right to life.

At Richard's inquest, the coroner emphasised that the investigations into his death were far broader than they would have been without the dedication and persistence of his family in ensuring questions were answered. For far too long the preventable deaths of so many patients with learning disabilities have not been investigated at all.

Is the breadth and depth of learning that can come from stories like Richard's just not recognised? Are the lives of people with disabilities not valued? Or are well-intentioned health and social care employees driven, in desperation, to minimise, distract and delay review in the hope of protection against a feared outcome? A health care culture characterised by anxiety inhibits the objective, dispassionate, reflective learning that is required to ensure that the NHS and social care deliver high-quality, equitable services to the people that need them, including our most vulnerable members of society. People like Richard; brothers, sons, uncles and friends.

What would it take for us to strive towards a system wherein insight, recognition and revision of problem procedures within the system are associated with pride and quality rather than fear (of exposure? of criticism? of shame?)? A reluctance to address inequalities or indeed a failure to recognise their extent risks perpetuating problem procedures as we cannot learn, we cannot revise and we remain doomed to reenact our mistakes, deepen our fears and perpetuate inequalities, remaining stuck.

Just as we need to see all patients (or people!) as fully human, we too as practitioners, employees, professionals need to work in a system where we too are seen and can see ourselves as fully human – fallible and therefore open to learning and doing our absolute best.

It is my hope that, by sharing Richard's story, people will feel empowered to question and adjust their practice when needed, to speak up and advocate when others need to do the same and to implement timely practice changes when systemic limitations become apparent, whatever settings we find ourselves in. Working proactively, flexibly and responsively with the 'whole person' in all that we do should help to reduce inequalities and unnecessary tragedies.

Emily Handley

FOREWORD

This book is a timely addition to the wealth of recent information about how inequality around the world and the recent austerity measures in the UK, which have most strongly affected the poor and disadvantaged in our society, are also detrimental to mental health. Despite calls for a 'parity of esteem', where mental health problems attract the same level of concern and resources as physical health problems, little has changed. In addition, some groups within society continue to be neglected and unnoticed, with repeated scandals coming to light of abuse and neglect, with institutions refusing to acknowledge their failures to protect vulnerable people, preferring to protect themselves and their own reputations. This book shines a fierce light into some of the areas of mental health that have suffered most from these inequalities, and yet seeks to open up a new dialogue, rather than take a purely critical stance.

My elderly mother has a photocopy of a prayer stuck to the inside of her larder cupboard door. Sometimes known as the 'Nun's prayer' by an anonymous author, it reminds her, each time she opens her larder cupboard, not to lecture the young, or to go on about her aches and pains. More importantly, perhaps, it encourages her to accept that she is sometimes wrong, with my favourite line of all, 'Teach me the Glorious lesson that I may be mistaken'. My mother is not doing so well in some of these areas, but she is always ready to admit that she may be mistaken, saying, 'Times have changed, and I am out of date now'.

Well my goodness, how times have changed over the last 50 years or so since the early development of the cognitive analytic therapy model. There is now more social and political awareness of the insidious and damaging affects of discrimination against and the oppression of less powerful groups in society; people with disabilities, people from minority ethnic groups, women, gay and lesbian people as well as people with mental health problems, but there is still a long way to go.

In developing cognitive analytic therapy as a model of therapy, which was potentially accessible to all and was respectful of the client's real-life experiences, Tony Ryle was a man ahead of his time. This openness and flexibility of the model has allowed CAT to update itself as new knowledge becomes available, and attitudes have changed. However, as this book emphasises, the individual stories that we hear from our clients can be so powerful, and so persuasive, that we lose sight of the social and political origins of their problems and need to be reminded of them over and over again. My hope is that just having this book on our bookshelves will function a bit like the anonymous prayer does for my mother. It will remind us all that we may be mistaken, and that our clients have 'glorious lessons' to teach us from their stories of growing up in times, or cultures that are different from ours: a reminder to question our assumptions about people, about the causes of their distress and difficulties, and about the best way to help them. A reminder that true collaboration results from a deep, authentic respect for the lived experience of the people to whom we seek to offer therapy, so that we can learn as much from them about their society and culture, and the world that they grew up in, as they learn from us.

The editors of this book, Julie Lloyd and Rachel Pollard, have already proved themselves to be both knowledgeable and passionate about these issues, through their own individual writings, previous book editing, and their past joint editorship of the *Journal of the Association for Cognitive Analytic Therapy*. They have assembled a rich and diverse group of therapists from the CAT community and have laid down a challenge to us all to examine our assumptions.

Alison Jenaway, Chair, Association of
Cognitive Analytic Therapy

1

INTRODUCTION

Cognitive analytic therapy and the politics of mental health

Julie Lloyd and Rachel Pollard

How far has cognitive analytic practice lived up to its initial radical agenda as restated by its founder, Anthony Ryle, in 2010? There is a tendency for radical ideas to drift towards the centre and sometimes even further and for previously radical discourses to become entangled with more conservative and authoritarian discourses (Parker, 1992). This could be seen as a measure of their success as values and beliefs once regarded as belonging to the left-wing radical fringes become accepted and even promoted by the mainstream. However, equally as dangerous, is the complacency and stagnation of the imagination that can follow when new ideas and progressive values become more widely accepted by and even embedded in conservative institutions.

Bringing politics out of the shadows

The relationship between the psychological and politics is troubled because from Freud onwards, psychotherapy's main concern was the private sphere confined to what is going on inside people's heads. For too long psychoanalysis and cognitive behavioural therapy (CBT) have located the causes of individual distress (and by implication the fault), in the mind of the suffering individual. As the various chapters in this book will show, what goes on 'inside people's heads' is very much a function of what is going on in the world around them. Therefore, it is a delusion of great folly to imagine that whatever context we work in, what we do as therapists can ever be untainted by 'politics'.

Therapists who claim to be outside politics are deluding themselves; even the most transitory human interactions take place in a political context, so therapists have to engage with the politics of the society in which they and their clients live. The pretence of non-engagement with these issues, is itself a political act of control that risks heaping sole responsibility on to our clients and their immediate families for their distress (see Figure 1.1).

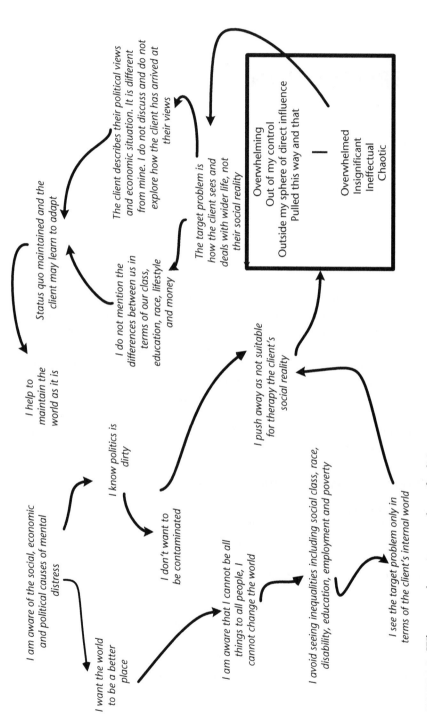

FIGURE 1.1 Why some therapists stay clear of politics.

These blockages collude with the neoliberal agenda that devolves all responsibility onto individuals and absolves the state and wider society from its mutual responsibility for the welfare of all its citizens. This leaves the social, political and material causes of poor mental health uninterrogated. Our engagement with people's sufferings as therapists inevitably confronts us with political and social issues because the forces they are up against are structural, not individual.

The limits to therapeutic dialogue

A primary aim of psychotherapy is to facilitate and encourage the client's freedom to speak and/or express themselves in other ways, particularly facilitating what otherwise could not be expressed, could not be thought about or could not brought into consciousness and integrated. Constraints on what can be expressed too often come from the political and cultural context concerning issues beyond the client's control that render the therapist's interpretations or techniques useless. Talking therapies that confine themselves to merely addressing the client's symptoms depoliticise pain from the outside by locating it inside.

The constraints on freedom of speech in the therapy room are echoed in the constraints that govern the politics of the provision of mental health services. When politics are barred from our formulations, we ignore the ways in which the inequalities that structure our society create misery and despair for so many people. In the UK, cuts to mental health services have eroded the space for freedom of speech and thought that psychotherapy potentially opens up. The alleviation of mental distress is no longer seen primarily as relief from suffering but as an economic problem to be 'managed' in the most cost-effective way.

The bio-medical model of mental ill health that informs government policies fails to address the actual causes of mental health in the circumstances of people's lives, causes that are gaining increasing recognition in non-governmental organisations. This is a paradigm shift in that mental health concerns are reconceptualised as a human rights issue and the application of the bio-medical model, particularly the use of psychotropic medicines and nonconsensual treatments are seen as human rights violations. Nevertheless, the UN Special Rapporteur in 2017[1] notes that:

> Public policies continue to neglect the importance of the preconditions of poor mental health, such as violence, disempowerment, social exclusion and isolation and the breakdown of communities, systemic socioeconomic disadvantage and harmful conditions at work and in schools. Approaches to mental health that ignore the social, economic and cultural environment are not just failing people with disabilities they are failing to promote the mental health of others at different stages of their lives.

Neoliberal politics peddles the myth of individual autonomy and self-determination, discounting the privileges that the rich and powerful were born into as contributing to their 'success' and blaming the poor and disadvantaged for their failure to gain a toehold on the ladder out of poverty and relative powerlessness. It peddles the myth that the causes of depression and anxiety are personal and attitudinal rather than socio-political. It peddles the myth that very brief 'psychological' therapy that is linear, prescriptive and 'delivered' by minimally trained mental health workers is sufficient 'treatment'. It serves as a smokescreen for forcing people into poorly paid insecure jobs when in poor mental and/or physical health often leading to homelessness, even greater degrees of poverty and worsening mental and physical health. Children in families affected are then left to carry a burden of economic deprivation and social disadvantage into their adult lives.

This places a straitjacket on freedom of expression for both client and therapist. The therapist's capacity to respond to clients as unique individuals has been severely compromised. Therapists are told to 'deliver' a prescribed model of therapy and clients forced to tailor their 'symptoms' according to the model of therapy being offered over which they have no or little choice. For many people, inhibitions due to anxieties and issues of trust are barriers to communication that take time to dismantle. For example, the survivors of trauma such as abuse, violence or torture, who risk finding themselves 'diagnosed' in ways that are considered amenable to 'treatment' by the limited range of therapies available, or as not eligible for therapy at all.

The reductive aims in commissioning public mental health services and resultant crisis in lack of service provision inevitably isolates and marginalises people further, as public interest is conflated with narrowly defined authoritarian economic interests that favour the rich.

The politics of psychotherapy

In order to destigmatise the need for mental health services, we need to challenge what Samuels (2015) has referred to as a two-tier system in which those who can afford to pay for it have access to counselling and psychotherapy while the poor and less powerful have to make do with very brief manualised treatment if they are lucky. The Health and Social Care Act 2012 passed by the coalition of the Conservatives and Liberal Democrats is one of the most singularly damaging pieces of legislation of recent times that forced an increasingly fragmented and market-led internal structure on the NHS in the UK. Predatory private companies such as Virgin Care, who avoid tax in the UK, by 2018 held over £2 billion worth of contracts and sued the cash-strapped NHS in Surrey when they lost a contract. The Private Finance Initiatives (PFIs) cost the NHS a further £2 billion every year despite a large fall in NHS spending as a share of GDP (gross domestic product). Cuts in NHS and local authority social services have had a devastating impact on what help therapists in the NHS can offer.

Since CAT began to be more widely practised in the 1980s, the political landscape has changed: The 'New Labour' governments of 1997, 2001 and 2005 advanced the neoliberal agenda of the Thatcher years, failing to address the housing shortage brought about by the sale of social housing, accelerating the privatisation of public services, failing to control the financial sector, pandering to the agenda of an expanding middle class and failing to represent the interests of the working class. During the same period, inequality became greater and as has been shown conclusively, the more unequal a society is the greater the extent of physical and mental ill health for everyone (Wilkinson, 2005). The politics of 'austerity' in which drastic cuts to public expenditure are made to 'balance the books' have further widened the gap between the privileged few and the majority who have seen their living standards and quality of life eroded. For those at the sharp end of the cuts it has led to the loss of their mental health and for some their lives due to increasing suicide rates (O'Hara, 2017). Psychologists Against Austerity,[2] have documented how government cuts have produced the psychological conditions for increasing rates of mental ill health while drastically reducing mental health provision relative to the need for it.

The economic context

> Capitalist economies are fundamentally unstable because of their inherent contradictions; one of these is that the unfettered drive for accumulation of wealth means that the social processes essential for the reproduction and maintenance of the labour force are overridden, effectively destroying its own conditions of possibility.
>
> *(Fraser, 2017, p. 24)*

State-managed capitalism, failed because of falling productivity – stagflation and because it promoted an androcentric model of social reproduction i.e. the bourgeois family and failed to draw on the labour potential of women and other minoritised groups (Fraser, 2017). The current neoliberal or global financialised capitalism is more pernicious in its effects on people and the environment. It is marked by higher levels of instability due to deregulation and as a result its internal contradictions are even starker. For example, while neoliberalism has been associated with a liberalisation of social attitudes in some countries, creating employment opportunities for a more diverse range of people as well as creating new consumerist demand, as Pankaj Mishra (2018, p. 18) points out, this has only benefited a few:

> Since the 1990s, the bonanzas of free trade and financial deregulation had helped breed greater tolerance for racial and sexual variety, primarily among the privileged – the CIA under Obama set up a recruitment office at the Miami Beach Gay Pride parade. Overt racism and homophobia had become taboo, even as imprisonment or premature death removed 1.5 million black men from public life. Diversification and multiculturalism among upwardly mobile, college-educated elites went together with mass incarceration at home and endless military interventions abroad.

This contradiction is even more noticeable when considered on a global scale when liberalisation of social attitudes towards LGBTQ people, women and ethnic diversity in some parts of the world seem to be matched by regressive attitudes and policies in others, despite the tentacles of neoliberalism reaching into all but the most remote corners of the planet. It is clearly not in the interests of capital to alienate large numbers of the potential workforce as well as the consumers of its products.

A Social Reproduction Theory (SRT)[3] approach would suggest that the policies of the current and recent governments in the UK have been peculiarly lacking in imaginative foresight when it comes to the welfare of the current and future workforce. The reduced availability of affordable quality childcare for working parents, the savage cuts in welfare benefits that have led to increasing levels of poverty for families with children, the failure of the state to address the housing crisis, the callous and often inhumane treatment of refugees are all examples of how the welfare of the current and future potential supply of labour is being vitiated. SRT regards the unpaid labour involved in reproducing and caring for the workforce as indivisible from labour in the monetary economy as the latter could not take place without the former. However even when this socially reproductive work is paid for it is undervalued, usually carried out by women and as levels of inequality widen both nationally and internationally outsourced to women from poorer households and poorer countries who increasingly staff our care homes and hospitals as well as caring for the children of wealthier families.

As mental health workers we are all involved in social reproduction in that our economic function is to restore people to the work place. The financial priorities of neoliberal capitalism mean that the satisfaction and individual fulfilment that mental health workers used to derive from their roles has been eroded, both due to the restrictive aspects of subordinating social and individual welfare to profits, alongside the deteriorating social conditions that adversely affect mental health in the population and the prospects for recovery. The dynamic non-linear processes that are involved in caring for and nurturing other people in hospitals, mental health clinics and care homes as well as schools and nurseries are now subject to meaningless attempts at economic quantification in a way that could be termed a *reification of process* by abstracting snapshots that have no meaning outside their given evolving context.

Many psychotherapists have lost their jobs in the NHS due to cuts in psychotherapy services and, despite government rhetoric about the importance of mental health, psychotherapy and counselling are extremely difficult for most people with mental health concerns to gain access to, unless they are able to pay for them. Those that remain are subjected to target driven 'micro-management' pushing them towards offering low cost brief therapies of 4–6 sessions or running psychoeducational groups. IAPT (the UK NHS front-line therapy service 'Increasing Access to Psychological Therapies') published data for mild psychological difficulties between 1 April 2014 and 31 March 2015; only 41.8% of referrals finished the course of treatment and of those, only 42.8% showed a reliable recovery assessed by questionnaire administered during treatment. Ali (2016) found that of 439 recovered participants following low-level CBT, 53% relapsed in a year, with half of these relapses occurring in two months after therapy had finished, and 80% after six months. These statistics suggest that even those lucky enough to gain access to NHS mental health services are being failed by the paucity of services on offer. Demand for psychotherapy will outstrip supply for the foreseeable future: In 2016, the government committed to a target of 25% of people in need of therapy to access it on the NHS by 2020, still leaving a scandalous 75% without treatment (UKCP, 2017). IAPT's remit is primarily to return people to work (Work and Health Programme, 2017). This psycho-educational industrialised sub-therapy is a long way from the emancipatory aims on which psychotherapy is supposedly based. For those 'lucky enough' to receive it, it often causes more harm than good, as people for whom such treatment is presented as a 'cure' for their mental distress, often feel an acute sense of failure and despair when this turns out not be the case.

The position of CAT

CAT is in an ambiguous position when it comes to responding to the current crisis in mental health provision and the diminished remit of the 'talking therapies'. Its original ethos; the right of everyone suffering from mental distress to have access to effective dynamically informed relational therapy in the NHS, has been seriously compromised by cuts to mental health provision. Different therapies are forced into competition with each other to see who can 'deliver' the required results for the least cost. This is fuelled by dubious research where the distinction between efficacy and effectiveness is not drawn, while the rising levels of inequality and social deprivation that are associated with rising levels of mental health remain unaddressed.

CAT therapists are sometimes faced with an unenviable choice; either to continue to work in a damaged and damaging organisation or to leave and work in the private sector with its attendant insecurity. At the same time the professional bodies representing psychotherapists face a choice to speak up and campaign against the cuts to mental health services and other policy decisions that adversely affect the most vulnerable and least powerful in our society or adapt to the prevailing ethos of privatisation and concentrate on protecting their members' interests.

As CAT developed, Ryle (1995), and the other therapists who were using and developing the model, further refined it to offer effective therapy to people whose psychological and emotional problems were more complex. This, in our view, led to CAT's social and political values of respect for each individual's unique experience being compromised by the need to conform to the bio-medical model in order to gain and maintain credibility in the NHS and with the commissioners of privatised services. Fozooni (2010) is rightly critical of elements in CAT that adopt an apparently unquestioning stance towards diagnostic classification and the DSM[4] distinctions between Axis 1 and Axis 2 disorders.

We believe that CAT should situate itself firmly on the political left and that the causes of mental distress are understood as being to a large extent the result of political and economic inequalities, even if these are subjectively experienced at the micro level of interpersonal conflict, neglect and abuse and the belief that effective treatment for mental health problems should be accessible to everyone, regardless of the means to pay for them. We don't believe that any type of therapy or therapist can claim to be beyond or outside politics and do believe that it is our responsibility as therapists and citizens to take politics seriously. However, psychotherapy does not have a good record of accomplishment in this respect as Anthony Ryle, the founder of CAT points out:

> Psychotherapists, however, seldom spell out how damaging individual values and assumptions may be derived from the past and present interests of the powerful, in part because they too are shaped by the same forces. And all too often psychotherapy theories reflect the ideologies and interests of the powerful. The Freudian superego, for example, is not a human universal, it is an internalized representative of the nineteenth-century European ruling class. The internalized forces of rebellion and protest are dismissed as the id, a disruptive remnant of our animal nature, dangerous and forbidden and needing to be repressed. What was seen to be universal and innate is the result of the internalization of the reciprocal class roles of ruler and ruled and as such both reflected and served to support the ideology of the capitalist culture of 19th and 20th Europe.
>
> *(Ryle, 2010, p. 7)*

Nevertheless, we don't claim to be speaking for all CAT therapists, and accept that it may, in theory, be possible to practice CAT and vote Conservative, although in our own experience we have yet to come across this rather rare and secretive animal!

Introducing the CAT model

Cognitive analytic therapy was a pioneer in the field of brief integrated relational therapies. There are now many different brands of integrated brief therapy and our aim is not to fall into the trap of trying to prove 'that mine is better than yours'. Like most therapists we have a personal and professional attachment to our own traditions, but research evidence from as far back as Rosenzweig's (1936) findings that 'all methods of therapy when competently used are equally successful' (p. 413), suggests that the skill of the therapist and the quality of their relationship with their client are the key to successful outcomes in psychotherapy, regardless of the model being used and it is not possible to know whether any positive outcomes from research projects were owing to specific or incidental factors (Wampold & Imel, 2015).

We start therefore from the position that other models are equally valid and all can gain far more from constructive criticism, cross-fertilisation and collaboration than from rivalry and competition.

Our hope is that this book will be of interest to anyone concerned about the politics of mental health regardless of the type of therapy they practice.

During and after training most therapists develop curiosity about other theoretical perspectives and practices and seek to learn from them and integrate elements of other models into their own practice, often seeking clinical supervision from practitioners from other traditions and having their own personal therapy with a therapist with a different background. CAT is itself an 'open' theoretical tradition with many of its practitioners having previous training in another type of therapy; knowledge and experience that they bring to their practice of CAT, while the theory and practice of CAT has been enriched by the absorption of ideas and insights from other traditions within psychotherapy as well as from developmental psychology, literary criticism, linguistics and philosophy. CAT also accommodates therapists who are 'scientific practitioners' and who uphold the importance of evidenced-based practice supported by research with statistically significant results alongside others who are highly critical of the politics of the 'scientist practitioner' tradition and its associated research methods. The authors of this chapter are both enthusiastic CAT therapists as the ethos of the model coincides with our own values as therapists and citizens, but we come from very different professional, theoretical and research backgrounds and practice CAT in very different ways working with very different client groups.

This introduction is not intended to be a comprehensive account of the theory and practice of cognitive analytic therapy (see Ryle & Kerr, 2002), but to provide an outline for those new to this type of therapy and to describe the concepts particular to this way of working psychotherapeutically that will be referred to in later chapters. We will also try to show how central concepts in CAT can be a theoretical basis for the understanding of the politics of mental health and mental health provision explored in this book. While the political, social and economic causes of mental ill health have been widely written about and discussed by psychologists and psychotherapists, they are rarely accounted for in the theories that inform practice (Ryan, 2017). Subsequent chapters will describe how CAT theory and concepts can be used to illuminate the causes of mental distress that originate beyond the immediate interpersonal environment of the affected individuals in a way that is relevant to therapists across a range of practice.

The ethos of CAT

As well as being a 'psychological' therapy, CAT is also 'social' in the micro sense in that there is a clear understanding of subjective experience and our sense of 'self' as being formed by our early experience of our relationships with other people and in the 'macro' sense in that our subjectivity is also infused by the societies we live in, our social class, our religious affiliations, our ethnic and gender identities, sexual orientation and our genetic make-up insofar as it affects our bodily characteristics and intellectual abilities and the social responses to these as well as the exigencies of life that lead to damage to the body and mind whether through accident, illness or crime.

Ryle and Kerr (2002, p. 217) describe the 'implicit values of CAT' as embodying 'a set of values and assumptions which are little celebrated in the individualistic, consumer-oriented societies of the contemporary Western World'. An important part of the politics of CAT is its commitment to the NHS and the principle of health care being available to all at the point of need. Ryle and Kerr (2002) note that despite the proliferation of treatment models, most psychologically distressed people in the UK still did not have access to effective psychotherapy and in the past 16 years this situation has deteriorated further.

For psychotherapy to be accessible it also must be practical for people to incorporate into their lives and also cost effective whether it is provided on the NHS or paid for by the patient. CAT was designed as a time-limited model of therapy partly with these considerations in mind but also and, as or more importantly, because it was claimed a time-limited intervention can be as or more effective. A course of CAT therapy is brief and intensive as opposed to long and extensive (Ryle & Kerr, 2002). However, the evidence for the equal or even increased effectiveness of brief therapy interventions is lacking and in making these claims CAT and other models making similar claims are positioning themselves politically to compete for limited NHS resources as well as those of private 'providers', conflating the interests of patients with those of the therapists treating them.

Ryle (1975) sought to demystify the process of therapy to make it more accessible and to eliminate the requirement of 'psychological mindedness' demonstrating how ordinary 'common-sense' psychology that many people use every day in their conversations with and about other people is not so far removed from the psychoanalytic defences elaborated by Klein, Fairbairn and Guntrip and redefined some of these in everyday language. The use of this language to describe what is happening in a therapy session serves both to demystify the role of the therapist, making the process of therapy more transparent and reduce, though obviously not eliminating, the power imbalance between therapist and client. CAT sees therapy as an actively collaborative project that involves not being with or doing to but 'doing with' (Ryle & Kerr, 2002, p. 2). However, like so many other therapies, CAT can be also be criticised for creating its own jargon; we will therefore try to keep technical terms to a minimum in this book and intend to describe only the essential concepts needed for a basic understanding of CAT.

The genesis of CAT: 'finding a common language for the psychotherapies'

Ryle's starting point was the unmet need for practical but in-depth mental health interventions among his patients in an inner-city GP practice and his frustration with what was available at that time, which he saw as either 'behaviourism and cognitive psychotherapy or the encompassing metaphoric jungle of psychoanalysis' (Ryle, 1987, p. 168). However, CAT is also indebted to these older traditions. While being critical of psychoanalysis for its apparent inaccessibility to most people who were in need of psychotherapeutic help, its apparent reluctance to understand its own theories and practices as politically and socially constructed and its neglect of those who were very ill or deemed not to be 'psychologically minded'. Ryle also acknowledged the considerable debt he owed to its unique insights into the importance of early experience in later psychological distress and how these relational patterns are reflected in the relationship between client and therapist:

> On the one hand I owe to it [psychoanalysis] my most profound insights into the psychotherapeutic process: on the other hand I am impatient with many aspects of its practices and with the complacency, conservatism and self-absorption of many of its institutions.
>
> *(Ryle, 1990, p. 221)*

Ryle was similarly critical of cognitive behavioural therapy (CBT) for its neglect of the relational and social dimensions of human experience and its conceptualisation of the person as a psychological monad. Traditional CBT[5] positions the suffering individual as suffering precisely owing to their views of what is happening to them, i.e. cognitive distortions or deficits, and not simply because of *what* is happening or has happened to them. Politically this is a conservative model because it fails to acknowledge the circumstances in people's lives that are the source of their distress. There is also covert class issue as CBT is far more likely to be offered to working-class people while psychoanalytic therapies were reserved for the middle classes (Ryan, 2017). Nevertheless Ryle was also similarly indebted to CBT for its crucial account of the sequential links between emotions, thoughts, behaviour and outcomes.

CAT stripped down to its essential elements is a psychoanalytic therapy conceptualised and described in cognitive language that seeks to understand individual distress in a social, historical and political context.

Many CAT therapists are clinical psychologists with a prior background in cognitive therapy. CAT has offered a way to deepen and extend their understanding and practice of psychotherapy through integrating insights from psychoanalysis, and more flexibility in the ways they are able to form relationships with their clients than is possible with a psycho-educational approach. Others coming from backgrounds in psychoanalysis, psychoanalytic therapy or existential/humanistic psychotherapy have found that the insights from these traditions can be harnessed more effectively when applied in a more focused, specific or practical way that takes into account the diversity of peoples' lived experiences and social reality.

Key concepts in CAT

One of Ryle's observations about the experience of people who were suffering from mental distress was that they were 'trapped' in ways of responding to their distress that served to exacerbate rather than alleviate it. For example, a person lacking in confidence might try to please people in an attempt to gain acceptance from others, only to find that other people then took them for granted and ignored their own wishes, making them feel unworthy of others' respect so their lack of confidence becomes more entrenched. This is called a *procedural sequence*. We all have procedural sequences that we follow in our everyday lives that mostly operate outside our conscious awareness and we only have cause to pay attention to them if they are a source of distress to ourselves and/or others.[6] These procedural sequences are understood as having been learnt in childhood as ways of adapting to the relational environment.

Another of Ryle's observations influenced by the object relations school of psychoanalysis is that as human beings we learn how to relate to other people and to ourselves from our very earliest experience of relationships with parents or caregivers and, as we get older, other significant people in our lives. If these relationships are mainly benign and supportive of the child's development, the child will be more likely to have a good relationship with themselves and go on to develop positive and rewarding relationships with other people in adult life. The opposite applies where the child's pre-dominant experience is, for example, of neglect, persistent criticism or abuse. Such a child is more likely to find it hard to accept themselves and experience difficulties in their relationships with other people and consequent mental distress in later life. These internalised relational templates are known as *reciprocal roles* (RRs). They are enacted between the other and the self, the self and the other and self to self. Obviously life is far more complex than that and most of us will have experienced a mixture of benign and less benign RRs growing up, but generally speaking the more flexible and adaptable our caregivers and significant others were in the way they related to us as children, the greater that range of RRs we are likely to have at our disposal to relate to other people as adults. And regardless of the way we were parented or cared for, as we grow older and relate increasingly to people outside our immediate families and come to understand how we are positioned and find ways to position ourselves in the wider society, we will encounter other RRs that will influence us in different ways.

A subjectively experienced 'role' involves memory, meaning affect and expectation (Ryle & Kerr, 2002). A reciprocal role has two poles or positions and describes a way of relating that tends to be self-reinforcing. Usually the more powerful or 'parental' position is uppermost and the child's response to this is in the lower position. Some examples are shown in Figure 1.2.

RRs are stimuli and the procedures are the active responses that result. A procedural sequence enacted by the child and caregiver will tend to maintain the RR and this is known as a *reciprocal role procedure* or RRP.

Restricting	Mocking	Demanding	Attentive
Controlling	Humiliating	Domineering	Thoughtful
I	I	I	I
Restricted	Exposed	Loyal	Cared for
Controlled	Worthless	Compliant	Safe
Anxious		Covertly Resentful	

FIGURE 1.2 How reciprocal roles are portrayed.

This bringing together of the procedural sequence with reciprocal roles is the core theoretical basis of CAT. In practice, this is translated into a *sequential diagrammatic reformulation* (SDR) or 'map'. This is a flow chart of the reciprocal roles that are a source of distress and the procedures that maintain them. Maps are drawn out in therapy sessions jointly, by clients and therapists working together. Their purpose is to encourage clients to stand back from their difficulties, externalise them and develop an increased capacity for self-reflection leading to enhanced self-awareness. For some clients this is an end in itself; for others it can help facilitate change as different ways of responding to RRPs that cause distress can be tried out.

Trans-diagnosis

In our view diagnostic labels often obscure rather than illuminate the origins and the subjective experience of mental distress.[7] There is a theoretical basis for a trans-diagnostic approach in CAT as a result of the incorporation of ideas from the Russian developmental psychologist, Lev Vygotsky, and the Russian philosopher and literary theorist, Mikhail Bakhtin.

Space does not allow for a detailed elaboration of these developments, but we will describe two ideas that have become key concepts in CAT, both of which are trans-theoretical and can be used across different therapeutic (as well as educational) contexts. The first of these is Vygotsky's (1978) concept of the *Zone of Proximal Development* (ZPD), which described the process whereby learning takes place initially, through interpersonal activity involving the acquisition of skills and concepts that acquire meaning, which are subsequently practised alone before becoming internalised (Ryle & Kerr, 2002). Vygotsky (1978, p. 86) summarised this as

> the distance between the actual developmental level as determined by independent problem solving and the level of potential development as determined through problem solving with adult guidance, or in collaboration with more capable peers.

The ZPD is applicable to all learning situations across the lifespan, it is dynamic and, as Ryle and Kerr (2002) suggest, implies a prospective as opposed to retrospective view of development and therapy.

The second of these is of these is the concept of the *dialogical self*, inspired by Mikhail Bakhtin and integrated into CAT theory as a result of the collaboration between Ryle with Mikael Leiman. This resulted in a theoretically rich and nuanced analysis of process in psychotherapy (e.g. Leiman, 1997, 2002; Leiman & Stiles, 2001) as well as a different way of conceptualising the 'self'.

A dialogical conception of self as a process in interaction with other dialogical selves understands psychotherapy as a human social practice not as a treatment to be 'delivered' according to theories that categorise, normalise or marginalise (Pollard, 2008). In CAT, this brought together the concept of different aspects of the self as different 'voices' speaking to each other from different positions or different points of view (Stiles, 1997) with the object relations' derived concept of RRs. This allows for a flexible, infinitely variable and non-pathologising description of phenomena that may in other contexts be classified as psychotic or personality dis-ordered. In contrast to some interpretations of the 'dialogical self' as being merely a metaphor for a collection of internal voices, in our view, Bakhtin's dialogism is a philosophical/ethical development of his phenomenological exploration of human interdependency (Hirschkop, 1999). Dialogism posits both the unique, irreducable aspects of human experience and therefore of each individual as defined by Cheyne and Tarulli (1999, p. 11):

> Dialogism . . . valorizes difference and otherness. It is a way of thinking about ourselves and the world that always accepts non-coincidence of stance, understanding and consciousness. In dialogism, the subversion by difference, of movements towards unity and the inevitable fracturing of univocality into multi-voicedness represents the fundamental human condition.

And also, the inter-subjective nature of human consciousness, the presence of the other in the self and our absolute need of the other and the other's need of us.

CAT as an aid to consultancy

As a CAT understanding of self is a relational and social one, it particularly lends itself to use as a consultancy aid with staff teams working in mental health and related settings, that pays particular attention to the interplay of transference and countertransference in therapeutic, caring and collegiate relationships (Kellett et al, 2014). By mapping the actual 'care plan',[8] i.e. the reciprocal role procedures (RRPs) or relational patterns that clients, staff and the organisation reenact with each other, staff can be helped to recognise their own part in both helpful and unhelpful or even damaging reciprocal role procedures and therefore try to avoid eliciting and reciprocating responses that cause or perpetuate distress. This is elic-ited by mapping a range of reciprocal roles procedures such as those that are longed for, those merely tolerated and those dreaded. Kellett et al. (2014) found that map-ping these RRPs had a significant impact on staff and organisations in their practice and relationships.

Conclusion

This section has attempted to give an overview of the ethos and politics of CAT and how they interact with clinical theory and practice as well outlining some of the key concepts that will be referred to in later chapters. A weakness in CAT is the lack of research into impact of the wider political and economic context on the mental health of people seeking treatment. In common with other models competing for validation in the NHS and with commissioners of private mental health services, CAT has attempted to prove its efficacy with research methods that could be seen as conflicting with its own ethos. This conflict of values seems to be an inevitable consequence of its commitment to the NHS and the principle of mental health services being available to all who need them. There is no easy way out of this conflict and within CAT opinions are divided as to whether the political necessity of certain types of research outweighs the ethical compromises that have to be made in order to gain and maintain credibility.

About the chapters in this book

The aim of this book is to draw attention to the real causes of and potential solutions to mental distress. We hope that the discussions in this book are transferable to therapists working with other models and schools, as our aim is not to evangelise for CAT, but to critique it and reposition it as a therapy of the left. CAT like other models and theories can be an invaluable framework that guides and contains therapists and clients but rigid adherence to any model or theory is primitive and harmful to patients as neither the theories or we have all the answers. Humility is an appropriate response to the limits to what we as therapists can do to alleviate the distress caused by harsh and unjust economic and political decisions.

This book challenges the socially divisive medical model through showing that human suffering is shaped and often caused by the political structures of the society in which we live. The complexity of mental health problems at macro and micro levels, their interaction with physical health problems and social, economic and cultural as well as geographical and environmental aspects of people's lives means that it is a gross oversimplification to research mental health and its treatment in isolation from social and political conditions.

Unlike many recent books on politics and psychotherapy, most of the contributors to this book are women. This is reflected in the practical clinical issues that are examined from a therapeutic and political perspective, recognising that 'politics' is so much more than the high-flown rhetoric of the still male-dominated leadership and intellectual commentators of the political left both within and outside psychotherapy, but is actually central to the work clinicians do with people in their work settings. Most of the contributors are clinicians working in the NHS and all have worked in the NHS in recent years.

Most of the chapters in this book are primarily informed by the authors' clinical work as well as their own lived experience. The different contributors discuss how CAT has been developed in working with different client groups; the survivors of sexual abuse, people with intellectual disabilities, people with long-standing complex problems, people in forensic settings and people with concerns related to gender and sexuality.

Chapter 2 is a powerful and penetrating critique of one of CAT's main theoretical constructs, reciprocal roles (RRs), relational interactions that are crucial to our subjectivity and a target for therapeutic interventions. The chapter shows how current therapeutic conceptions of reciprocal roles are inadequate to understanding the unequal balance of power in the distressing reciprocal role procedures

(RRPs) that many people find themselves caught up in and that they are powerless to change as a result. It describes how as therapists we need to take more account of the complex and multi-layered world that people live in and acknowledge the constraints that this places on the capacity of people to change. Chapter 3 develops the theme of the role of power or the lack of it in people's 'coping strategies' and discusses how Pierre Bourdieu's concepts of symbolic power and symbolic violence can further our understanding of the threat people both experience and fear when stepping outside their position in the social hierarchy and advocates for more involvement in mental health services for people whose expertise is grounded in their own experience of mental distress.

Chapters 4 and 5 discuss the role of economics and the material conditions of life in mental health. Chapter 4 describes the interaction between the development of cognitive analytic therapy and political/economic changes over the last 40 years and proposes a trans-theoretical ethic, derived from the work of Mikhail Bakhtin, as an alternative to developmental accounts of subjectivity where people's assigned roles in the social political world can be interrogated and challenged. Chapter 5 moves from the macro role of the super-rich global elite and their impact on economic conditions and the deleterious effects of inequality on health to the micro-personal implication of these and particularly how they affected staff and patients in an NHS service under threat.

Chapter 6 discusses how the suffering caused by economic inequality and deprivation, as well as other forms of trauma, is handed down from one generation to the next. Illustrated with case material the author shows how CAT-informed consultancy can help different staff teams working with the same family to avoid replicating original trauma in their interactions with their clients.

Chapter 7 describes some of the inequalities endemic in the lives of people with learning disabilities, including premature mortality and limited access to health and social care services. A moving and powerful letter written to the NHS using the CAT reformulation framework offers the opportunity for readers to understand and engage with the structural neglect and marginalising of people with learning disabilities.

Chapters 8 and 9 continue exploring another aspect of this theme in the cultural, historical and social underpinnings of our responses to being challenged by the behaviour of another within health and social care settings. It looks at how we can end up responding in kind to behaviour that is challenging, owing to the distress it causes us. The second of these two chapters describes examples of how using a CAT framework can assist. Chapter 10 describes concerns about shortcomings in how the political agenda 'Transforming Care' is being implemented with regard to offenders who have learning disabilities; a structural neglect that take us full circle back to many of the issues raised in Chapter 7.

Chapter 11 charts the social and political history of responses to child sexual abuse that has profoundly influenced the attitudes of psychotherapists. This is an example of where the personal is definitely political. Because there are dramatic and significant changes in political and social attitudes towards survivors of child sexual abuse, which are allowing previously silenced voices to express themselves, both the authors write from the dual position of NHS mental health workers who are also survivors of child sexual abuse.

Chapter 12 continues the theme of how political and social attitudes affect the stance taken by psychotherapists exploring the inter- and intra-personal issues associated with gender diversity, including the conflicting attitudes of governments, the medical profession and society. Chapter 13 develops the idea that our gender identity is socially constructed throughout our life experiences. This can lead to patterns of relating to ourselves and others that we may assume are 'natural' or 'typical' of the way men or women are, that also constrain us. The chapter offers practical ways in which these issues can be acknowledged and addressed in therapy.

Chapter 14 offers an original analysis of the politics of psychotherapy as well as society in general from a Girardian perspective. René Girard's insight into human psychological and political processes are profound but underutilised in psychotherapy, perhaps because they cast an unflattering light on our real motivations and desires and yet these same desires and the insecurities they give rise to are ruthlessly exploited by neoliberal capitalism, making all of us its willing accomplices. This chapter suggests how Girard's central concept of mimetic desire could be integrated into CAT understandings of our human subjectivity.

Chapter 15 explores the theme of what it means to be the beneficiary of racial privilege as a therapist; how being 'white' affects a person materially and in terms of positioning and entitlement. Remaining silent in the face of this becomes a form of collusion. Chapter 16 moves outside the UK to explore the experience of working in Italian mental health services from a CAT perspective. The authors bring their own personal experience as Italian citizens and clinicians in the health service together with a fascinating historical, cultural and political analysis of the social and mental health issues they encounter in Italy. Writing within and from the perspective of a very different but also closely related European culture casts an interesting light on the influence of political and social context on the provision of mental health services.

Chapter 17, the final chapter in the book, brings together many of the issues described in earlier chapters placing these within the context of how psychotherapy training perpetuates the many inequalities, power differentials and unconscious political biases that therapists internalise and replicate in their work if these are not acknowledged and brought out into the open.

Notes

1 UN (2017) report on the right of everyone to the enjoyment of the highest attainable standard of physical and mental health.
2 http://psychagainstausterity.wordpress.com.
3 SRT is a Marxist feminist analysis of capitalism that looks at the complexities of everyday life both in and outside the work place with a particular focus on how labour is maintained and reproduced. Labour rather than commodities is regarded as the primary focus. It is sometimes seen as a Marxist alternative to intersectional analysis of social relations under capitalism according to class, gender, race, sexuality and disability

4 *The Book of Woe* (Greenberg, 2013) describes how the development of DSM involved inventing constructs (rather than listing material realities), which act to reduce and reify complex human relationships into categories that legitimise the power used as an instrument of control as well as offering the appearance of scientific and impartial credibility to psychiatry and psychology.

5 CBT, now more commonly referred to as cognitive therapy, has developed more nuanced and complex ways of working since Ryle was writing in 1990 and the so-called 'third wave' of cognitive therapies such as 'acceptance and commitment therapy', 'mindfulness-based cognitive therapy' and 'dialectical behaviour therapy' have integrated concepts and practices from other modes of psychotherapy that take more into account the social complexity of emotional and psychological distress.

6 Common procedures can be identified by use of the 'Psychotherapy File' (see the Appendix), alongside other common ways in which we limit ourselves, such as snags and false polarisations, known as dilemmas.

7 Although patients sometimes want a diagnosis as it 'legitimises' how they feel and acts as a 'ticket' for mental health services so clinicians must proceed with sensitivity and respect for how patients wish their mental health difficulties to be referred to.

8 When CAT therapists refer to a 'care plan' they mean the actual interactions of staff with clients and each other, not the official Care Plan as defined by the organisation.

References

Ali, Shehzad (2016). Behavioural research and therapy. BPS Digest, 13 June, University of York. https://digest.bps.org.uk/2017/06/13/false-economy-half-of-low-intensity-cbt-clients-relapse-within-12-months (Accessed 02/04/18).

Cheyne, J. A. & Tarulli, D. E. (1999). Dialogue difference and voice in the Zone of Proximal Development. *Theory and Psychology*, 9, 5–28.

Fozooni, B. (2010). Cognitive analytic therapy: A sympathetic critique. *Psychotherapy and Politics International*, 8(2), 128–145.

Fraser, N. (2017). Crisis of care? On the social reproductive contradictions of contemporary capitalism. In T. Bhattacharya (ed.), *Social reproduction theory*. London: Pluto Press.

Greenberg, G. (2013). *The book of woe: The DSM and the unmaking of psychiatry*. New York: Blue Rider Press.

Hirschkop, K. (1999). *Mikhail Bakhtin: An aesthetic for democracy*. Oxford: Oxford University Press.

IAPT (2014–2015). Psychological therapies: Annual report on the use of IAPT services: England 2014/15. http://content.digital.nhs.uk/catalogue PUB19098/psyc-their-ann-rep-2014-15pdf (Accessed 17/06/17).

Kellett, S., Wilbram, M., Davis, C. & Hardy, G. (2014). Team consultancy using cognitive analytic therapy: A controlled study in assertive outreach. *Journal of Psychiatric and Mental Health Nursing*, 21, 687–697.

Leiman, M. (1997). Procedures as dialogical sequences: A revised version of a fundamental concept in CAT. *British Journal of Medical Psychology*, 70(2), 193–207.

Leiman, M. (2002). Towards semiotic dialogism: The role of sign mediation in the dialogical self. *Theory and Psychology*, 12(2), 147–280.

Leiman, M. & Stiles, W. B. (2001). Dialogical sequence analysis and the Zone of Proximal Development as conceptual enhancements of the assimilation model: The case of Jan revisited. *Psychotherapy Research*, 11, 311–330.

Mishra, P. (2018). Why do white people like what I write? Review of *We were eight years in power: An American tragedy* by Ta-Nehisi Coates (2017). *London Review of Books*, 40(4), 17–20.

O'Hara, M. (2017). Mental health and suicide. In V. Cooper & D. Whyte (eds), *The violence of austerity*. London: Pluto.

Parker, I. (1992). *Discourse dynamics, critical analysis for social and individual psychology*. London: Routledge.

Pollard, R. (2008). *Dialogue and desire: Mikhail Bakthin and the linguistic turn in psychotherapy*. London: Karnac.

Rosenzweig, S. (1936). Some implicit common factors in diverse methods of psychotherapy: 'At last, the Dodo said, "Everybody has won and all must have prizes"'. *American Journal of Orthopsychiatry*, 6, 412–415.

Ryan, J. (2017). *Class and psychoanalysis landscapes of inequality*. London: Routledge.

Ryle, A. (1975). *Frames and cages: The repertory grid approach to human understanding*. London: Sussex University Press.

Ryle, A. (1987). Cognitive psychology as a common language for psychotherapy. *Journal of Integrative and Eclectic Psychotherapy*, 6(2). www.acat.me.uk (Accessed 02/04/18).

Ryle, A. (1990). *Cognitive analytic therapy: Active participation in change, a new integration in brief psychotherapy*. Chichester, UK: Wiley.

Ryle, A. (1995). *Cognitive analytic therapy and borderline personality disorder: The model and the method*. Chichester, UK: Wiley.

Ryle, A. (2010). The political sources of reciprocal role procedures, reformulation. *Journal of the Association for Cognitive Analytic Therapy*, 34, 6–7.

Ryle, A. & Kerr, I. B. (2002). *Introducing cognitive analytic therapy: Principles and practice*. Chichester, UK: Wiley

Samuels, A. (2015). *A new therapy for politics*. London: Karnac.

Stiles, W. B. (1997). Signs and voices, joining a conversation in progress. *British Journal of Medical Psychology*, 70, 169–176.

UKCP (2017). Members' circulation June 2017.

UN Report on Mental Health (2017). www.ohchr.org/EN/Issues/Health/Pages/SR RightHealthIndex.aspx (Accessed 29/03/18).

Vygotsky, L. S. (1978). *Mind in society: The development of higher psychological processes*. Cambridge MA: Harvard University Press.

Wampold, B. & Imel, Z. (2015). *The great psychotherapy debate: The evidence for what makes psychotherapy work* (2nd ed.). London: Routledge.

Wilkinson, R. G. (2005). *The impact of inequality: How to make sick societies healthier*. London: Routledge.

Work and Health Programme (2017). www.gov.uk/work-health-programme (Accessed 25/09/18).

2

RECIPROCAL ROLES IN AN UNEQUAL WORLD

Hilary Brown

This chapter explores the impact of inequality on reciprocal role procedures and questions what balance we should aim to achieve between attending to the internal worlds of our clients and acknowledging the wider social systems in which these are embedded. In CAT theory we tend to focus on early reciprocal roles that are internalised by patients from interactions with their primary caregivers, sometimes forgetting how relationships take place against a backdrop of increasing inequality and insecurity.

There is pervasive evidence (Toye, 2011; Wilkinson & Pickett, 2009) that unequal societies generate more troubled and troubling societies across a range of criteria. The model of unchecked capitalism that has allowed this to happen is unsustainable for the planet and the people who inhabit it (Raworth, 2017). Reciprocal roles clarify these findings as, in conditions of more extreme inequality, relationships of exploitation or dependence exceed those characterised by mutuality. Our relationships, suffused by notions of superiority and inferiority, make us relate upwards or downwards with little room for manoeuvre.

These insights usually remain outside the therapy room, unacknowledged in the therapeutic alliance. Instead, the suffering caused by inequality is addressed as if it were a product of the person rather than a by-product of unstable reciprocal roles set up within and between current social hierarchies. Unmanageable feelings of envy, deprivation, humiliation and disconnectedness arise out of skewed interactions and the procedures that individuals fall back on to cope as they seek to persuade themselves that they, and their loved ones, matter. Sometimes actions arising from such pervasive and unmanageable feelings lead people into active resistance to defend against capitulation, at other times they scapegoat people they consider having usurped their rightful place or sink into alienation and depression. When there is nothing to 'be done' they may become involved in compulsively seeking solace through addictions or maintaining illusions, shoring up islands untouched by the outside world in the form of idealised relationships with partners or children that inevitably frustrate or disappoint. All these strategies have outside edges and come under threat.

Psychotherapy seeks to square this circle as individuals reach out for meaning and for relief but when they walk through the door of the therapy room they may find their difficulties pathologised, 'explained' in purely personal terms or their histories reduced to narratives about their particular significant others. It is easy to see how a person might come to blame themselves as a result of this downward delegation of responsibility and feel stigmatised because they need to seek help (Smail, 1987/2015). A more empowering stance would be to redefine the therapeutic task as one of helping the person to come to terms with the way political realities have shaped their personal narratives and to reach out for new, active ways of coping.

Inner and outer worlds

Our work as therapists sits at the intersection between different pressures, as we seek to help our patients separate what is internal and open to change as opposed to external and outside our control. Treating harsh realities such as unwarranted deprivation as if they were personal choices or internal brakes is like recognising symptoms but making a wrong diagnosis. Locating difficulties in the person also risks prescribing a course of treatment that doesn't work because it is aimed at the wrong problem.

Many individuals come to feel worthless in similar ways, and well-defined groups of people share the same fate in ways that provide evidence of this misreading of cause and effect. Examples include the epidemic of depression and anxiety currently being experienced by young women subject to relentless social comparisons through social media and the disproportionate conviction and incarceration of young Black men in the US and in the UK due to pervasive discriminatory, and persecutory, practices. Data like this assumes some mental health issues arise as a direct response to unequal and disadvantageous treatment rather than the result of coincidentally similar parenting techniques. Families operate within a social context and within a matrix of more global inequalities: their role is to mediate between social pressures and individual development and the more unfair those external realities are, the harder their job.

Ryle and Kerr (2002, pp. 6–21) posited that curiosity and experimenting were at the heart of being human and that in favourable circumstances a person would learn about how to relate and achieve through a simple process of trial and error. They inferred that patients seeking therapy might be employing faulty strategies in which their 'aim-directed' behaviour went awry. They mapped procedures where a person's goals were inappropriate, or their actions did not produce the hoped-for results; they noted where their evaluation of feedback led back on itself to confirm unhelpful beliefs and assumptions. The result for patients was often a failed strategy but closed to revision, like being in a hole but continuing to dig oneself in.

They described three kinds of procedures that had the tendency to stall; first, where a person failed to canvas a range of options and instead operated as if there were only two, equally extreme and 'bad' courses of action. This they termed a dilemma; sometimes described as a false or polarised choice, or as black and white thinking. The second procedure they described as a trap, a vicious cycle or self-fulfilling prophecy wherein the outcome serves to confirm the person's initial pessimistic expectations, so they end up more firmly entrenched in negative beliefs about themselves and other people than when they started. The third procedure that leads back in on itself they named as a snag, describing it as a process whereby a person goes a long way towards reaching an appropriate goal but stumbles at the last hurdle, as if they feel that they do not deserve success and/or that it will bring disapproval or envious attack from important people in their life. They related all of these strategies to personal beliefs and behaviours, acquired in the context of repeated interactions with significant attachment figures. They thereby described a comprehensive process of personal learning that could lead a person to feel constrained, unable to break out of old patterns and doomed to repeat the same mistakes.

But turning our eyes outwards we reframe these unhelpful procedures seeing them arising as a result of external pressures and not only, or even primarily, as a consequence of relationships within the family or of processes within the person. Individuals may have been very disadvantaged within their families, but their well-being may also have been compromised by poverty and marginalisation, rammed home through repeated unequal interactions at home, at work, within public services and in their dealings with official agencies.

When we take these wider force fields more fully into account, a polarised choice might be forced rather than false, if society paints certain groups into a corner an individual might be thrown back on despair or aggression where there is no safe middle ground. In societies that hold on to rigid gender roles, for example, a woman may only have two options – conform or escape. A trap might sum up a situation in which there are hoops to jump through that you simply do not have the wherewithal to jump, for example when working long hours does not allow you to live debt free.

Refugees fleeing war, for example, in Syria or Mynamar are faced with unthinkable choices or dilemmas with terrible consequences however they decide: being bombed or shot in their own homes or the risk of drowning at sea and/or disease and destitution.

Women who experience domestic abuse are more likely to be killed when they try to leave, so they are literally, not metaphorically, *trapped* if they stay with their violent partner, but at heightened risk if they leave. In some cultures, women are not allowed to make autonomous decisions and although progress is being made, a policy of aggressively reversing reproductive rights is being pursued. Women, especially those who do not have the potential to be financially independent, face a situation where they either comply or are exiled from family or community. It might then be for the therapist to sit with them while they think through whether to make the best of a situation or to take an enormous risk to leave. Emilion and Brown (2016, p. 120), training CAT therapists in India, urged them to encourage (literally) those women who considered their lives to be in danger to leave despite the strong cultural expectations against doing so. In Western countries too, victims of domestic abuse may have to be actively supported to act drastically to secure a safer outcome for themselves and for their children.

Snags might also be actual, not merely perceived, operating as explicit prohibitions or more hidden threats. In communities riven by inequality, success may lead to real, and not feared, envious attacks. It makes sense to consider these procedures in the light of tangible social inequality and to explore with our clients how far they believe they can safely change. Inequality potentially fractures families so social cohesion cannot be maintained even within the family network. Clients fear that success will be envied rather than celebrated and this led one of my clients to hide the fact that she had been offered a new job because she believed that her sister would feel bad about her achievement. Her sister at that time was in a minimum wage, 'dead-end' job and her feelings of envy and worthlessness were triggered by the fact that other members of the family were in a more fortunate situation. My client decided not to take the new job but by then the damage had been done. This snag was not located in her internal dialogue but in real, external interactions and a sense that she would lose her sister if she pursued her own goal.

Learning inequality in the family

Children are inevitably unequal, relying on their parents and other caregivers to use the power they hold wisely. Holding an outside-in stance in CAT, we see how important it is to meet the inexperience and vulnerability of children with kindness and protection, but poverty in a sea of plenty goes against the humane order of things and leaves in its wake envy, anger and unrest, at a group as well as at an individual level. Within a loving family such discrepancies cast a shadow, but in one marked by personal instability or aggression it lights a long fuse and ignites explosive states.

From the outset, children have inboard detectors of injustice: the cry 'It's not fair' can be heard at picnics and at computer screens across the planet. Children struggle with difference unless there are good reasons why a rule for them is not a rule for everyone. Siblings who have had to give ground to a brother or sister who came too soon after them, or whose special needs trumped their own need for nurture, often come into therapy to revisit these issues as adults because the fallout from these perceived injustices seems to be one that festers, rather than dilutes, over time. Children learn who is valued and who is not inside and outside the family, and they struggle to understand this unfairness whether they eventually occupy roles that are privileged, comfortable but insecure or those that feel diminishing and depriving.

Parenting is especially sensitive to inequalities but the gamut of parenting advice is rarely focused on people living in states of extreme deprivation, as for example in bed and breakfast accommodation or in camps for refugees who have fled for their lives enduring harsh and dangerous journeys.

In CAT we learn about the role of parents in 'enculturating' children (Vygotsky, cited in Ryle & Kerr, 2002, p. 39) incrementally by drawing the infant into the shared signs and language, but also into the system of rules and values, that govern the society, acclimatising them to any injustices that they are likely to face and suggesting strategies for accommodating these, whether by complying or by resisting. Sometimes a 'wayward' child will be bullied into conforming by an otherwise caring parent because they fear the consequences for that child of standing out, others will support their child's own predilections while cautioning them against being open outside the family. Parents may therefore be parenting in defiance of society's prevailing norms or in conformance with them; they may double-down on societal rules or subtly undermine them.

When Ryle (1975) began to explore what he later developed as the model of 'reciprocal roles' he set aside the everyday economically framed unequal interactions between passengers, customers and patients with their ticket collectors, fishmongers and doctors, on the assumption that family relationships are different and more salient in forging our sense of self than these everyday interactions within our workplaces and communities. But our early and most intimate relationships are held within, not operating outside, economic and social realities. Families are always located at a particular nexus in the social hierarchy, determining the outlook, resources and degree to which they and their children will be supported and/ or scrutinised. Mothers and fathers not only bring different personal resources to their early interactions with their children, but are separately and together able to call on different levels of public resource such as housing, health care and assistance with childcare, to cushion the demands of parenting.

Parents' own experiences colour the hopes and aspirations they hold for their children as well as inevitably shaping their skills and styles of interaction. They may consciously model themselves on their own parents or they may act from a part of themselves that felt short-changed by the care they received for themselves in childhood. If they live in a community that expected to succeed they will pass this on to their children together with their own sense of achievement or disappointment. A sense of decline in the social status of one's ethnic group/social class may chafe and lead to resentful or harsh messaging: a child might be told, 'If I could do it why can't you?' or they may be invited to scapegoat others as being responsible for everything their situation seems to lack. If their community 'fits in' or 'stands out' that will be communicated to the child along with clear messages as to how much leeway they will have, and about whether they should seek to challenge authority or if they can risk deviating from accepted norms.

Where families have been scattered by migration, economic pressure or generational conflict, they may find themselves parenting without support in communities that have no shared wisdom about how to cope. Home should be where the heart is, but home may dissolve in the face of debt, eviction or violence and then where is a person's heart and where is a child's stability?

When we take this more outside-in (as opposed to inside-out) view, it becomes clear that what goes on in the relationship between parents and children is a function of their social positioning as well as of their personal competence, narratives, attachments and desires, which is why, as Samuels (2001, p. 28) asserted, 'Individuals live not only their own individual lives but also the life of the times'. The potential repertoire of reciprocal roles that they will be allowed to engage in will be shaped by social pressures as much as by patterns of communication within their family of origin because families mirror power imbalances in wider society.

Extreme inequality makes childhood more treacherous, most notably for children brought up in poverty, but also for children of plenty who fear envious attack or resentful alienation. In societies where class or caste is unacknowledged, individuals are encouraged to see their achievements or difficulties as the product of their own efforts, talents, determination and motivation and not to turn their critical eye back on to the lack of resources, discouragement, exclusions and barriers that have blocked their path or made theirs, or others' personal journeys more hazardous. These wider currents should be there in a person's reformulation and on their map (SDR), to help them make sense of their own particular childhoods and of their own particular parents. The most personal of interactions that shape our childhood selves have never been unadulterated by social positioning or material considerations – they could instead more helpfully be seen as being forged *in* them and *by* them.

Learning about difference

Infancy is a time of intense, significant relationships with our primary caregivers when we learn about our self-worth, are exposed to role models, self-management skills, self-care and emotional regulation; all infused by the material world and the social hierarchies that hold us and constrain us. Later when we meet the world independently through playgroup and school we learn from and place ourselves in relation to our elders, peers and their families. We note differences, challenge the notion our own families are 'normal' or have universal value systems. Difference and inequalities appear through numerous interactions and comparisons mediated by our caregivers and amplified by social media. We may already have encountered people being 'written out of our lives' or being 'written out of the lives of others' because we or they come from the wrong kind of family, the wrong class or the wrong neighbourhood, Some wealthier parents delegate aspects of their childrearing to working-class women, to nurseries staffed by low-paid workers or to boarding schools and their children from a young age will already be learning whether and how these people fit in, are valued or set aside.

Rigid demarcations in the outside world affect the growing person's internal world because weighted differences, on grounds of gender, sexuality, class and race, distort the processes of internalisation, identification and anticipation in the family circle and act as filters for what is allowed in. The simple model of a reciprocal role with one pole consisting of an enactment observed and copied by the child and the other representing their crystallised response state, does not hold water against this backdrop. A response state might be so paralysing that a person gets caught in it but the enacting state, when performed by someone who is different and more powerful or more highly valued can mean that the child or young person may be explicitly told that certain types of interaction are off limits to them. For example, in societies that encourage or enforce gendered stereotypes, girls do not learn in parallel to their fathers in a way that says, 'you too could do this' they are still likely to be told, 'this is what girls should be like to be acceptable to men', 'be my little princess', 'use passive, seductive, ways of getting what you want not active ones', 'don't be angry, men do not like angry women' and 'do as I say and not as I do'. When lodged in her internal world these messages translate into anxieties and body-image issues, into self-policing and self-deprecation. Other-control is eventually experienced as self-control and a 'natural' desire for a partner who, in his ability to dish out selective approval and disapproval, confirms the girl's depleted sense of agency and reinforces the norms that are practised in the wider society.

Garry Younge (2018, p. 1) writes about a prominent politician who occupies a senior office of state, despite very public mistakes, gaffes and sexual scandals, by drawing on the privilege that accrues to him on account of being male, privately educated and well connected. He describes just one instance of the gulf that would open up between his experiences and those of a black woman aspiring to progress to such a role pointing to a time after this man had been fired from an internship at the prestigious *Daily Telegraph* newspaper 'for making up quotes', writing as if he had been a black woman and who was subsequently given a job on the *Telegraph*'s leader-writing team. Younge points out that black women would not be given second chances in this way and would be collectively condemned if one woman was to 'make up quotes' as if they were from a white man and if she were to succeed as a journalist would be seen as an exception. Quite apart from this, Younge writes that to his knowledge the *Telegraph* has never had a black political columnist of any gender.

What might seem at first glance like a career trajectory driven by individual qualities are actually class and race privileges. When he offends, even when his mistakes have had dire consequences for others, he invites his audience to consider it a bit of a laugh, *and they do.* Younge is right to point out that a black woman could not possibly succeed in politics using this blueprint. To paraphrase, she would not be given as many leg-ups, handouts, shout-outs or ways back, instead she would get more put downs, cold shoulders, raised eyebrows, Internet trolling, body shaming and encouragement to stay in, or get back to, 'her place'.

Successful strategies/procedures are dependent on shared perceptions of how men and women of different classes and ethnicities can and should behave and on the ability to work within or bend these to the service of differential goals. Employment roles vary with women often being recruited into vaguer positions as helpmates to men, 'work-wives' whose job includes unspecified 'emotional labour' (Hochschild, 1979) including the need to mollify men who occupy roles with proper agency (Filipovic, 2018). Women must dress in certain ways and temper their assertiveness, not to breach norms that pertain to them as women, not as workers (Gay, 2018).

Some people, catapulted by particular talents, single mindedness, shocking events or lack of conformity, take issue with implicit norms, naming them and stepping outside, while others knuckle under and work within them. In Western liberal democracies our rights to step aside, for example on the grounds of sexuality or other inclinations, have been secured, at least for now, but wherever rigid demarcations are imposed, on and in our communities, they will lodge in the internal world until other-control becomes manifest as self-control. In these ways, gender and class inequalities get under the skin, limiting a child and young person's horizons and putting barriers across his or her path long before he or she comes to perform these identities for themselves.

Power at the heart of reciprocal roles

Our bread and butter, as CAT therapists, is to focus on the early roles that are enacted within the family and particularly on those that come to act as a template for later relationships, leading us to expect, enact, elicit and respond in particular ways and to manage any difficult feelings engendered through these roles using 'procedures' that combine beliefs, behaviour and the potential for change. CAT boils down complex processes of interaction into a two-dimensional process that has an active and a responding part. CAT theory traces how a child internalises these relationships, incorporating them into their own internal dialogue, transforming other-to-self interactions into a self–self dialogue that underpins how we later elicit or avoid engagement with others – that is the self–other component of our behaviour.

We envisage these roles as a central part of a person's mental furniture and consider that we are all likely to operate from both active and responding role positions, as if a person learns what it feels like to be related *to* in a certain way but also sees and learns *how* to relate in that way to others. Changing from one pole to the other, for example by rejecting a bullied victim position and switching into a more dominating, bullying state, becomes a way of coping and fending off unmanageable feelings. Alternatively, a person may switch between responses, angrily defiant one moment and cringingly crushed at another. When responding to a parent or caregiver who is unpredictable and/or unsafe, a child will struggle to find a steady way to be and hence to find a stable sense of themselves. From these positions children learn procedures that protect them and allow them to survive, but many years later arrive in a therapist's office seeking to move beyond these straitjackets. Held hostage by their own ways of coping they cannot find a way out of their resulting unhappiness and restriction, as if they have developed an internal version of Stockholm syndrome, obeying rules that they now issue to themselves and being afraid of words or actions that were forbidden in another time. Therapy might help them challenge these old rules and open up other strategies including asking for help or learning to stand up for oneself or self-soothe in ways that are not harmful.

Although culture is seen as an important context for the internalising of roles in CAT we should be more explicitly exploring how far these roles are skewed according to race, gender, sexuality, class and other social signifiers. As therapists we look for, and try to name, role reversals and especially to bring the doing role into awareness if it is drowned out by the more feeling-laden 'done to' mental and emotional states. But unequal power within, and beyond, the family distorts processes of internalisation. Role reversals may not be possible as a strategy for managing painful subjective experiences or allowed as a route out of damaging realities. Entrenched ways of reacting are as likely to reflect prevailing social messages as historical personal ones and the more forceful and damaging these external messages are (West, 2017), the more they will travel across the membranes that keep a person's internal world apart from the outside world, and the more they infiltrate the person's internal dialogue. So, it is easy to see how, for example, gender or racial oppression undermines a person's confidence and flexibility.

In many cultures, a man may be able to move from being dominated at work to being dominant within his family structure where a woman would not be able to make that transition. Her strategies for dealing with being dominated would have to be less overt and challenging. She may have to take in a sense of herself as a bad or as a failed woman/wife or daughter because she is not allowed to occupy the top pole of this reciprocal role. She may, like many women who joined recent movements to name their experiences of sexual harassment and assault by powerful men, have to 'bide her time'. Similarly, in communities divided by race or skin colour, the latitude afforded to members of the dominant group may not be extended to those who are relatively oppressed or disadvantaged. Their behaviour and options are more heavily scrutinised and policed so that the judged do not, or cannot, become the judges (Emilion & Brown, 2016). Sullivan (2006, p. 173) terms this 'hierarchical' or 'asymmetrical' reciprocity and he considered these roles to be 'reciprocal but not equivalent' because social conventions do not allow every individual to play both parts, exclusions operating on the basis of gender, class and ethnicity. An overt claim to racial privilege and entitlement is back on the agenda of many Western countries as if this would, could or should reinstate the reciprocal role of privileged/superior to disadvantaged and looked down upon that has been challenged by recent upheavals in cultural norms, global economics and technological change.

Recognising the importance of social hierarchies in opening up, or closing down, the repertoire of potential role positions a person is allowed to operate from is essential if we are to understand how class, gender and racial stereotypes are formed, how men and women are shaped differently by economic realities and gender-based violence and to validate the ways in which people try to maintain stability in insecure workplaces or manage tension in their neighbourhood's interactions with law enforcement officials. Marginalised communities necessarily evolve ways of expressing resistance and defiance because people on the receiving end of oppression have no choice but to accommodate to power in their choice of reciprocal role positions remaining vigilant in order to survive.

These processes are universal, but the fact that excluded groups not only fare badly but that more unequal societies flounder, lends weight to the evidence that external inequality seeps inwards before it is projected out again. As therapists we tend to encounter people who, as adults, do not have a sufficient range of role positions to help them function but also, we see people whose roles are contradictory, fragmented or intense. Internalising reciprocal roles takes more than mere observation – it requires an identification that may not be possible across the barrier of these differences. A daughter whose father is a bully will not learn how to act in a bullying way because his behaviour will have been a display of how a man can act to a woman, not of how a woman can exercise her own power.

Extreme, publicly sanctioned versions of disrespect and dehumanisation are the precursors to many atrocities. Lifton (2017) has written about the process of moral corruption in relation to Nazi doctors, psychologists engaged in the torture of people incarcerated at Guatanamo Bay and more recently in relation to Donald Trump. In 2017, Lifton wrote that,

> [e]xtreme ideologues do much to create a malignant normality, which comes to pervade most institutions, including medical ones. Then ordinary people who work in those institutions adhere to that normality, often aided by bits and pieces of the extreme ideology. The prevailing normality can be decisive *because it excludes alternatives and provides strong pressures for destructive behavior.*
>
> *[My emphasis]*

He named this process 'malignant normality' and described how individual citizens adapt to expectations that at another time they would have resisted or repulsed. Society-wide dilemmas are created that limit the options for ordinary people to influence the outcomes of political, and resultant personal, struggles.

Factoring power dynamics into reciprocal roles

When social context is put back into the naming of reciprocal roles, the underlying inequalities in power and access to resources, whether material or emotional, become starkly apparent. This should lead us to question the notion that a patient will inevitably have access to both poles. In CAT we refer to the distinction between 'magisterial', that is imposed, interactions, for example instructions, orders or threats, and 'Socratic' interactions that are more dialogic, tentative and consensual (Jellema, 2005, p. 5). Reciprocal roles as they are played out in the family, in therapy and in society at large, seem to fall into three groups and their impact is more easily appraised if these power dynamics can be named.

1. First, there are 'top-heavy' roles, where power lies exclusively in the enacting pole. These interactions may start out as encouraging or containing, but can slip into infantilising, patronising, coercive or abusive styles of relating. The recipient of such treatment has limited options and tends to capitulate or collapse, which we sometimes describe as feeling 'crushed', or to explode and unsuccessfully retaliate. The predominant feelings are humiliation, resentment,

anger or dependence and it can be difficult to switch roles particularly if the perpetrator draws on social power that the victim cannot claim, as for example if the perpetrator of sexual violence presents as an alpha male, which their victim, whether female or male, cannot and probably would not want to emulate. Victims of these top-down roles can easily be triggered by later events to feel intolerably worthless and crushed. People who have been bullied or belittled, being in no position to turn the tables on their actual harasser(s), sometimes find others who are even more vulnerable than they are, on to whom they visit these harmful ways of behaving. Acknowledgement of the original abuse releases a person from the need to repeat these behaviours and interrupts the cycle.

Gender-based violence, for example, is not a reciprocal role that women can viably get out of by becoming violent to men; they are far more likely to become violent to themselves as a way of coping and of trying to elicit care from others. Tellingly, male victims of sexual abuse by men are more likely to become abusive themselves (if they are not helped) than female victims who cannot step into this position.

2. At the other end of the spectrum, are reciprocal roles that represent the attempts of those without power to organise and elicit the input they need. These are 'bottom-up' roles, they are not responding to, so much as seeking input from others in states of increasing desperation. When they try to assert their needs, they find that they can only get a response by manipulating indifferent others into caring for them, presenting in intense or emotionally demanding ways that are as likely to provoke rejection as to be successful. Their appeals may produce an initial response but over time, the 'giver' is left feeling coerced and put upon as if they had no choice but to attend to the individual; this leads them to step back or to avoid so that the person experiences themselves being rejected and ignored repeatedly. From these underdog positions we see reciprocal roles that include trying to please others, putting a lot out to get a little back, trying to self-soothe or to regulate themselves by eating, drinking, spending or other addictions, but then giving up and blaming themselves for their failure. These are individuals who attune to and try to read the minds of others leaving them little room to be mindful of their own needs, attending to others even when those others exhibit mental states that are unstable or extreme.

Within families these are the roles that Winnicott referred to when describing a 'parental' child, one who with limited developmental and/or material resources took care of the parent's needs, attempting to keep their world stable and viable. Alice Miller (1987) describes how children under threat of violence 'take the blame' for violence even when it has been arbitrary or prompted by their ordinary needs and not by faults or unnecessary demands, because this position maintains a hope that by contorting their sense of self they can 'manage' their unpredictable environment. This also occurs at a societal level – think of a single mother trying to feed her children healthily while owing money to payday loan companies. Marginalised groups within society find themselves 'desperately seeking' fairness, justice and stability and finding that the world turns its back on them.

As Scanlon and Adlam (2011, p. 137) state:

> The implication here is that we have a need for there to be victims of violence, power differentials and relative deprivation in order that 'we-the-included' can have a more secure sense of our own well-being in relation to 'them the excluded, the dis-eased'.

Commenting on both the violence or indifference of the current mechanisms for keeping people in their place and the intransigent refusal of some people to be on the receiving end of this so-called 'help', they describe how '[t]he envy and the shame born of such profound, yet relative, social disadvantage can be psychologically and emotionally crippling and the emergent violence is born of the experience of having been, and continuing to be, psychologically violated'.

3. In the middle ground, we find consensual relationships of mutuality and reciprocity. These roles are more fluid, equitable and 'reciprocal'. Both poles are available to each person and each person is equally influenced by the other, taking turns and acknowledging the gift of the other's presence in their lives. The initiator sets up open-ended conversations in which challenges can be issued and received, clarification sought and both parties respected.

Although emotional deprivation occurs across the spectrum of material wealth, it is concentrated by poverty, instability and displacement. Understanding that not all reciprocal roles are equal, or indeed reciprocal, helps to account for the high levels of intergenerational (di)stress that occur in unequal societies. By decontextualising reciprocal roles and portraying individuals as equal players even when they are not, CAT theory risks collusion with a form of victim-blaming that deflects us from seeing the real sources of painful mental states and hopeless procedures in external social structures rather than in individual pathology. The already broken are thereby re-categorised as inherently damaged, sometimes to be stigmatised and sometimes to be pitied but rarely to be fully respected.

In CAT, reciprocal roles can be grouped into 'top-heavy' or 'desperately seeking' ways of relating in contrast to more equal open-ended and mutual ways of operating. We have colloquial expressions for these skewed forms of relationship: the 'do as I say not as I do' bluster of the bully, the 'give and take' of the mutually respectful interchange, the 'banging your head against a brick wall' that leads to desperation and the 'trying to get blood out of a stone' that sums up the plight of a person whose escalating attempts to draw others into their orbit are met with absence, indifference or withholding. Drawing reciprocal roles with an arrow showing the direction of pull, or with different size poles at each end, helps to make clear where the energy was and where the pain originated from. Drawing *unbalanced* reciprocal roles against the backdrop of social inequality helps a patient to move towards understanding and perhaps forgiveness. Three things need to find their way into our conversations and on to our maps – a historical context, an understanding of the family's class and a sense of the power dynamics that pull at the heart of each reciprocal interaction.

What are the current contours of inequality?

Recent research points to increasing levels of inequality and less social mobility than in previous generations. Numerous studies point to the long-term and pervasive social effects of inequality in terms of increased national rates of suicide, early pregnancy, familial abuse, incarceration and depression (see Wilkinson & Pickett, 2009) and at an individual level in terms of poor health outcomes and early mortality (Hayward & Gorman, 2004). 'The Long Arm of Childhood' (Hayward & Gorman, 2004) links familial socio-economic conditions and educational attainment to later 'lifestyle' decisions such as smoking, drinking and exercise; to different tendencies towards risk-taking, deferred gratification, sense of agency and control; and to exposure to second-hand smoke, poor nutrition, infection and marital violence, all of which have been shown to contribute to premature morbidity and mortality.

While achievement in adulthood can mitigate these early disadvantages, many people find it impossible to escape from the distressing and constraining hold they continue to represent, leading them into stressful and dangerous working environments that further exacerbate their risk. Socially excluded groups are ten times more likely to die early than the general population (Townsend, 2017), or that middle-aged men from disadvantaged backgrounds are twice as likely to be single as those from rich families, (Institute for Fiscal Studies, cited in Elliot, 2017). Gay men experience higher rates of depression and suicidality (Lee et al., 2017), young gay men being at particular risk (Paul et al., 2002) and those with lower educational attainment and incomes also faring worse (Dotinga, 2017), demonstrating the tangible impact of cumulative layers of social exclusion.

Difficult family circumstances provide the context for adverse child experiences, a conceptual measure that has been shown to act cumulatively as a predictor of physical and mental ill-health in adulthood (Lanius et al., 2010). Hence psychotherapy could be characterised as a life-course approach to *mental* ill-health, exploring its sources and, through the reparative relationship, attempting to (re-) build resilience. These studies demonstrate the equivalent (and often comorbid) physiological damage sustained by our patients amply demonstrates the need for long-term sustaining interventions that go beyond individual therapy and that address poverty and housing inequality, access to supportive employment and income support, options for social inclusion and concerted advocacy in support of their rights and access to resources.

The extent of these disparities, even in wealthy countries and their pervasively undermining impact on individuals and on the social fabric, cry out for change. Hayward (cited in Townsend, 2017), labelled those who are socially excluded as 'canaries in the mine' pointing to 'something toxic in our society'. As therapists we must decide where the boundaries are between the past and the present, the internal and the external, but we should never leave individuals in distress carrying the blame for what can be shown to have been the cumulative effect of difficulties over which they had, and continue to have, very little control.

How more unequal societies lead to more unmanageable feelings

Solid mental health seems to rely on stability and the ability to move between manageable states, but when extremes make it difficult for a person to keep themselves steady they may switch between experiencing themselves as entitled to control others or feeling needy and wanting. Recent research suggests that this uneven ground is not only a function of individual families failing to find or keep a foothold, but reflects growing inequalities across our society that separate out winners from losers, distributing resources unfairly and leaving many desperately trying to keep things steady at the expense of others, or sinking into quicksand. It is as if some are held hostage by controlling relationships or community norms, whereas others are abandoned with no one to address their needs or to map their pathways through life.

Many of the reciprocal roles that we name in therapy have their origins in these unequal social structures and these are translated into distress and anger that is re-enacted in the personal sphere. When life paints a person into a corner they feel the shame and disappointment of that at the same time as they harbour an ambition to prove something that cannot always be achieved. Disappointment seeps in. The same cycle is replayed in the next generation leading to more hopes dashed and more disappointment. So, we can see that role positions are situated at the junction between the political and the personal, they are shaped by gendered expectations and linked to class, ethnicity, privilege and/or social status and these structures cement a person into roles that appear to be personal but are borne out of unequal power and unfair access to resources.

Inequality in the relationship between the therapist and their clients

Class is therefore a crucial component of the therapeutic relationship, alongside race, gender and sexuality because the patient cannot help but hear the therapist from a positioned role.

Ryan (2017, p. 120) talks about the ways in which working-class therapists may be invited to feel 'lesser' by patients from higher social classes and the converse may be experienced by the patient of a 'posh' therapist, who they perceive to be unable to appreciate the precariousness of their uncomfortable world.

Theoretically, psychotherapy has been ambivalent about placing responsibility for mental distress at the door of unequal social structures moving instead through cycles of 'understanding' and 'blaming' individuals for their predicament. Freud was silent about race, class and austerity as the tides of Nazism washed up against his doorstep, an omission that might have contributed to his having lost two of his sisters to the Holocaust and to the lateness of his decision to leave Vienna. Persecution is one of those coercive reciprocal roles that leave little room for a flexible response but that cannot be addressed by denial or self-belief. His views on racism were underdeveloped and his narratives removed class or inequality from the equation under the guise of 'analysability'.

Ryan (2017, p. 48) critiques Freud's early case studies in which material relating to working-class carers and servants, who often had more day-to-day contact with children than their mothers, was blanked out. The work of low-income carers a century later, those who augment parental care in homes and day nurseries, may continue to be written out of personal narratives with important individuals being designated unworthy of a place in the person's story. Their absence often goes un-noted and their losses, when they leave are 'ungrievable' (Ryan, 2017, p. 48). This pattern of rendering class invisible within psychotherapy and psychotherapeutic theory persists, but was there from the beginning in Freud's writing, hampering the growth of psychotherapy by unhitching the internal from the external.

How might these issues disrupt the therapeutic alliance? Money may come into private practice as an area of negotiation, but also as a currency for emotional exchange over and above the financial transaction. A sense of relative deprivation may be triggered by payment putting the therapist in a depriving role. Sometimes this provides a window into past trauma and childhood stories of want come to the fore. Deprivation also brings a focus on small and immediate things, as opposed to the making of links or mapping of the past. Why would someone want to map their childhood when they are concerned about whether they have enough money for their bus fare home?

Returning CAT to its radical social roots

Ryle's (1975) seminal 'shortest account of object relations theory' harked back to a time when interaction between genders and classes was structured and predictable, when people could fall back on accepted and expected 'order' that allowed them to relate to people from different places in the social hierarchy without friction, for example, 'in being a traveller to a ticket-collector, a shopper to a fishmonger, or a patient to a doctor, we regard the other, and expect to be regarded by the other, largely in terms defined by the reciprocal roles' (p. 53). These limited and prescribed roles gave rise to routinely repetitive and condescending interactions, of inequality infused with class and race prejudice. Things have moved on, reliev-ing some pressures while extenuating others. The new social agility has brought wealth and opportunity to some, while others have been left standing on the side-lines. Psychotherapists should name these external pressures otherwise they locate a person's difficulties in the personal past when, on deeper consideration, their 'symptoms' would be more accurately portrayed as responses to social dislocation in the present and in the real world. How far can we acknowledge these political realities within therapy without jeopardising our credibility as 'neutral' and technically proficient practitioners? Ahmadi (2011, p. 15) sums up these tensions saying,

> As a woman and a therapist working in frontline services, I have often struggled to find my position in such dilemmas. I have always endeavoured to help patients to find a balance between a narrative focusing on painful, intimate experiences and a narrative to help us both to define our role in relation to the powerful historical and social forces contributing to the patient's difficulties of living.

Can our clients 'get better' if the source of their pain lies in the present as opposed to the past, and is instigated by structural inequality instead of inadequate parenting? Susie Orbach (2016) stated that, 'Like works of literature, which introduce us to characters with increasing complexity and depth, the psychoanalytic endeavour involves the analyst and analysand in a quest to understand a multi-layered inner world.' Radical, social therapies such as CAT, must provide a template defining our task more broadly as the inner world is inextricably created in, and out of, external forces, mediated by individual caregivers certainly, but never impervious to the impact of culture and economics. We might define our task to include a quest to help our patients understand the impact of 'a multi-layered *external* world' on their personal experiences. To reframe a feminist axiom, not only is the personal political; the political becomes personal. Rhona Brown (2010) refers to this quality as 'psycho-political literacy and validity', which should be an integral part of our training and supervision. Doherty (2017, p. 214) argues that, 'when clients are having powerful dysregulated emotional responses to the political situation, we can help them unpack how it connects to their personal journeys' and he speaks of a hope that even in the current political climate, we can act as an 'incubator for empowered citizenry in a democracy where we're neither victims nor flame-throwers'. He sums up the aspirations of this chapter by urging us to integrate our roles as citizens and as therapists. We are all diminished by structures that create winners and losers instead of equals. Inequality is therefore one of the things that matter and one of the things we should mind about. We should never stop wondering about the therapist's role in a world where home can come to seem like 'a shark's mouth' (Shire cited in Bausells & Shearlawe).

Bibliography

Ahmadi, J. (2011). What are the most dominant reciprocal roles in our society? *Reformulation, Journal of the Association of Cognitive Analytic Therapy*, Summer, 13–17.

Bausells, M. & Shearlawe, M. (2015). Poets speak out for refugees: 'No-one leaves home, unless home is the moth of a shark': Five young London poets who have written about displacement and identity reflect on the refugee experience. *Guardian*, 16 September. www.theguardian.com/books2015/spe/16/poets-speak-out-for-refugees (Accessed 18/08/18).

Brown, R. (2010). Situating social inequality and collective action in cognitive analytic therapy. *Reformulation, Journal of the Association of Cognitive Analytic Therapy*, Winter, 28–34.

Doherty, W. (2017). New opportunities for therapy in the 'Age of Trump' chapter. In B. Lee (ed.), *The dangerous case of Donald Trump: 27 psychiatrists and mental health experts assess a president* (pp. 209–216). New York: Thomas Dunne Books.

Dotinga, R. (2017). Gay men's suicide risk rises as income falls. Health Day Victoria Texas. www.gulfbend.org/poc/view_doc.php?type=news&id=193314&cn=9 (Accessed 09/03/18).

Elliot, L. (2017). Men from poor families twice as likely to be single, IFS study finds. *Guardian*, 11 August.

Emilion, J. & Brown, H. (2016). Intercultural supervision: Acknowledging cultural differences in supervision without compromise. In D. Pickvance (ed.), *Cognitive analytic supervision* (pp. 109–122). London: Routledge

Filipovic, J. (2018). Donald Trump and his work wives. *New York Times*, 20 January.

Gay, R. (2018). Roxane Gay on clothes in the workplace: I have never been good at dressing like a woman. *Guardian*, 19 February. www.theguardian.com/lifeandstyle/2018/feb/19/roxane-gay-clothes-workplace-female-employees.

Hayward, M. & Gorman, B. (2004). The long arm of childhood: The influence of early-life social conditions on men's mortality. *Demography*, 41(1), 87–107. https://pdfs.semanticscholar.org/e28d/125b9bde84c1b04c99a63d9e67aa358d6c48.pdf (Accessed 06/03/18).

Hochschild, A. R. (1979). *The managed heart: Commercialization of human feeling*. Oakland, CA: University of California Press.

Jellema, A. (2005). An animal living in the world of symbols. *Journal of the Association of Cognitive Analytic Therapy*, Autumn, 6–12.

Lanius, R., Vermetten, E. & Pain, C. (2010). *The hidden epidemic: The impact of early life trauma on health and disease*. Cambridge: Cambridge University Press.

Lee, B. (ed.) (2017). *The dangerous case of Donald Trump: 27 psychiatrists and mental health experts assess a president*. New York: Thomas Dunne Books.

Lee, C., Oliffe, D., Kelly, M. & Ferlatte, O. (2017). Depression and suicidality in gay men: Implications for health care providers. *American Journal of Men's Health*, 11(4), 910–919. https://doi.org/10.1177/1557988316685492.

Lifton, R. J. (2017). Malignant normality. *Dissent* [online magazine]. Spring 2017. www.dissentmagazine.org/article/malignant-normality-doctors (Accessed 06/03/18).

Miller, A. (1987). *For your own good: The roots of violence in child-rearing*. London: Virago.

Orbach, S. (2016). The poetry of psychotherapy. *Guardian*, 29 October.

Paul, J., Catania, J., Pollack, L., Moskowitz, J., Canchola, J., Mills, T., Binson, D. & Stall, R. (2002). Suicide attempts among gay and bisexual men: Lifetime prevalence and antecedents. *American Journal of Public Health*, 92(8), 1338–1345.

Raworth, K. (2017). *Doughnut economics: Seven ways to think like a 21st-century economist*. London: Random House Business Books.

Ryan, J. (2017). *Class and psychoanalysis: Landscapes of inequality*. London: Routledge.

Ryle, A. (1975). Self-to-self, self-to-other: The world's shortest account of object relations theory. *New Psychiatry*, April, 12–13.

Ryle, A. & Kerr, I. (2002). *Introducing cognitive analytic therapy principles and practice*. Chichester, UK: John Wiley.

Samuels, A. (2001). *Politics on the couch, citizenship and the internal life*. London: Profile Books.

Scanlon, C. & Adlam, J. (2011). Defacing the currency? A group analytic appreciation of homelessness and other inarticulate speech of the heart. *Group Analysis*, 44, 131–148.

Smail, D. (1987/2015). *Taking care: An alternative to therapy*. London: Karnac.

Sullivan, S. (2006). *Revealing whiteness: The unconscious habits of racial privilege*. Bloomington, IN: Indiana University Press.

Townsend, M. (2017). Britain's socially excluded 10 times more likely to die early. *Observer*, 12 November.

Toye, J. (2011). Equality, inequality and reciprocal roles. *Reformulation, Journal of the Association of Cognitive Analytic Therapy*, Winter, 44–48.

Wachtel. P. (2014). An integrative relational point of view. *Psychotherapy*, 51(3), 342–349.

West, H. (2017). In relationship with an abusive president. In B. Lee (ed.), *The dangerous case of Donald Trump: 27 psychiatrists and mental health experts assess a president* (pp. 244–261). New York: Thomas Dunne Books.

Wilkinson, R. & Pickett, K. (2009). *The spirit level: Why more equal societies almost always do better*. London: Random House.

Younge, G. (2018). Boris Johnson's white privilege: Imagine he was a black woman. *Guardian*, 2 March. www.theguardian.com/commentisfree/2018/mar/02/boris-johnson-white-privilege-black-woman (Accessed 07/03/18).

3

PUTTING THE SOCIAL INTO PSYCHOTHERAPY

Implications for CAT

Teresa Hagan, Nicola Armstrong and Jan Bostock

The challenge

We consider how cognitive analytic therapy (CAT) can accommodate the experience of past and ongoing social and personal adversity that is pervasive in the lives of so many people who seek help in the form of psychological therapy. It is important to take Fatimilehin's (2017) challenge to psychological therapy seriously, especially her questioning of the universality of concepts, ideas and theories. We cannot assume that psychological concepts and therapy recommendations are always applicable or appropriate to all groups of people who may seek help from mental health services, and serious attention needs to be given to their position in the social world. We take a critical look at the apparently common-sense notion of coping strategies as commonly used in CAT and ask: What is considered to be healthy or harmful? Who decides on this judgement? Once these questions are raised, closer analysis shows that they are not straightforward but require further elaboration and dialogue.

In order to explore the concept of coping strategies, some of which are considered to be 'problem procedures' in CAT terms, we consider some of the ideas outlined by Smail (2005), Bourdieu (1984) and Ryle (2010), as well as considering the influence of service user perspectives (Spring, 2015). Their work emphasises the need to situate therapy within a social context and can help us consider what this could mean in practice. The analysis brings into focus the reality that effective coping strategies are dependent upon one's position in society, that we may have been overly influenced by white, Western middle-class norms in our understanding of procedures for coping and that we need to think further about our use of language and its implications for the validation we hope to provide in therapy contexts. We suggest that for many people, coping strategies in situations of abuse and adversity are best understood as survival strategies. We think this helps in sense-making with different groups of people seeking help, those with and those without access to significant and important resources, and also explore whose interests are being served. We need to emphasise the importance of a shared understanding that is attuned to a person's social position and perspective and to challenge unquestioned psychological expertise.

Coping strategies in therapy and CAT

It is assumed that we all agree on what makes coping strategies helpful, and much of our day-to-day work with those seeking help involves some version of working with these to name, change and/or improve them. A main therapeutic tool in CAT is the shared understanding through reformulation in which therapists seek to provide genuine validation and a compassionate understanding of a person's difficulties and the patterns of thought, behaviour and feeling, which can be observed and then expressed as problem procedures.

Within CAT, what are regarded as dysfunctional formative relationships and neurobiological vulnerability are thought to combine to lead to psychological distress and associated difficulties, particularly social and relational problems with the self and others through the development of reciprocal roles (RRs) and their associated reciprocal role procedures (RRPs), which in turn can then serve to exacerbate psychological distress. The aim is to address these using reformulation, which aims to provide a validating narrative. A range of factors are regarded as important: biological, familial, cultural and also organisational (see Kerr et al., 2012).

The work of therapy is to name and then recognise reciprocal roles and procedures so that clients will not resort to the historical, defensive, avoidant or symptomatic problem procedures e.g. soldiering on, placating or illness behaviours (Kerr et al., 2012), as these are regarded as maladaptive. For some people seeking help, e.g. those offered diagnoses such as 'emotionally unstable personality disorder', 'psychopathology is conceived as procedural enactments of RRs and associated dialogical voices and a tendency under stress to dissociate into self-states'. CAT works by 'developing a therapeutic relationship in which the client can internalise new RRs leading to new perceptions of self and interacting with others by recognising and revising maladaptive RRPs' (p. 293). The identified RRPs, which are drawn out in sequential diagrammatic reformulations (SDRs), are the current habitual coping procedures. Naming the RR enactments is seen as illuminating and validating showing how these and patterns of coping (the RRPs) reinforce initial formative experiences in vicious cycles. Does conceiving of such habitual coping as maladaptive sufficiently understand the function of such patterns in people's survival? We question whether this could underplay their strengths (see Bradley, 2012).

The aim of CAT is to help the client to reflect on habitual patterns of coping and the Psychotherapy File is used to highlight procedures in the form of traps, dilemmas, and snags (Kerr et al., 2012). Through therapy, it is hoped that new benign reciprocal roles experienced through therapy will have been internalised. It is also acknowledged that 'whilst the relationship is an important aspect of therapy, this is rarely in itself enough to effect significant change' (p. 294). 'Insight helps them [clients] to reduce/contain intense states which lead to desperate coping behaviours (procedures)' and it is acknowledged that clients may also need 'active supportive assistance to deal with problems associated with these coping behaviours' (p. 292), for example substance misuse.

CAT has become a broad umbrella under which a variety of approaches to the understanding of mental health problems are voiced, ranging from the privileging of the more psychiatric/treatment models by e.g. Kerr et al. (2012) to those with a more social materialist perspective e.g. Brown and Msebele (2011). This is in keeping with the spirit of dialogue encompassed within the model and its founder (Ryle, 2010) always encouraged dialogue and innovation in developing the model, even though it has to be acknowledged that some of these approaches do not sit well together. Tensions such as these, however, can be regarded as helpful, laying the ground for more development. When we focus on the impact of historical and current social adversity in people's lives we can make a number of observations.

The impact of social adversity and the importance of trauma-informed approaches

It is assumed, but rarely spelled out in therapeutic writings, that people seeking help in adulthood have significantly changed their position in the world from their childhood, making their habitual patterns of coping no longer relevant or necessary. When meeting with people who continue to endure adversity in their daily lives, this assumption requires revision. One obvious example would be when working with people who are enduring abusive situations, such as domestic violence, where attempting to change RRPs that developed in response to adversity may be a significant and even an endangering challenge.

Childhood exposure to adversity has been linked with a range of serious physical health conditions (chronic lung and heart diseases, liver disease, autoimmune diseases, chronic pain, gastrointestinal problems, gynaecological difficulties and sexually transmitted infection) (Sweeney et al., 2016). Early trauma can have a particularly negative effect on children's development and functioning. Chronic exposure to toxic, prolonged, interpersonal stress is likely to affect children's neurodevelopment and immunological systems due to their state of hyperarousal, and the consequent allostatic load on them physically. There is a greater prevalence of histories of abuse and neglect for people with mental health problems than those in the general population. It has been suggested that half of mental health service users have experienced physical abuse, and more than one-third sexual abuse (Mauritz et al., 2013, cited in Sweeney et al., 2016).

Associated mental health problems include depression, anxiety disorders, memory and attention difficulties, eating disorders, sexual problems, personality difficulties, dissociative problems, substance misuse, post-traumatic stress, bipolar disorder and psychosis (Sweeney et al., 2016). These are linked with the experiences of terror, shock, potential self-blame and powerlessness, which can occur and be associated with both hyper- and hypoarousal, hypervigilance and dissociation. Hence the importance of attending to the embodiment of psychological distress and the impact of social disadvantage, discrimination and adversity.

Taking seriously the long-standing and current array of adverse experiences described by many of those seeking help draws attention to the key roles of humiliation, deprivation and fear in the development and maintenance of coping/survival strategies. Many of these include the helpless damaging and vicarious experiences, which children have to endure as a result of their position in society. These may include:

- helpless witnessing of the repeated humiliation of parents at the hands of welfare agencies, employers, educational and health services;
- repeated insecurity because of homelessness and insecure tenancies;
- hunger as the limited household income is whittled away towards the end of the week;
- being singled out as in receipt of free school meals;
- queuing with others at food banks;
- witnessing your parents struggle to be heard by teachers/doctors;
- being aware that teachers may not like or respect you and have little if any confidence in your talents and abilities;
- being bullied at school for poor clothing and not having 'cool' clothing;
- witnessing your parents' disappointment as they do not get the job they have worked towards;
- enduring noise around your home and having to walk through stinking litter and excrement left throughout the thoroughfare to your home;
- fear of being on the street of your home where violence and assaults are commonplace;
- enduring cold when the meter runs out of electricity or gas;
- trying to appear 'fine' to anyone in authority (and your family) in order to preserve the status quo;
- caring for and constantly worrying about your family members who are disabled and require high levels of assistance for the accomplishment of ordinary routine tasks of living;
- walking past the many facilities to which you are denied access e.g. family gyms, swimming pools, tennis clubs, dance classes;
- experiencing exclusion from the many 'opportunities' on offer at school, which require 'a parental contribution' or possibly worse, offers of special assistance to pay your fare from some charitable fund;
- repeatedly being told 'no' to requests for the many high-status goods advertised for 'cool' kids such as trainers and computer games, which contributes to your status among your peers;
- seeing your parents having to defer to those with power over them.

These experiences differ according to the position of being in a visible minority, where the continued role of institutionalised racism, classism and sexism deny access to good highly valued jobs and positions in society. Different groups in society, dependent upon their access to power, control and resources often continue to experience into adulthood similar experiences to those in childhood.

These experiences are day in and day out, repeated and familiar and in therapeutic writings it has to be acknowledged that we appear to know little about how anyone is meant to cope effectively with them. What would a healthy/adaptive coping strategy look like? These pain-filled experiences are described by many people seeking help in their struggle to build their confidence and sense of purpose. These are the adverse experiences that accumulate and lead to the development of coping or survival strategies. We should never underestimate the costs involved for adults seeking help in their re-telling of these experiences, and the attendant feelings of humiliation, shame and fear for themselves and for those close to them.

The impact of such adversity leads us to consider the ways in which people survive constant threats to their safety, security and self-esteem. Having a 'threat' system primed to act could be as important and helpful in adulthood as it was when it developed in childhood. This is especially pertinent for those who experience verbal/physical attacks and constant undermining in social conditions of homophobia, racism and sexism. It may be necessary to be able to block out feelings in order to cope and the 'placation trap' can be seen to be especially useful to those with little, if any power and control in their lives. This has been found to be apparent for those trapped in domestic violence where 'status quo' survival strategies seem the safest. In conditions where there is no recognition that abuse is unacceptable and where there is ineffective protection against further abuse, there is a lot to risk losing in standing up to abuse (Bostock et al., 2009).

We suggest that rather than being seen as maladaptive, procedures or coping strategies developed in the light of such ongoing experience of adversity and threat, are more helpfully expressed as *survival strategies*.

The fit between survival strategies and one's position in the social world

The insights of Vygotsky (1978) have illuminated to some extent the developmental processes of RRPs as acquired from the culture in which one is embedded. But such thinking has had little, if any influence on the power dynamics relevant to therapy. It is unusual in CAT to find any reference to linking procedural sequences to social positions occupied by those seeking help.

The writings of Bourdieu (1984) can be particularly helpful in deepening our understanding of survival strategies and what can be involved in trying to understand and change these. He offers insights that are not readily visible in the theorising used by CAT, offering a set of concepts that can be used to help and specifically drawing attention to power relations that make up the social world.

Each of us occupies a position in society in which we carry on our daily business in any number of key areas: home (if we have one), work (if we have a job), organisations we have to deal with and our neighbourhoods and communities (if we have one). These are referred to by Bourdieu (1984) as 'fields', namely sets of specific complex social relations.

In each of the fields, we may occupy dominant/subordinate or other positions depending upon our access to power and resources in that field. In carrying on our daily business, we develop a certain 'disposition for action' that is conditioned or overdetermined by our position in the field (so, for example, a man could be subordinate at work but dominant in the home.)

This disposition, combined with every other one we develop through our everyday engagement with the world, which Bourdieu (1984) calls our 'practice', will eventually come to constitute a system of dispositions – known as 'habitus' – that can be viewed as 'the sea we swim in'. Dispositions are 'a sense of the game', a partly rational but partly intuitive understanding of our social world and of the social order in general. They are a practical sense, giving rise to opinions, tastes, tone of voice, facial expression, typical body movements, mannerisms and preferences and are therefore key to understanding the development and maintenance of habitual coping/survival strategies.

The dispositions are to be regarded as conditioned responses to the social world, becoming so ingrained that they come to occur spontaneously. Bourdieu (1984) shows that these dispositions will typify our position in the social world. It therefore follows that some will be shared by people occupying similar positions. He theorises that in going about our everyday lives, we usually tend to also reproduce and legitimate the forms of social hierarchies that are in evidence, e.g. domination and subordination. This would include adopting/adapting to the common opinions prominent in each field that are experienced as self-evident. This can cloud from consciousness even the acknowledgement of other possible power relations and some apparent contradictions (such as when women find themselves joining in the oppression of other women) become understandable and almost predictable. If Bourdieu is correct, then it would be expected, for example, that women will be subject to sexist and demeaning views of women in general and find themselves with conflicted and conflicting feelings towards themselves and other women.

The writings of Bourdieu are not to be regarded as a totally deterministic view. He stresses that no field in which we take part can be completely stable but that given their power to imprint upon us the way to be, there will be measureable and hard to shift continuities in society, e.g. the consistent 'failure' of certain social groups to 'succeed' in the education system, and even 'artistic' preferences that have been shown to display concordance with social position. Such processes are regarded as a main means by which inequalities in society are maintained.

Children internalise these dispositions at an early age. They guide the young towards their 'appropriate' social positions, the behaviours that are 'suitable' for them and foster aversion to other behaviours. When we feel something is 'right', the world is in order, we know how to be in a social situation to the extent that we would not be able to articulate what we are doing, we just do, like riding a bike. The opposite then is also the case when we can find ourselves in a situation (or field) where we feel quite out of place and we don't know the rules, we do not know what to expect.

Some people seeking therapy are all too familiar with what therapy is all about, while for others it can be experienced as an unknown quantity. These dispositions are 'cognitive structures, internalised, embodied social structures' (Bourdieu, 1984, p. 470) becoming natural to the individual. We act according to our 'feel for the game', where our psychological strategies and expectations would be referred to as a part of the game that we adapt according to our habitus, being the field in which we take part e.g. the education system or the family.

We develop strategies that are adapted to the needs of the social worlds we inhabit, and these are unconscious (below consciousness) and act on the level of a bodily logic, like knee-jerk reactions. This would mean that changing our survival strategies cannot be achieved through voluntary agency alone, e.g. trying hard. Survival strategies that comprise schemes of perception, thought and action, develop and are maintained in response to the objective conditions encountered. This shows the importance of paying attention to the conditions in which people live.

Social adversity and the scope of psychotherapy

Some therapeutic approaches encourage us to acknowledge and map the adverse ongoing situations that people live with; for example, those experiencing racism (see Brown et al., 2011), sexual abuse (Hagan & Gregory, 2001) and to explicitly talk about the scope for change and access to power and influence (Bostock, 2017). In her teaching, Dhanjal (2014) relates the experience of working with people in the army where the room for manoeuvre can be very limited. Others have also acknowledged the sheer levels of difficulties faced by some client groups, and suggest adding in other approaches to address difficult memories, for example, somatosensory approaches (Ogden, 2006) desensitisation or eye movement desensitisation and reprocessing (EMDR). The challenge of reintegration and rehabilitation is frequently not addressed in CAT, and there is some recognition that some clients may benefit from multidisciplinary team input and longer packages of care, extended follow-up and support including social rehabilitation (Kerr et al., 2012, p. 296 ff). There has been little, if any development of systematic ways in which to incorporate the material realities of the social world into reformulation and the crucial impact of snags, which can be viewed as systemic and external.

Ryle (2010), the founder of CAT, urges us 'to recognise the harmful effects of both current and internalised historical and social factors' and warns us not to join the *sleepwalkers* and to attend to the ultimate as well as the intimate influences on well-being, noting that otherwise we are working with at best partial formulations. He outlines how CAT has moved steadily from the individual to understanding the social formation of individual personality and warns that we may fail to identify powerful but less obvious contemporary influences, noting that to question one's place in the world requires one to understand how, and in whose interests, one's personality has been shaped. These social forces may be challenged by the ideas of the articulate few, but they also engender the distresses, which bring people to psychotherapy. Psychotherapists seldom spell out how individual values and assumptions may be derived from the past and the present interests of the powerful, in part because we too are shaped by the same forces. Subversive or rebellious ideas tend not to be considered, voiced or acted upon.

Exits may include replacing a passive acceptance of the ideas of the socially dominant with an exploration of an infinitely rich and complex critical and oppositional dialogue. If we restrict our attention to the immediate family or friends and leave wider social forces off the agenda, we distort reality and cannot share or validate the reality of people's social and psychological lives. Social and historical forces form aspects of the self or dispositions that may feel innate or 'given' because, in most cases, they have never been articulated, let alone questioned. In our work as psychotherapists we should recognise and name them. We live in a dangerous and unhappy world and are well placed to know some of the human costs even though we have no claim to know the solutions (Ryle, 2010).

The thoughtful and challenging comments from Ryle above resonate with ideas to be found in both Bourdieu (1984) and Smail (1997) and encourage us to look outside of individuals in order to make sense of their survival strategies. We need to cease to rely on what seem to be exclusively internalised theories, which have been privileged in the therapy world (Hagan & Gregory, 2001). Bourdieu in particular has helped to articulate what we think of as the socialisation process, the process whereby a child internalises the social world in which they are born, adopting the meanings and language that surrounds them and consequently developing strategies that are attuned to their world. Where their world is particularly harsh, these strategies will be pertinent to their survival and some authors, e.g. Spring (2015), speak of dissociation as 'a sane response to some very insane things'. Recognising the reality of this with those seeking help can be experienced as validating and sane-making. For many people in abusive situations coping is about surviving in a world when they fear not surviving. It is about getting through at that moment in time in the best way possible, with no time or opportunity to rationalise, to challenge their thinking, and balance the long- and short-term benefits. Dissociation is an understandable response to dangerous circumstances. If this is not acknowledged, people can feel pathologised rather than understood.

How can CAT meet some of these challenges?

Understanding symbolic violence

Therapists and clients alike have developed their habitus/system of dispositions and any group holding power over another can enact a form of 'symbolic violence' over those with less power and resources. This highlights the need for us to be reflexive, and to pay attention to the effects of our own position in service provision (as therapists, therapy clients and/or experts by experience). We need to explore our own reciprocal roles and how these can affect understandings of others who do not occupy similar positions, noting, for example, that professional jobs in psychology and psychotherapy do tend to be dominated by the white middle class.

Re-formulation that accounts for adversity

In contexts where reformulation reveals particular formative and current cultural contexts that are beyond the remit or power of mental health professionals to address or modify, it is suggested that 'sociocultural micro-mapping' may be important in identifying and acknowledging the impact of such influences and how they might affect attempts to offer therapy or social assistance. Formulations that go beyond the intrapsychic and offer a broad understanding that accounts for social, physical and psychological influences on distress can be incorporated into CAT re-formulations (Bostock, 2017).

It is also acknowledged that in the absence of social support, social purpose, identity and meaning, some people are 'beyond the reach or remit of psychotherapy services in the NHS as presently constituted' (Kerr et al., 2012). The power-mapping work of Hagan and Smail (1997) has been referred to as one example of sociocultural micro-mapping that can help to highlight domains of power and powerlessness. But this has not been integrated into the reformulation process in CAT or wider clinical psychology practice. While the CAT Psychosocial Checklist (ACAT, 2004) is intended to provide a means of discussion, it does not provide a systematic model to understand and acknowledge adversity and its ongoing impact in a person's life and survival strategies. The checklist seems to assume an awareness of psycho-political realities that may not be available to people seeking help, and it also seems to assume that key characteristics such as gender or ethnicity cannot also be experienced as sources of pride and value (even within cultures that may denigrate some).

However, it is within the scope of CAT to re-formulate in the light of an understanding of how power has been used in an individual's life, what threats they have and still experience, and how the settings in which they live may perpetuate threat and power abuse. This analysis can inform a shared understanding of how these influences have been and are embodied, and how they translate into their dispositions for action and survival strategies.

In Figure 3.1 we show one way of incorporating the distal and powerful influences of the wider social world on the way in which reformulations can be constructed. One of the main difficulties is that the more distal influences are much less visible in our day-to-day lives, but may be very powerful. Distal and societal forces are experienced via proximal fields and where there is exposure to abuse, discrimination, adversity and entrapment, we detail how reciprocal roles are enacted and linked with psychological costs. Reciprocal roles and procedures are societally and culturally driven and influence relationships that are experienced as proximal, personal and individual. These are a part of our habitus, the dispositions that encompass procedures or survival strategies such as appeasing, soldiering on and self-protection through avoidance, dissociation and hypervigilance. We give

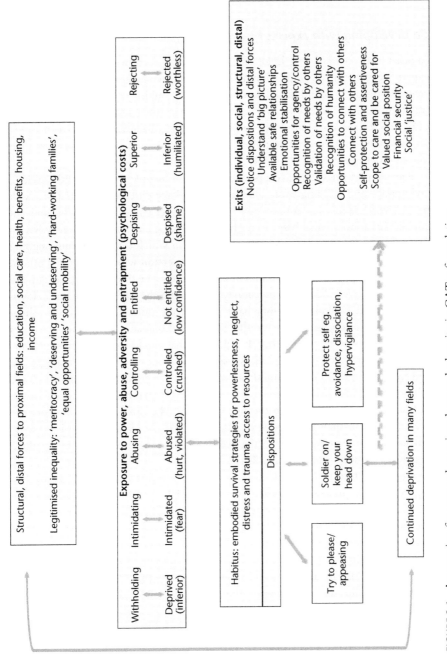

FIGURE 3.1 Accounting for past and ongoing abuse and adversity in CAT reformulation.

examples of exits that are social as well as individual and illustrate the need for benign and enabling relationships in order that individual exits can be developed.

Co-developing with experts by experience

Another way forward that holds much promise is working in partnership with experts by experience and developing ideas around working collaboratively in services and research. Brandon and Armstrong (2013) outline an extremely important way to bring into focus a range of aspects of service provision that could be more validating for those seeking help, namely working collaboratively between a person who uses services, carers/families/friends and those who provide services with the acknowledgement of genuinely shared expertise.

Peer support roles can have a positive impact on people engaging with services, giving hope and building trust. They are able to have different conversations with people who use services as they have less power over clinical judgements and can connect on a more equal basis. In terms of what has gone before, they may have a key role in developing benign/supportive fields in which those enduring ongoing adversities could gain some resources such as connection with like-minded others, supportive social bonds, friendship, mutuality and cooperation. It also opens up the possibility to give collective expression to articulating alternative views (see below).

Berger and Luckmann (1966) have persuasively outlined the way in which social institutions have a 'facticity' that defines and regulates what takes place and that also gives a sense of authority. It is possible that psychological therapy modalities could learn much from experts by experience about what survival strategies are and aren't effective in preserving their well-being. We could develop a rich source of knowledge with people who have been enabled to maintain their mental health or recover their mental health through adversity. We can acknowledge here the contributions to such knowledge that have been made by those who have written about their experiences, texts that many people using our services have valued (examples would include Spring, 2015).

Co-production needs to extend to evaluations and research into the psychological therapy processes in order to understand how power operates from the perspective of people using services. Service user and carer researchers with participatory and emancipatory methodological frameworks support more openness and can enrich the quality of information and how it is collected, analysed, interpreted and written up. These ideas also demonstrate why diversity is so important in mental health care and therapy contexts, to ensure that what we are discussing with people who use psychological therapy is reasonable or even possible in the context within which they live.

Comparing distinct survival strategies

There could be value in explicitly comparing people occupying different positions in society – those who are constantly and almost consistently receiving positive affirmations and approval in whichever field they occupy, and those who are constantly and consistently receiving negative feedback. Key reciprocal roles and their related procedures that are likely to be in evidence would include: valuing to valued, undermining to worthless, rewarding to rewarded, withholding to deprived. Those occupying valued positions in society through the repeated experiences of being valued and rewarded (both in the past and currently), are likely to develop distinctly different coping/survival approaches from those occupying less valued positions, coping with repeated experiences of being devalued and deprived. Learning conspicuous consumption (the tastes of luxury, Bourdieu, 1984) would apply to one group, while learning to do without (the tastes of necessity) would apply to the other. Both can be seen as having an important impact on self-compassion.

Notions of 'dependence'

There is a current emphasis in mental health care on encouraging people seeking help to develop 'better' coping strategies in order to achieve self-reliance, independence and self-help as worthy goals. This requires further critical understanding that CAT can facilitate. If we were to lay out the many and varied examples of other-reliance, interdependence and other-help enjoyed by those in comfortable positions, the matter can become clearer.

It has become commonplace and unquestioned for members of the more privileged groups in society to show high levels of dependence on others over whom they have power and influence, to secure both paid and unpaid support. For example, significant help is routinely secured with childcare, driving, organising, shopping, cooking, cleaning, laundering, gardening, dog walking, exercise, money management, fitness and relaxation. Reliance upon and control of others would seem to be a powerful approach to coping, which is not available to all in society. Some groups can also be seen to adopt further strategies to maintain their positions through the preservation of family wealth, the allocation of significant/unearned resources to their offspring, the development and maintenance of networks of influence and control and the courting of the influence of others in authoritative/ valued positions to access and maintain generous pay and allowances.

These assets show the extensive material and social resources that can be secured and deployed by those with power and also, by contrast, the poverty of cultural and practical supports available to many others seeking help. Mapping out the day-to-day experiences of those with significant power and resources, may tell us much about what is desirable/needed to maintain well-being and help us understand the persistence of lower mental health among those who are relatively deprived. It may also illuminate the potential costs involved for the privileged, such as unrealistic expectations of entitlement that can alienate people from others and set the stage for social isolation and constant anxiety to maintain one's favoured position. Divisions of this sort can lead to a lack of real empathy for others, a tendency to bully and exploit others and the consequent costs on both sides.

Validating survival strategies

What are the conditions within which a person might be able to change/improve their strategies? What would be required to maintain their mental health? Entirely intrapsychic coping strategies that can be recommended through therapy may be of use to those who are comfortable but will be of limited, if any, use to others. Some strategies that are more likely to be consistent with occupying a relatively power-less position in the social world come to mind, such as 'soldiering on' whereby a person may need to keep their head down. This may be costly in terms of self-confidence, physical, mental and emotional exhaustion, but practically useful (and required) in their exposed social position. To pathologise this as a dysfunctional coping strategy would be ignoring and invalidating their experience.

People can find themselves in low paid and low status jobs requiring many hours of work, feeling guilty about their absence from their children and homes and in positions where they are required to defer to their employer/s, take up an inferior to superior role, server to served, neither of which is likely to build high levels of self-esteem or self-compassion. It may be the case that we stand in need of having a lot to learn from those occupying deprived positions in society about what are effective ways to cope. How can one maintain one's self-confidence and belief in such circumstances? How can one deal with persistent devaluing in the media? Are there ways of maintaining one's well-being on very limited means? We also should consider how we learn about the destructive and overpowering strategies that are in the repertoire of those with whom we live in hierarchies of power, in order to build social environments that are more enabling of people's well-being.

The promotion of benign fields

It follows then, that we may need to ask whether or not a person has access to any validating/supportive 'field' in which to change/develop their coping strategies. There is the possibility that working with others facing similar difficulties could offer at least one 'benign field' in which clients are enabled to gain a better under-standing of their difficulties in a validating setting. Guy Holmes' (2010) group work illustrates how people from different backgrounds can explore psychological and social theories to understand and cope with various aspects of their lives such as toxic mental environments, coming off psychiatric drugs, sharing what leads to the experience of depression. These groups also offer the chance of having painful experiences recognised and validated, and sharing mutual encouragement and ideas and support for acting to change difficult situations.

It also may help us to acknowledge the difficulties that can be faced by people once discharged from therapy in 'maintaining' their gains if they do not have access to 'fields' outside of services that promote this and also the real difficulties of doing 'homework' between therapeutic sessions. In setting expectations in therapeutic work, we may also need to acknowledge that people learn to want what conditions make possible for them and not usually to aspire to what is not available to them.

Spring (2015) describes the need for 'a place where you can think and feel and begin to mentalise, to move from victim to resilient survivor', which she found in therapy. It may also help us to come to terms with the limitations of an individual therapy approach for others. Support through the Internet may also be a means of building more amenable shared fields that support people and offer alternative ideas that may not otherwise be easy to articulate.

Embodiment

These ideas bring into focus the importance of recognising the embodiment of coping strategies (e.g. in trauma work the notion that the body remembers, see Van der Kolk, 1994) and just how difficult it can be for a person to try something different that requires them to ignore/overcome all that their body is telling them. Bourdieu (1984) stresses how imprinted these can be and in therapy it has often been a struggle to reframe good self-care as not being a luxury, while everything in some people's lives tells them that it is. Therapeutic work with embodiment may complement the verbal bias of CAT and help people to become more attuned to being compassionate towards themselves, an idea that is often unfamiliar to people using mental health services.

Concluding comments

There is a need for us to question the assumptions that underlie our work, a need to develop a more coherent understanding of the processes by which strategies are developed and maintained, and the circumstances in which they can be changed or improved. We need to guard against setting people up to fail in their therapeutic work by taking full and explicit account of what could be possible. And we need to be alert to the ongoing subjugating discourses and practices that may impinge upon them while also bearing in mind their strength to build on.

The ideas of Bourdieu (1984) and Smail (2005) can enrich CAT re-formulations when people's dispositions for action, and the embodiment of these, are viewed with reference to an understanding of the complex social relationships in their immediate environments. These are influenced by the assumptions and practices in their wider worlds, predicated on their access to power. Such considerations help to describe a bigger picture in relation to what may have and still is influencing feelings and responses. This is fundamental to a more attuned psychological therapy.

Understanding and validating people's strategies for survival in the light of these considerations is important. It may take time and a change to being in a safe situation in order to make it feasible to gain a new perspective on particular ways of getting through life. There needs to be a clear discussion of alternatives that resonate with the person seeking help, and we need to create the opportunity for sensitive conversations. However, from a service user perspective, enabling people to view themselves in relation to their strengths, skills and abilities as opposed to the usual position of feeling fractured, broken, disordered and a problem is vital.

Such a strength-based approach is possible in CAT and may enable people to envisage connecting with others to gain more power over their lives, so long as there are sufficiently benign conditions.

We can generate valuable knowledge by working co-productively with experts by experience. In a social world of unequal access to power and resources (the context within which a person resides), we cannot take for granted that the types of strategies likely to be helpful to one group are going to be helpful to another. Psychological therapists have a responsibility to articulate what people need, for example; 'routine and stable daily access to a set of benign experiences at home, in public spaces and at work, along with confidence in an adequate welfare state' (Sen, 1998, cited in Pilgrim 2017, p. 35). However Ryle's (2010) caution remains pertinent in that we should not pretend to know more than we do. We need to take a humble and open approach to ensuring we understand and address the social as well as the psychological with CAT, while accepting the limitations of therapeutic power.

Bibliography

ACAT (2004). CAT psycho-social checklist. www.acat.me.uk. www.acat.me.uk/refor-mulation.php?issue_id=14&article_id=237 (Accessed 08/12/17).

Berger P. & Luckman, T. (1966). *The social construction of reality: A treatise in the sociology of knowledge.* New York: Anchor Books.

Bhattacharya, S. (2014). The lifelong cost of burying our traumatic experiences. www.newscientist.com/article/mg22429941-200-the-lifelong-cost-of-burying-our-traumatic-experiences (Accessed 31/10/17).

Bostock, J. (2017). Understanding power in order to share hope: A tribute to David Smail. *Clinical Psychology Forum,* 297, 13–17.

Bostock, J., Plumpton, M. & Pratt, R. (2009). Domestic violence against women: Under-standing social processes and women's experiences. *Journal of Community and Applied Social Psychology,* 19, 95–110.

Bourdieu, P. (1984). *Distinction: A social critique of the judgement of taste* (English translation). London: Routledge.

Bradley, J. (2012). A hopeful sequential diagrammatic reformulation. *Reformulation, Journal of the Association of Cognitive Analytic Therapy,* Summer, 13–15.

Brandon, T. & Armstrong, N. (2013). Is there a pathway to recovery through care coordi-nation? Service User Research Steering Group. www.rwire.co.uk (Accessed 08/12/17).

Brown, H. & Msebele, N. (2011). Black and white thinking: Using CAT to think about race in the therapeutic space. *Reformulation, Journal of the Association of Cognitive Analytic Therapy,* Winter, 5–8.

Brown, R. (2011). Flowers by the window: Imagining moments in a culturally and politi-cally reflective CAT. *Reformulation, Journal of the Association of Cognitive Analytic Therapy,* Summer, 6–8.

Dhanjal, R. (2014). Lecture notes. DClin Psy Community Psychology Module, Sheffield University (available through T. Hagan).

Fatimilehin, I. (2017). Working across boundaries in services for children, young people and families. *Clinical Psychology Forum,* 297, September.

Hagan, T. & Gregory, K. (2001). Group work with survivors of childhood sexual abuse. In P. Pollock (ed.), *Cognitive analytic therapy for adult survivors of childhood sexual abuse* (pp. 190–215). London: Wiley-Blackwell.

Hagan, T. & Smail, D. (1997). Power-mapping 1: Background and basic methodology. *Journal of Community and Applied Social Psychology*, 7, 257–284.

Holmes, G. (2010). *Psychology in the real world: Community-based group work*. Ross-on-Wye, UK: PCCS-books.

Kerr, I., Bennett, D. & Mirapei, C. (2012). Cognitive analytic therapy for borderline personality disorder. In J. Sarkar & G. Adshead (eds), *Clinical topics in personality disorder clinical* (pp. 286–307). London: RCPsych Publications.

Mauritz, M., Goossens, P., Draijer, N. & van Achterberg, T. (2013). Prevalence of interpersonal trauma exposure and trauma-related disorders in severe mental illness. *European Journal of Psychotraumatology*, 4. www.ncbi.nlm.nih.gov/pmc/articles/PMC3621904.

Ogden, P., Minton, K. & Pain, C. (2006). *Trauma and the body: A sensorimotor approach to psychotherapy*. New York: W.W. Norton.

Pilgrim, D. (2017). The necessary ambivalence of David Smail: A critical realist reflection. *Clinical Psychology Forum*, 297, September.

Ryle, A. & Kerr, I. (2002). *Introducing cognitive analytic therapy*. Chichester, UK: Wiley.

Ryle, T. (2010). The political sources of reciprocal role procedures. *Reformulation Journal of the Association of Cognitive Analytic Therapy*, Summer, 6–7.

Smail, D. (1997). *Illusion and reality: The meaning of anxiety*. London: Constable and Company Ltd.

Smail, D. (2005). *Power, interest and psychology: Elements of a social materialist understanding of distress*. Ross-on Wye, UK: PCCS Books.

Spring, C. (2015). Recovery is my best revenge: My experience of trauma, abuse and dissociation. https://carolynspring.co.uk/recovery-is-my-best-revenge-overcoming-trauma (Accessed 25/08/17).

Sweeney, A., Clement, S., Filson, B. & Kennedy, A. (2016). Trauma-informed mental healthcare in the UK: What is it and how can we further its development? *Mental Health Review Journal*, 21, 174–192.

Van der Kolk B. A. (1994). The body keeps the score: Memory and the evolving psychobiology of post-traumatic stress. *Harvard Review of Psychiatry*, 1(5), 253–265.

Vygotsky L. S. (1978). *Mind in society: The development of higher psychological processes*. Cambridge, MA: Harvard University Press.

4

THE DE-RADICALISATION OF CAT

A regressive interaction of economics, theory and practice?

Rachel Pollard

In some respects psychotherapy as currently practised confers more benefits on its practitioners, in terms of financial rewards, status, personal fulfilment and ambition than it does on the people in receipt of it. However progressive we might consider our politics to be, those of us that are paid are still parasitic on society's injustices and imperfections while those of us who work for little or no money are exploited. The closer we are to the people at the sharp end of injustice and inequality the more aware we become of these contradictions and the more it affects our own mental health and ability to practice according to our own values.

This chapter discusses the interactions between economics and mental health. While contemporary economists acknowledge the psychological influences on people's economic behaviour, psychotherapy theory, including CAT, rarely if ever take explicit account of economic conditions and how these affect mental health. This is a stark omission given that deteriorating levels of mental health in the population are strongly associated with the prevalence of neoliberal economic policies that have led to widening inequalities in the distribution of wealth and power in society. I will discuss how the development of CAT has interacted with economic conditions and the extent to which the values of CAT have been compromised by harsh economic realities. I will then consider how a practice of psychotherapy informed by the ethics of the Russian philosopher, Mikhail Bakhtin, could potentially offer a space beyond theory in which we could, alongside our clients, find the freedom to think for ourselves. There is a growing awareness of and anger about the effects of government policies on mental health among psychotherapists and psychologists but what happens in the therapy room is unlikely to lead to significant political change without political action outside it. And even for those therapists disinclined towards political campaigning, the very least we can do is not perpetuate the insidious values of neoliberalism in our work and instead provide a space where people can question the roles society has assigned to them and the values associated with those roles.

Psychotherapy under neoliberal capitalism

Twenty years ago the general atmosphere among the small CAT 'community' was one of enthusiasm and optimism. Since then the political landscape has changed. The hoped for fairer and more just society that ushered in the years of 'New Labour' after 18 years of Tory rule evaporated with the anger and disillusion that set in after the disastrous 2003 Iraq war, along with the realisation that the Blair government was considered by many to be merely a political variation on Thatcherism.

It may be significant that CAT was devised around the same time that neoliberalism as a political and economic doctrine was tightening its grip on Western 'democracies'. The importance of this economic doctrine and the policies that emerge from it cannot be underestimated in the effects it has on everyone globally and nationally. More an ideology than a rational research-led approach to economic policies, neoliberalism has elevated the 'economy'[1] high above the welfare of the people the 'economy' is supposed to serve. Neoliberalism was originally based on a theory of human subjectivity that asserted that all human activity is based on rational economic self-interest and that with minimal interference by the state, the free market would maximise efficiency in all aspects of economic activity. The subjects of neoliberalism cultivated themselves so as to maximise their capacity to compete in the market for jobs, material goods and status. There is no recognition of human value or subjective experience beyond economically productive activity, reducing human beings to units of production and consumption.

In the 1970s, economics was a social science, primarily concerned with human behaviour and welfare; economic policies were formulated and evaluated according to the affects they had on people's lives. The dominant economic model then was J. M. Keynes' *General Theory of Employment, Interest and Money* (1936) in which state intervention in the economy was seen as both desirable and necessary to ensure high levels of employment and investment in key industries and social welfare, even at the expense of running a deficit. Keynesian economic policies, sometimes referred to as state-managed capitalism, were adopted widely by governments after World War II and although the 'General Theory' is not a Marxist theory or even a theory of the left, its policies are associated with more state spending on welfare and state ownership of industries of national importance, such as transport and energy. Crucially Keynes recognised the interdependence of each country on other countries in a global economy and how it was in the interests of the stronger economies to support the weaker ones.[2] Keynes fell out of favour during the 1970s as Western economies failed to maintain full employment or control inflation. This was a result of the US President Nixon's decision to end the fixed exchange rate between the dollar and other currencies and the post-war support for struggling European economies. This meant a return to floating exchange rates leading to widespread economic instability. Orthodox Keynesians attributed the failure of governments to stabilise their economies to insufficient state intervention in the economy but were sidelined in favour of the monetarist Chicago school of economists who redefined the study of economics as an 'objective science' rather than a branch of social science concerned with human welfare. This led to government policies focusing on maximising market efficiency by tinkering with the money supply rather than by investment in jobs and services. Economics as it is taught in universities now has become a branch of applied mathematics that studies the markets and is no longer concerned with economic policies as a way of achieving desirable social goals (Earle et al., 2016). The idea that economics is an 'objective science' best left to experts has led to a dangerous split between economic decisions and political outcomes. Economic policies are always political in their intent and effects and should be subject to democratic oversight. Yanis Varoufakis (2016) writes that, 'The notion that money can be administered apolitically by technical means alone is a dangerous folly of the grandest magnitude' (p. 97). This misguided faith in the markets and technical adjustments to the money supply means that government emphasis is on deregulation, reducing taxation, reducing spending on welfare and leaving the financial sector free to maximise profits with minimal government interference. The global financial crisis of 2008 and the era of 'austerity' that followed were a direct result of irresponsibly managed, unregulated financial institutions. However, 'austerity' is also an economic policy that lines the pockets of the very rich at the expense of the poorest and most vulnerable people in society (Cooper & Whyte, 2017). The result of nearly 35 years of predominantly neoliberal policies has been increasing levels of inequality of wealth and life opportunities. The denationalisation of state-owned industries, the selling off of social housing, costly private finance initiatives, the often disastrous privatisation of NHS services, the commercialisation of higher education, the increasing prison population, zero hours contracts, the closing down of psychotherapy departments and their replacement with IAPT services are all policies that stem from neoliberal ideology. It is entirely in keeping with neoliberal government to have taken the advice of an economist, Richard Layard, with regard to improving the nation's mental health.

While the markets are left unfettered by state interference, those workers still employed by the state are subject to increasing regulation and micromanagement in which professional knowledge and values are subordinated to managerially defined 'targets' defined in terms of financial efficiency. Neoliberalism has given rise to a managerial culture that privileges profit above all else and in which managers lack the knowledge that informs the work of the people they manage, substituting notions of 'evidence-based practice' and 'clinical governance' (Smail, 2017) for clinical judgement. Privatisation of public services has also led to a breach of trust between workers and managers formerly bound together by a common purpose, to be replaced by a climate of fear in which employees at all levels try to 'cover their backs' while the services they are able to provide suffer as does staff morale. In terms of its effects on mental health, neoliberal government both promotes the social and economic conditions that lead to increasing levels of mental distress and dismantles the services that could help to alleviate it while, at the same time, promoting narrowly defined and prescriptive definitions of mental well-being.

Since the 1980s the new science of behavioural economics has emerged in which psychology is used to explain and predict economic behaviour, the myth of rational economic behaviour having been exposed by Kahneman (2011) and others.[3] Governments were urged to take advantage of the cognitive biases that inform human decision-making to influence the behaviour of the population. So called 'Nudge' units, were set up by the coalition government in the UK in 2010 and by the Obama administration in United States staffed by behavioural economists to persuade people to behave in more 'socially responsible' ways such as drinking and eating less, exercising more and saving for retirement, all behaviours that save governments money. The mathematics of behavioural economics have now been mapped to the extent that algorithms are increasingly used by governments and major corporations to predict, manage and manipulate peoples' behaviour, a process that takes advantage of the 'big data' collected by, for example, Amazon, Google and Facebook.

So micromanagement of employees has also extended to the micromanagement by stealth of individual citizens in all aspects of their lives including their mental health. This is one of the contradictions of neoliberalism in that it both devolves responsibility from the state to the individual while also intrusively undermining our rights to privacy and autonomy. Collective responsibility for all is replaced by individual responsibility in which the strong and privileged thrive and those disadvantaged by virtue of poverty, class, ethnicity, health or disability, gender or sexual orientation are left to struggle and blamed for their failure to overcome the odds that have been stacked against them.

The government's 'Work and Health Programme' (2017) links receipt of welfare with health services and therapy: the purpose here is clearly to prioritise the interests of the 'economy' over the welfare of its citizens. Mental health interventions offered through IAPT then become another form of intrusive micromanagement that involve 'Techniques, instruments, obsessive measuring: so that psychotherapy in the twenty-first century has become a parade of psychotechnologies' (Sanders, 2014). This leaves no place for therapy that allows for therapists to build a relationship and engage with the harsh realities and depth of suffering in their clients' lives.

CAT theory and practice

No theory emerges independently of the political context that gives rise to it. The acknowledged influences on CAT were the unmet need for psychological therapy and the perceived inadequacy of other therapeutic models to meet that need. CAT was intended to offer accessible but in-depth psychotherapy to people who had been previously excluded from it[4] and where it was needed without imposing any preconditions on the nature of their mental distress. However, from a Foucauldian perspective, the power and usefulness of psychological theories lies in what they produce, that is forms of subjectivity that lend themselves to the individualised self-responsibility necessary to meet the evolving labour and consumption requirements of free market capitalism. From this perspective there was nothing radical about

CAT's stated aims, which, according to Ryle and Kerr (2002), were promoting individual autonomy and self-responsibility through the revision of repetitive and maladaptive patterns of thought and behaviour.

CAT initially situated itself, politically, to the left of psychoanalysis that was seen as excluding the majority who needed it, from psychotherapeutic help, not least because only the relatively well-off could afford to pay for it and the length of treatment meant that the numbers that could be seen in NHS services were small. Ryle (1995) argued that by attributing their patients' difficulties in changing patho-logical styles of relating to innate faults in the patient such as a 'weak ego', 'envy' and 'excessive death extinct' and by failing to acknowledge the external circum-stances of their lives, some psychoanalytic formulations actually hinder rather than promote integration and the capacity for self-reflection. Ryle was similarly criti-cal of cognitive behavioural formulations and treatment protocols that addressed 'dysfunctional' thoughts and behaviours as if they were something innate to the individual rather than originating in their social environment. However in propos-ing CAT, a much briefer (psycho-educational as well as exploratory) model of therapy that linked intra-psychic phenomena with interpersonal experience, Ryle was also positioning CAT for a role in a market led NHS.

The brevity of CAT relative to psychoanalytic psychotherapy was and contin-ues to be one of its main selling points. In what has become a competitive market place for contracts in the privatised NHS, one of CAT's claims as discussed by Nehmad (2017) is that it is the most cost-effective therapy for treating patients with 'borderline personality disorder'. From the beginning CAT was a therapy intended for use in the public sector across a wide range of presentations and diagnosis. This ideal has been severely compromised by the cuts in mental health provision in the NHS and the increasingly regulated and circumscribed conditions in which therapy is offered. A consequence of CAT's commitment to the NHS involved 'competition' with other models of therapy and the need to 'prove' itself through research and by promoting CAT among other mental health professions, to encourage the recruitment and training of therapists in CAT. This process has been intensified by the privatisation of mental health services and the competition for usually short-term contracts.

CAT training was originally intended to be accessible to workers in a range of mental health and related settings, but as fewer employers are willing to fund train-ing and course fees are beyond the means of many modestly paid workers, CAT has become increasingly dominated by the relatively privileged professions of psychia-try and clinical psychology, a restraint on class diversity within the organisation. Paradoxically it is CAT's radical departure from the practices of psychoanalysis that made it attractive to professions and institutions whose agenda is to contain and manage suffering rather than address the causes of it. In keeping with the agenda of becoming a mainstream therapy in the NHS, CAT has also been relatively uncritical in its failure to question the usefulness of psychiatric diagnostic categories (Fozooni, 2010). One reason for CAT's failure to challenge psychiatric diagnosis is to gain credibility with the powerful medical model that is dominant in NHS mental health services. This of course serves the neoliberal agenda by attributing the causes of mental distress to individuals and their families rather than to a society that demands conformity to the self-serving values of the wealthy and powerful.

CAT as a relational therapy: a new restrictive definition of psychological health?

In focusing almost exclusively on the relational aspects of development and subjectivity, CAT is part of a broader current in psychotherapy sometimes referred to as 'the relational turn'.[5] Many commentators see this development as a progressive one due to the emphasis on the actual experience of patients and the authenticity required of the therapist in a co-created and collaborative therapeutic relationship.

There is nothing particularly radical about the way human development and psychological distress were originally theorised in CAT, with its reliance on object relations theory, although it did claim to go further in that the meanings internalised from patterns of relating and communicating with other people reflect the values and structure of the wider culture (Ryle & Kerr, 2002).

The CAT focus on the relationships between the client and other people as well as their relationship with the therapist, mapping transference and countertransference, is distinctly psycho-educational. Rather than being encouraged to correct their negative thinking, patients are encouraged instead to change the way they relate to other people and themselves, with the therapist assuming the mantel of expert in human relating, from a benevolent but nevertheless paternalistic position, entirely in keeping with neoliberalism and its devolution of responsibility on to individuals for their mental health. This leads to therapists giving undue priority to their patients' willingness or capacity to learn how to relate in a way the therapist considers appropriate and to reflect on that process, as the yardstick of their patient's progress towards better mental health. There is a covert political agenda here in which the power of the therapist to define the goals of 'treatment' is seldom acknowledged.

From this perspective CAT promoted an instrumental approach in which relationships with others are used to further individual goals and also gives rise to a different set of pressures to conform. It also excludes or marginalises people who are not neuro-typical, have intellectual or learning disabilities and even those whose preferred relating style is more introverted than the current norm, people who can easily feel overwhelmed and swamped by the pressures to relate and for whom solitude is a vital component of mental well-being. It may be significant that the diagnosis of 'social anxiety disorder' entered the DSM for the first time in 1980 – a pathology defined according to the complex relational demands of living in socially mobile and socially insecure societies characterised by free market capitalism and the demise of settled communities.

Although CAT claims to be a comprehensive theory that integrates the findings of theory from different schools of psychotherapy, developmental psychology and observational research (Ryle & Kerr, 2002), no theory of human development and self-hood can embrace every aspect of subjective and intersubjective experience, so perhaps what is significant is what they choose to emphasise and what they leave out. In CAT relationships are conceptualised as dyadic and vertical with the more powerful half of the dyad usually occupying the upper position. This oversimplifies the relational experience of most of us as it does not accommodate the actual complexity of family group dynamics and those in the wider society (e.g. see Ugazio, 2013), nor it does not account for gendered issues or the development of sexuality and the discovery of sexual difference.

In discarding the interpretation of the unconscious in favour of an understanding of inter-subjective processes and phenomenological experience and rejecting the significance of the Freudian drives in psychic life at a theoretical level, relational therapies also deny the reality of corporality in human life and relationships as well as the existence of any individual experience that is not mediated by relationships (Mills, 2005). A further and far more important criticism of relational therapies is that they totally fail to account for the role economic circumstances play in the subjective well-being of clients and therapists and how it is in the 'interest' of therapists to promote models of mental health that ensure their own incomes (Smail, 2017). Whereas neoliberalism has no concern for the individual beyond their capacity to participate in productive economic activity as a worker and consumer, relational psychotherapy along with all other models fails to account for the impact of economics on subjectivity.

Dialogical CAT: a missed opportunity?

The most significant theoretical development in CAT was the integration of the concept of the 'dialogical self' derived from the work of Mikhail Bakhtin (Leiman, 1997). This represented a further refinement and elaboration of what is understood as the relational formation of self and the thoroughly social nature of subjectivity. The dialogical self is a complex metaphor (Pollard, 2008) that can be inferred from the patient's talk and their interactions with the therapist. Dialogical positions can be mapped out from a close analysis of the patient's speech known as dialogical sequence analysis (DSA) (Leiman, 2004). This allowed for a more nuanced exploration of the patient's subjective and relational experience and the reconceptualisation of reciprocal roles and the Kleinian defences as different 'voices' talking to each other (Stiles, 1997) in a way that is less pathologising.

Nevertheless 'dialogical CAT' remained within a normative developmental framework, despite Bakhtin's emphasis on indeterminacy and unfinalisability, in which the relative power of the therapist, the role of psychotherapy within the wider social context and the failure of models of psychotherapy to account for their own existence remain unchallenged. The dialogical self is often divorced from its wider social context and is, by omission, disembodied; a self without gender, sexuality or desire, pitched at a level of abstraction to render it uncontroversial (Pollard, 2008). Similarly to other relational theories it fails to account adequately for individual agency and the limits to individual agency as well as the core experience of being 'me' as opposed to anyone else.

Internally persuasive discourse and embodied dialogical subjectivity

If dialogism is abstracted from its context in Bakhtin's phenomenology then it becomes a description of speech, rather than a philosophical idea concerned with the nature of meaning (Hirschkop, 1999), and the 'dialogical self' is merely a collection of voices talking to each other. I have never found this particularly useful as a therapist. While many clients find it helps to identify aspects of inner speech as something they've internalised, absorbed or copied from someone else and not properly belonging to them, this doesn't necessarily help them challenge or reduce the power of this 'voice' and the suffering it causes. An example given by Leiman and Stiles (2001) in which DSA is used to illuminate the therapy of a 42-year-old woman presenting with depression fails to account for the wider social, historical and economic context in which women are and have been marginalised and oppressed. An exclusive focus on speech or discourse can become merely another tool for assessment within a normative developmental framework without any reference to the social and political context of the client's life.

I suggest that if one of Bakhtin's most important but less discussed concepts, *internally persuasive discourse* can be cultivated, then a therapeutic interaction with the potential to transform the way people understand themselves and their place in the world becomes at least possible. Internally persuasive discourse is defined as the opposite of 'authoritative discourse', a monological discourse that is spoken from a single closed perspective (e.g. the discourse of neoliberalism). By contrast, internally persuasive discourse can encompass multiple perspectives and contradictory ideas and propositions and rather than resolving them in a dialectical synthesis continues to throw up new contradictions. It requires open-mindedness and a willingness to listen without prejudgement. It is the antithesis of dogma and received wisdom or what Bakhtin termed 'theoretism' – there is no authority or theory that can tell us what to think as opposed to thinking for ourselves. To do otherwise is an abdication of responsibility or what Bakhtin termed an 'alibi for being' (Bakhtin, 1993). To exercise responsibility we must allow for the human subject to have free will, however circumscribed this may be, which is difficult to reconcile with a self that is entirely at the whim of immediate relational and distal social forces.

Crucial to a critical appreciation of Bakhtin's phenomenology is the recognition that dialogue is always between two or more embodied subjects. While the dialogical self is an abstraction, the embodied self is material, specific and unique. For Bakhtin, it is the body that defines the self and distinguishes it from other selves, not just because all bodies are different but also because our bodies/ourselves occupy a particular position in space and time unique to us. There is no transcendental position that can escape the reality of embodiment.[6] The narrative structure of each human life is distinct and different from that of everyone else and it is this that allows us all to perceive and evaluate our perceptions from our own vantage point in the world and exercise a degree of free will[7] and the responsibility that follows from that with regard to how we conduct our lives. From this perspective, psychotherapy must be able to move beyond 'the relational' to facilitate each patient's exploration of their own unique experience and perceptions; to cultivate an internally persuasive discourse resistant to closure by the dominant authoritative discourses that claim to know what is best for us.

As we can only know our own experience from the confines of our own bodies we are dependent on the perceptions of others to enable us to comprehend the bigger picture. There are ethical implications consequent upon the uniqueness of each individual: as each person's experience and point of view is unique to them and as each act like each word is unique and unrepeatable, these cannot be governed or justified by appealing to either transcendent ideology or norms, rules or theories. The uniqueness of our position means, as Holquist (2009) observed, that we have an *ontologically imposed* responsibility for the evaluation of what we perceive and, by implication, the actions that follow from that. Put more simply, we have a moral duty to 'break the rules' when our evaluation of the specifics of a particular situation demand that we do so (Pollard, 2012).

Internally persuasive discourse requires the disinterested 'outside' perspective of another person. 'Outsideness' is Bakhtin's phenomenological description of how we are positioned in relation to other people in the social world. It is an attempt to capture the asymmetry between our inner experience of ourselves and other peoples' experience of us and vice versa. What we can see and how we evaluate and understand what we see is constrained by where we as embodied subjects are positioned in relation to other people and objects in the world. This is not so much a limitation as an opportunity for creative activity, as we all possess an excess or surplus of seeing in relation to another in that we can see what they cannot see and they can see what we cannot see. Interiority or introspection is not a very reliable or useful way to get to know ourselves as our subjectivity is both unique to us but also dependant on the perspectives of other people to give meaning to our own experience: 'I myself cannot be the author of my own value, just as I cannot lift myself up by my own hair' (Bakhtin, 1990, p. 5). Outsideness therefore goes beyond intersubjectivity and implies interdependency, which as Hirschkop (1999) observes involves a moral responsibility towards others. It is also a horizontal rather than a vertical concept as everyone has equal access to outsideness and the surplus of seeing and this should be used in such a way that equates to 'a fully realised and thoroughly consistent dialogic position, one that confirms the independence, internal freedom, unfinalizability and indeterminacy of the other' (Bakhtin, 1984, p. 63).

Ethics or theory?

This partial appropriation of Bakhtin in CAT theory in which the dialogical self is uprooted from its philosophical and phenomenological origins also sidestepped the tension between CAT as a scientific practitioner model of therapy governed by theory-driven techniques 'delivered' by therapist/experts and dialogical CAT as an open-ended conversation between two embodied subjects, or the tension between experience and form. This tension cuts across different modalities and even each therapist as we struggle with the need to give form to our own and other's experience and the conflicting desire to approach each person we meet without pre-judgements (Pollard, 2011). Once we have a theory in mind, it is almost inevitable that we will be biased towards what confirms our theoretical hypothesis and discount that which does not. Theories can be eagerly reached for when our sense of ontological security is lacking (Cayne & Loewenthal, 2011) and theories about people are always invented by the powerful to explain the experience of the less powerful.

From an ethical perspective the outside position of the therapist is vital, being able to offer the clients a different perspective they can either use or refuse but never assuming to know what their client's experience is or what is best for them. As Brown (2010) highlights, individualised psychotherapy interventions often fail as they assume wrongly that individuals, on their own, have the power to change themselves and their circumstances. Like other forms of psychodynamic and humanistic psychotherapy, CAT can overstress what is going on 'in the room' while neglecting the significance of the patient's history as well as the impact of politics and economics in the origins of reciprocal roles. CAT, while being more accessible to more people, can also become a means of closing down a dialogue rather than opening it up. A particular concern, therefore, is how to oppose the centripetal forces that seem to operate when a model of psychotherapy becomes successful and embedded in institutional settings with conservative agendas.

Bakhtinian ethics – an ethics of a non-categorical imperative?

One of Bakhtin's concerns was the apparent paradox of human interdependency; the distinctiveness that each person possesses in relation to every other person, that makes us both unknowable to but also dependant on other people. While all CAT therapists have to work within a structure subject to regulations and codes of ethics these are necessarily principles that apply to all therapists and all clients. Ethics in practice involves a focus on the particular according to the unique and unrepeatable interactions and circumstances surrounding each therapeutic encounter or what Beasley-Murray (2007) refers to as the 'ethic of a non-categorical imperative' (p. 84). Of particular importance for all therapists are the ethical issues involved in the use of theory to give form to human subjectivity. The competition between different models of psychotherapy as well as being a market-driven phenomenon is also a struggle for values that can reflect conflicts in society. As Holloway (1999) suggests, ethical concerns can become entangled with the seductiveness of power and control so that the most powerful determine the prevailing values. The centralising forces of neoliberalism have led to a situation where practice is driven by techniques derived from questionable research designed to achieve predetermined goals of questionable therapeutic value and the centrifugal forces that reflect the complexity and diversity of human experience are ignored.

Conclusion

When evaluating the question asked by the title of this chapter, the most important consideration to bear in mind is that of complexity. Politics often involves polarisation and the adoption of rigid inflexible positions. It would be lazy and inaccurate to conclude that CAT had sold out to conservatism and neoliberal values by adapting to market conditions and it is almost inevitable that previously radical discourses become institutionalised and drift towards the centre but that can also be seen as a measure of their success. Even so, what we are able to do as therapists is a messy compromise between what we aspire to and the constraints of our work settings. Nowhere is this more true than in the NHS. While most CAT therapists are ideologically committed to the principle of mental health care, adapted to the need of each individual, being freely available to all who need it, the NHS at present falls far short of this ideal; an ideal that is being torn apart at the seams by privatisation, inadequate funding, poor managements and the conservatism of the predominant 'medical model'.

As neoliberal ideology has tightened its grip on public services and even insinuated itself into professional associations, the scope for therapists to think independently and practice according to their own values and exercise their own responsibility from a position of outsideness has to be defended and fought for. Nevertheless there are many therapists working in the NHS and other settings who continue to strive against the odds to provide a service to their clients according to the needs of each individual and not according to the diktats of neoliberal government and managers charged with implementing their policies. Individually and collectively they are cultivating their own internally persuasive discourses and endeavouring to enable their clients to do the same. Several of the chapters in this book describe the way this work is being done in varied settings with different groups of clients, using CAT, as one way among many, to help their clients towards better mental health and towards finding a position where they can exercise more power to enhance well-being in their own lives and that of their families in an unfair and unequal world.

Notes

1 What we mean by the 'economy' is ill-defined and little understood and increasingly left to 'experts', yet it affects us all in every aspect of our lives.
2 If Keynes' warning not to punish the Germans at the Treaty of Versaille had been heeded, the rise of Hitler and World War II and its aftermath that is still very much a feature of current global politics may never have happened.
3 Of course those conversant with psychoanalytic theory have always known this, as did Shakespeare and most philosophers and writers of literature prior to Shakespeare and since!
4 As Ryan (2017) notes, working-class people were far more likely to be offered CBT, a form of psycho-education, designed to correct negative and dysfunctional thoughts and behaviours and excluded from more in-depth and longer-term psychoanalytic therapy. When I worked in the NHS psychoanalytic psychotherapists offered four session assessments to screen out those not deemed 'psychologically minded enough' to benefit from

psychoanalytically informed therapy, a process people who were rejected for therapy often found deeply distressing.

5 The term 'relational' can give rise to some confusion as humanistic and existential therapies have always regarded the relationship as paramount. In psychoanalysis in the UK it is associated with a focus on 'object relations' rather than drives and the work of Winicott, Fairburn and Klein. It is not always clear whether it refers to developmental aspects of selfhood or the therapeutic way of working or both. It can also be used to distinguish psycho-educational and technique-driven therapies from other models.

6 Lakoff and Johnson (1999) demonstrate that even the most abstract or spiritual ideas cannot be expressed without recourse to metaphors derived from bodily experience.

7 By free will I mean the freedom to think for ourselves and make our own judgments independently of all the myriad social pressures in the contemporary world. It is different from power, which is of course very unevenly distributed among people.

References

Bakhtin, M. M. (1984). *Problems of Dostoevsky's poetics*. Minneapolis, MN: University of Minnesota Press.

Bakhtin, M. M. (1990). *Author and hero in aesthetic activity: In art and answerability, early philosophical essays*. V. Lipianov (trans.), M. Holquist & V. Lipianov (eds). Austin, TX: University of Texas Press.

Bakhtin, M. M. (1993). *Toward a philosophy of the act*. V. Lipianov (trans.), M. Holquist & V. Lipianov (eds), Austin, TX: University of Texas Press.

Beasley-Murray, T. (2007). *Mikhail Bakhtin and Walter Benjamin: Experience and form*. London: Palgrave.

Brown, R. (2010). Situating inequality and collective action in cognitive analytic therapy. *Reformulation: Journal of the Association of Cognitive Analytic Therapy*, Winter, 28–34.

Cayne, J. & Loewenthal, D. (2011). Post phenomenology and the between as unknown. In D. Loewenthal (ed.), *Post-existentialism and the psychological therapies: Towards a therapy without foundations*. London: Karnac.

Cooper, V. & Whyte, D. (2017). *The violence of austerity*. London: Pluto Press.

Earle, J., Moran, C. & Ward-Perkins, Z. (2016). *The econocracy: The perils of leaving economics to the experts*. Manchester, UK: Manchester University Press.

Fozooni, B. (2010). Cognitive analytic therapy: A sympathetic critique. *Psychotherapy and politics international*, 8(2), 128–145.

Hirschkop, K. (1999). *Mikhail Bakhtin: An aesthetic for democracy*. Oxford: Oxford University Press.

Holloway, R. (1999). *Godless morality: Keeping ethics out of religion*. London: Canongate.

Holquist, M. (1984) *Dialogism, Bakhtin and his world*. London: Routledge.

Kahneman, D. (2011). *Thinking, fast and slow*. London: Penguin.

Keynes, J. M. (1936). *The general theory of employment, interest and money*. London: Macmillan.

Lakoff, G. & Johnson, M. (1999). *Philosophy in the flesh: The embodied mind and its challenge to western thought*. New York: Basic Books.

Leiman, M. (1997). Procedures as dialogical sequences: A revised version of a fundamental concept in CAT. *British Journal of Medical Psychology*, 70(2), 193–207.

Leiman, M. (2004). Dialogical sequence analysis. In H. J. M. Hermans & G. Dimaggio (eds), *The dialogical self in psychotherapy*. Hove, UK: Brunner-Routledge.

Leiman, M. & Stiles, W. (2001). Dialogical sequence analysis and the Zone of Proximal Development. *Psychotherapy Research*, 11(3), 311–330.

Mills, J. (2005). A critique of relational psychoanalysis. *Psychoanalytic Psychology*, 22(2), 155–188.

Nehmad, A. (2017). CAT and borderline personality disorder. *The Psychotherapist*, Summer, 33–35.

Pollard, R. (2008). *Dialogue and desire: Mikhail Bakhtin and the linguistic turn in psychotherapy*. London: Karnac Books.

Pollard, R. (2011). Ethics in practice: A critical appreciation of Mikhail Bakhtin's concept of 'outsideness' in relation to responsibility and the creation of meaning in psychotherapy. *American Journal of Psychotherapy*, 65(1) 1–26.

Pollard, R. (2012). Great time: From Blade Runner to Bakhtin. *Reformulation: Journal of the Association of Cognitive Analytic Therapy*, Summer, 32–34.

Ryan, J. (2017). *Class and psychoanalysis: Landscapes of inequality*. London: Routledge.

Ryle, A. (1995). Defensive organisation or collusive interpretations? A further critique of Kleinian theory and practice. *British Journal of Psychotherapy*, 12(1), 60–68.

Ryle, A. & Kerr, I. B. (2002). *Introducing cognitive analytic therapy, principles and practice*. London: Wiley.

Sanders, P. (2014). Ordinary stories of intermingling worlds and doing what is right: A person-centred view. In D. Loewenthal & A. Samuels (eds), *Relational psychoanalysis and counselling: Appraisals and reappraisals*. London: Routledge.

Smail, D. (2017). Understanding the social context of individual distress. In R. Tweedy (ed.), *The political self: Understanding the social context for mental illness*. London: Karnac Books.

Stiles, W. (1997). Signs and voices: Joining a conversation in progress. *British Journal of Medical Psychology*, 70, 169–176.

Ugazio, V. (2013). *Semantic polarities and psychopathologies in the family: Permitted and forbidden stories*. R. Dixon (trans.). London: Routledge.

Varoufakis, Y. (2016). *And the weak suffer what they must? Europe, austerity and the threat to global stability*. London: Bodley Head.

Work and Health Programme (2017). www.gov.uk/work-health-programme (Accessed 25/09/18).

5

THE MADNESS OF MONEY

The super-rich, economic inequality and mental health

Lawrence Welch

Introduction

Psychotherapists are not taught about economics or the effects of economic policies on people's welfare beyond a general understanding that economic deprivation is associated with poorer mental as well as physical health. However, economics is a central factor in the interactions between people as monetary exchange enables the products of the diverse activities of individuals to become available to others. While money plays a major role in our daily lives it generally operates in the background while triggering powerful unconscious 'fast brain' (Kahneman, 2011) responses.

Since the global financial crisis of 2008, we have learnt that economics cannot be safely left to the 'experts' i.e. the mathematicians and statisticians; 'number crunchers', that governments have come to rely on for formulating policies and predicting their outcomes. Economics, once known as the 'dismal science', has recently become 'sexy' and economists such as Thomas Piketty (2014) have graphically highlighted to a wider readership the pronounced tendency of capitalist economies to lead to greater concentrations of wealth among a very few and widening levels of inequality threatening widespread instability unless governments intervene. The shocking statistics of the disparity in wealth and income between the super-rich global 'elite' and the rest of the population are worsening as times goes on.[1] In the UK, income inequality means the richest 10% of the population have an original income 24 times higher than the poorest 10%. Wealth inequality is even starker, with 10% of households owning 47% of the total wealth whereas the poorest 50% own a mere 8.7% (Equality Trust, 2017a).

According to the Equality Trust (2017b), on average, the chief executive officers (CEOs) of the UK's largest 100 companies (the FTSE 100) take home around 190 times what the average employee takes home.

This runs alongside huge tax avoidance where every year multinationals avoid paying huge sums in taxes: according to the Inland Revenue £5.8 billion was lost to tax avoidance in 2017 (Marriage, 2017). Wilkinson (2005) and Wilkinson and Pickett (2009) give a powerful account of how income inequality affects those people with the lowest incomes in a rich society; negatively affecting social relationships, mental and physical health and leading to increased levels of obesity, violence, imprisonment and reduced social mobility.

There is a gaping hole in the major theories that have led to the different schools of psychotherapy currently operating in the Western world. This gaping hole is how economics, or the material conditions of life affect us as individuals psychologically and emotionally. As David Smail (2017) points out, psychotherapy in its varying forms has become a major commercial success story, but the subject of money is hardly mentioned. Smail suggests that there is repression on an industry-wide scale, operating as if money cannot be openly referred to in polite circles.[2] Even in private practice where the client pays the therapist, the subject of money is, according to Ryan (2017), rarely part of the therapeutic discourse. Smail traces the origins of this 'repression' to Freud whose letters reveal considerable anxiety as well as shame about lack of money and his fear of not making enough and goes so far as to suggest that this fear could have led to the retraction of the seduction theory:

> Could it be that Freud's gradual shifting of the burden of blame for his patients' 'neuroses' from the fathers and uncles of his 'hysterical' female patients to, eventually, themselves (via, incidentally the lower orders in the household – the servant girls) might have been something to do with who was paying his bills?
>
> *(Smail, 2017, p. 5)*

If that was the case, then Freud and psychoanalysis has even more to answer for in terms of the immense, unrecognised and fiercely denied suffering of thousands or even millions of children since who have been sexually abused (the politics of society's changing attitudes towards child sexual abuse over the last 50 years are discussed in Chapter 11 of this volume).

In this chapter, I will describe how contemporary economic conditions characterised by extreme levels of inequality in the distribution of wealth globally and nationally directly or indirectly affects the lives of the population. I will go on to discuss how this affects patients and mental health workers in the NHS and how CAT can help to further our understandings of how money affects us all in our working and personal lives.

The super-rich and us

Capitalist economies depend on the surplus value of people's labour, the surplus being taken up by the employers, owners and shareholders of the various businesses that comprise 'the economy'. This means that the interests of owners and share-holders are always in conflict with the interests of workers. Trade unions have traditionally fought for and represented the interests and rights of workers, their key bargaining tool being collective action and the power to withdraw the labour on which capitalists absolutely depend. However, there has been a steep decline in union membership since the 1970s, particularly in the private sector, partly owing to the decline of heavy manufacturing industries. This decline is associated with a relative decline in the share of the economy paid in wages and fewer employment rights leading to increased job insecurity and reduced income for many workers.

From a psychological perspective, Marx described the cultural hegemony of capitalism in which we mostly fail to question the supposed inevitability of exploitation and termed it 'false consciousness'. Central to the concept of hegemony (the dominance of one class in society over the rest) is the, nowadays, subtle coercion required to ensure that the labour requirements of capital are met. According to Perry Anderson (2017), this lies in lifestyle expectations that can only be met by commodities in which the inner and spiritual life of the individual are ignored. We are not only enslaved as workers but also as consumers under the illusion that we work and consume of our own free will. This willing participation can blur the basic conflict of interest between the owners of the means of production and the workers who produce profits for them.

So-called austerity policies ostensibly implemented to reduce the national debt have the most damaging effects on the poorest people in society while the wealth of the very rich often increases during economic downturns, as wages are depressed and assets are moved around to whatever sectors in the economy are most profitable.[3] Nowhere is this clearer than when considering that the wealth of Jeff Bezos, the owner of Amazon and at the time of writing the richest person on the planet with a net worth of over $100 billion dollars, is made through the exploitation of thousands of underpaid, overworked employees many of whom in the United States are reliant on Medicaid, food stamps and housing subsidised by US tax payers (Sanders, 2018). In the UK thousands of working households are similarly dependant on food banks and welfare benefits. There is something appallingly wrong with a global economy where the richest have wealth that for most of us is unimaginable, while the majority of the people who create their wealth, live in conditions of absolute or relative poverty. A contemporary example in the UK of how the material interests of the richest 10% is in direct opposition to the interests of the rest of the population is the shortage of housing: homelessness, overcrowding and corrupt landlords for the poorest are matched by inflated house prices and increased wealth for the owners of property in areas of high demand.

While professing concern for inequality, the global rich are unwilling to take any action that reduces their own wealth and power: 'They are loath to pay a living wage, but they will fund a philharmonic orchestra. They will ban unions, but they will organise a workshop on transparency in government' (Milanovic, 2018). What follows enumerates some of the ways in which the activities and selfish greed of the super-rich adversely affect the welfare of the rest of the world's population.

The material affects

1. The direct exploitation of workers in the companies they own or have shares in.
2. The indirect exploitation of citizens nationally and globally by tax avoidance and pollution of the environment that reduces the quality of life for everyone else and depletes tax revenues that could otherwise be spent on health, welfare, education and recreational facilities for all.
3. Related to this are the effects of the activities of the super-rich on climate change both in terms of the industries they own and the high consumption life styles they both enjoy and promote as desirable.
4. The global arms trade is possibly the most extreme example of how wealth is created for a few at the expense of the suffering of some of the world's poorest and most vulnerable populations.
5. The global tobacco industry relies on the exploitation of not only the people who work in it but also the millions who consume its products.
6. The pharmaceutical industry similarly exploits sick people who are dependent on its products while, from a mental health perspective, inventing 'disorders' for which its medications then become essential.
7. The concentration of wealth globally and nationally in the hands of a few individuals and big corporations that are not democratically accountable to anyone other than shareholders distorts the distribution of power among people so that national governments have reduced capacity to govern in their own national interests.
8. Democracy is further undermined when these corporations control and manipulate access to information
9. Social media owned by a handful of super-rich individuals globally has a complex relationship with the people who use it and its influence in the world socially and politically is both beneficial and harmful. However, its material consequences and how it makes its money is selling the data of its users to businesses, who are then further exploited by targeted advertising designed to get us all to consume more by stimulating insatiable desires.

In summary, the unequal distribution of wealth and the activities of those who own a disproportionate share of the world's material resources leads to or exacerbates poverty, disease, displacement, homelessness, lack of education and employment, lack of opportunity, disruption to family life as well as supporting authoritarian regimes who oppress their citizens, and, for women particularly, rape and other forms of sexual exploitation as well as slavery.

The effects of inequality on health

It does not take a genius to work out that the suffering the activities of the super-rich cause in the lives of vast numbers of the population also leads to poorer physical and mental health. For example, Marmot's (2015) study of the civil service found that those at the lower end of the inequality gap were four times more likely to die than those at the top in a given time period and this was after other factors affecting health were controlled for. These were people employed by the civil service and not living in conditions of destitution or poverty, but nevertheless suffering the psychological stress of being at the bottom of the 'pecking order'. According to a study by the University of Washington, life expectancy in the United States, a country that ranks high on inequality scales, varies by as much as 20 years[4] between the poorest and richest areas, while in the UK, relative social and economic disadvantage is associated with not only reduced quality of life, but also with a substantially reduced life expectancy (Wilkinson, 2005). Wilkinson (2005) refers to this phenomenon as 'social toxicity':

> Our reflexivity as human beings, the way we experience ourselves partly through other's eyes, is . . . the highway through which the social gets into us. No wonder then that it is the main gateway by which the psychosocial gets under the skin to exert such a powerful influence on health.
>
> *(pp. 92–93)*

The adverse effects of poverty and social deprivation on mental health have been widely researched and documented (James, 1998; Pilgrim & Rogers, 1993; Sennett & Cobb, 1972; Smail, 1993; Wilkinson, 2005; Wilkinson & Picket, 2009). As well as the obvious disadvantages that relative poverty and powerless confer, there are other psychological stresses that affect all but the most powerful and entitled in societies with steep inequality levels as discussed in Chapters 3 and 4 of this volume.

In recent years, these psychological stresses have for many younger and more vulnerable people been exacerbated by social media that both facilitates and temporarily pacifies social anxieties. Those of us who use social media are also 'working' unpaid for the companies that own the platforms by providing them with our data.

There are also more subtle influences at large that insinuate their way into our conscious and unconscious assumptions and affect the values that govern how we live our lives. Perhaps the rot set in when Peter Mandelson, now Lord Mandelson, a former Labour government minister, announced that 'New Labour' was intensely relaxed about people getting 'filthy' rich, if they pay their taxes (Jones, 2012). The problem is that most of the 'filthy rich' go out of their way not to pay taxes, as the 'Paradise Papers' and 'Panama Papers'[5] have shown. But also it is illustrative of a shift of political values away from the post-war ethos of the welfare state and collective responsibility administered through national and local government paid for through taxation to ensure the welfare of the most vulnerable in society (whether the very young or very old, sick, disabled or unemployed), towards a more individualistic ethos where profits are prioritised over people.

The effects of privatisation in the NHS

Privatisation by stealth of the NHS threatens to destroy a fundamental service to the whole population without any democratic mandate (Davis et al., 2015; Pollock, 2004).

When profits not people are the priority, services are cut, there is downward pressure on wages and poorer employment conditions for staff. The use of taxpayers' money to outsource NHS services to private businesses is eroding the principles on which the NHS was founded. To give just one example, Virgin Care, part of the Richard Branson empire, secured 400 contracts worth £1 billion in 2016–2017. This is a company that pays no tax in the UK as its parent company Virgin Holdings is based in the British Virgin Islands, a tax haven.[6] Another company, Care UK, a major private 'provider' is also a donor to the Conservative party. These companies are not democratically accountable to NHS service users but to their shareholders, so unprofitable contracts are withdrawn without notice leaving seriously ill patients without vital treatment. Privatisation has led to administrative costs rising from 5% of the NHS budget in the 1980s to 14% in 2005 and is now likely to be much higher (Paton, 2014). A consequence of the complex range of interconnected bodies involved in NHS funding and the increasing levels of dysfunction are high vacancy rates for staff (Kotecha, 2017). Private companies have taken advantage of this by providing private services enabling those who can afford to pay to avoid long waits for NHS GP and other services. This process of creeping privatisation in many cases leading to failing and inadequate services has led to a two-tier health service where those with money or private health insurance receive high-quality health care when needed, whereas those without often languish on long waiting lists.

Nowhere is this more keenly felt than by patients on long waiting lists for NHS mental health services. In mental health the two-tier service means that those who can afford to, pay for psychiatric treatment, psychological therapies, psychotherapy and counselling privately, as the NHS is unable to meet the demand for mental health care. This process is driven both by trained mental health workers being made redundant or unable to find paid employment in the NHS and would-be patients unable to obtain access to the support or therapy they need as well as inequality of income and wealth.

From the political to the personal and how using CAT can bridge the gap

We are all shaped by our immediate proximal experiences as well as wider societal and political forces. My own personal experience of anxiety about how others perceive me and 'getting things wrong' was, I think, triggered by my mother's experience of wanting to throw me out of a porthole as an infant on a ship to South Africa, where my father was going to work as Church minister. I was being a 'demanding' baby while my father and sister were seasick. I only learned about this incident much later in life when my mother told me. This anxiety continued despite my mother being a very caring parent who I deeply admired. Both my parents were strongly anti-apartheid but holding these views and expressing them was not without risk in South Africa in the 1950s and 1960s. These early experiences contributed powerfully to my political awareness and involvement in left-wing groups after I returned to the UK to avoid conscription, but also left me with life-long anxiety at the micro level.

Translating this experience into the NHS work setting, I felt a deep commitment to the work itself both in terms of one-to-one relationships with patients whose stories I was always interested to hear and make sense of and also to the other members of staff where we shared a collaborative purpose. Despite my position as a consultant psychotherapist, I had major difficulties with my manager who I experienced as highly forceful and uncollaborative. I had a visceral sense of anxiety when I thought she was around in the building I was working in, which I was aware of but found hard to manage. I could discuss the challenges with others who had similar experiences and it was helpful to know my experience wasn't entirely personal, but we were unable find a joint strategy to bring about change.

The situation got much worse when a more senior manager told us our service had to be downsized. Ironically, the 'downsizing' was the Care Commissioning Group's (CCG) solution to the fact that the service's waiting lists were too long owing to referral rates having increased by 86% between 2010 and 2013, while staff levels were down owing to four unfilled psychology posts. While the obvious answer to this was to increase the number of clinical staff to meet the increased need, the CCG's answer was to impose a performance-managed industrial model with non-clinical managers setting performance targets for professionals where throughput and outcomes assessed by tick boxes became the priorities for the service rather than direct patient care. This industrial model is now prevalent throughout NHS mental health services as private providers compete to outbid each other for lucrative contracts. To add to staff distress, through feeling under pressure to compromise their personal and professional values, there is an additional pressure of increased job insecurity as posts are cut or services shifted to other 'providers'. A report by the New Savoy partnership in March 2017 found that depression and reduced well-being among psychologists employed in the NHS had increased considerably due to pressures of work and that these workers were among the most stressed in the working population as a whole.

I found the experience of our service being cut, being forced to compete for my own job and being unable to provide the level of care for patients that I believed was needed, traumatic. It highlighted the importance for me of psychotherapists discovering ways of managing the underlying tensions between the personal and political, particularly as the struggles that many patients face are similar. I found that conceptualising my own experience as a complex range of overlapping reciprocal roles, some entirely personal from my past and some operating in the present as a response to changing conditions at work and in the political sphere, helped me to make sense of my subjective experience (see Figure 5.1). Sharing these reflections with colleagues helped us find common ground while also respecting our

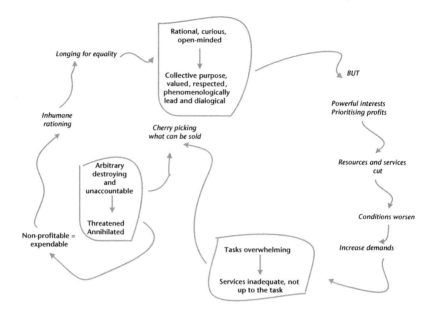

FIGURE 5.1 Selling health care.

individual differences. It also emphasised the importance of collective action and strong union representation.

A powerful tool in helping us to grasp how patients manage their own struggles exists when finding ways of naming the tensions we can face individually and reflecting on what can be done about them. There are many layers to the process. We need to find ways of talking to colleagues about the tensions we may struggle with at work in a dialogical way rather than getting trapped in conflicts where we can feel dismissed or become dismissive, ourselves. This in turn must be articulated to management, even when we feel it is unlikely our views will be heard. Alongside this we need to expand our knowledge about the wider economic and political issues, which are central to shaping our experience without feeling overwhelmed by the complexity of these. As a result of personal reflection and dialogical discussions with similarly affected colleagues, we wrote a counter proposal to the Trust's argument for cuts. The downsizing inevitably continued but at least two of the posts were retained as a result. At a time of great uncertainty for staff and patients alike this small victory renewed our faith in the potential of collective action.

Important in this process is developing a sense of personal *equality* and individuality as human beings rather than unconsciously moving into a place where those in power can be experienced as 'superior'. We have to raise our consciousness of the extent to which the 'social' gets inside us particularly if our relative 'powerlessness' as employees is compounded by our class, gender, sexuality, ethnicity or disability. If we can feel equal, we can then recognise more strongly how, for many of us, the powerfully unconscious response to our own perceptions if they differ from others is to feel we have got it wrong in relation to a critical other. There can be no doubt that cultivating a sense of human equality with the people and institutions that oppress us is easier to achieve collectively. Solidarity with others in a similar position to ourselves can be a huge source of strength as many sufferers from mental health problems have found when they become part of 'user' movements. A felt sense of equality can give us the strength to tolerate uncertainty, acknowledge we don't have all the answers and that we might be mistaken. We need to maintain a sense of *curiosity*, which means that however convincing the view we currently hold, it will at some time in the future be open to question. As Staemmler (1997) says, we need to become comfortable with not knowing in order to be open to new ideas and the possibilities offered by other perspectives. The sense of equality and curiosity both require the development of the observing eye where we 'notice' our immediate responses to the other and find ways of giving ourselves time for reflection and testing out different perspectives.

Curiosity about what motivates capitalists and managers will also be central to developing a place where methods for confronting inequality can be expanded into more effective means for widening the debate about the issues and thinking about how to bring about change. Alongside this is curiosity about what leads some people to be so accepting of the commands from above. A further curiosity is about what triggers masses of people to come together and fight for change. If we can develop a better awareness of these issues we then need to discover how best to communicate it so that, for example, the divisions that inevitably occur when people experience things differently, do not override the need for collective action.

Notes

1 See https://inequality.org/facts/global-inequality (Accessed 26/01/18).
2 While some psychoanalysts do attach significance to the 'fee' this is a purely psychological significance rather than one that reflects the material aspects of the relationship between patient and analyst.
3 There is an ideological agenda being pursued here to reduce the role and responsibilities of the state in the provision of welfare benefits.
4 www.theguardian.com/inequality/2017/may/08/life-expectancy-gap-rich-poor-us-regions-more-than-20-years (Accessed 26/01/18).
5 The 'Paradise Papers' refer to over 13 million documents leaked to reporters from the *Guardian* in 2017 documenting tax avoidance arrangements for numerous global companies and wealthy individuals. The 'Panama Papers' were leaked by a Panamanian law firm in 2015, again to *Guardian* newspaper journalists and concern tax avoidance arrangements dating back to the 1970s.
6 For a more detailed discussion see www.nhsforsale.info/private-providers/virgin.html (Accessed 26/01/18).

References

Anderson, P. (2017). *The H-word: The peripeteia of hegemony.* London: Verso.
Davis, J., Lister J. & Wrigley, D. (2015). *NHS for sale: Myths, lies and deception.* London: Merlin Press.

The Equality Trust. (2017a). www.equalitytrust.org.uk/scale-economic-inequality-uk (Accessed 05/03/18).

The Equality Trust. (2017b). www.equalitytrust.org.uk/sites/default/files/.../WealthTracker 2017.docx_.pdf (Accessed 05/03/18).

James, O. (1998). *Britain on the couch: Treating a low serotonin society.* London: Arrow.

Jones, O. (2012). Foreword. In *Why inequality matters.* The Equality Trust. http://classonline. org.uk/docs/Why_Inequality_Matters.pdf (Accessed 05/03/18).

Kahneman, D. (2011). *Thinking, fast and slow.* London: Penguin.

Kotecha, V. (2017). Sustainability and transformation plans: Five key questions for planners. The Centre for Health and the Public Interest (CHPI). https://chpi.org.uk/wp-content/ uploads/2017/06/STPs-5-key-questions-FINAL-2017-06-18-.pdf (Accessed 05/03/18).

Marmot, M. (2015). *The health gap: The challenge of an unequal world.* London: Bloomsbury.

Marriage, M. (2017). £5.8 billion lost. *Financial Times.* www.ft.com/content/00de4f00-b754-11e7-8c12-5661783e5589 (Accessed 09/02/18).

Milanovic, B. (2018). Dutiful dirges of Davos. *Global Policy,* 24 January. www.global policyjournal.com/blog/24/01/2018/dutiful-dirges-davos (Accessed 10/02/18).

New Savoy Partnership (2017). www1.bps.org.uk/.../news/new-savoy-partnership-charter-and-survey-results (Accessed 10/02/18).

Paton, C. (2014). At what cost? Paying the price for the market in the English NHS. Centre for Health and the Public Interest. www.chpi.org.uk/wp-content/uploads/2014/02/ At-what-cost-paying-the-price-for-the-market-in-the-English-NHS-by-Calum-Paton. pdf (Accessed 10/02/18).

Piketty, T. (2014). *Capital in the twenty-first century.* Cambridge, MA: Harvard University Press.

Pilgrim, D. & Rogers, A. (1993). *A sociology of mental health and illness.* Buckinghamshire, UK: Open University Press.

Pollock, A. (2004). *NHS plc: The privatisation of our health care.* London: Verso.

Ryan, J. (2017). *Class and psychoanalysis: Landscapes of inequality.* London: Routledge.

Sanders, B. (2018). Lets wrench power back from the billionaires. *Guardian,* 14 January. www.theguardian.com/commentisfree/2018/jan/14/power-billionaires-bernie-sanders-poverty-life-expectancy-climate-change (Accessed 24/01/18).

Sennett, R. & Cobb, J. (1972). *The hidden injuries of class.* London: Norton.

Smail, D. (1993). *The origins of unhappiness: A new understanding of personal distress.* London: HarperCollins.

Smail, D. (2017). Understanding the social context of individual distress. In R. Tweedy (ed.), *The political self: Understanding the social context for mental illness.* London: Karnac Books.

Staemmler, F. (1997). Cultivated uncertainty: An attitude of Gestalt therapists. *British Gestalt Journal,* 6(1), 40–48.

Wilkinson, R. (2005). *The impact of inequality: How to make sick societies healthier.* London: Routledge.

Wilkinson, R. & Pickett, K. (2009). *The spirit level: Why more equal societies almost always do better.* London: Allen Lane.

6

THE INTERGENERATIONAL TRANSMISSION OF THE ADVERSE EFFECTS OF INEQUALITY

Josephine F. Discepolo Ahmadi

Introduction

The impact of inequality on mental and physical health has been well documented in recent years including how economic disadvantages and social deprivation can be handed down from one generation to the next. The advantages children from wealthy families enjoy through better education, career opportunities, social connections, inherited wealth, property and frequently an endowment of confidence and entitlement are well known. These advantages are matched by corresponding disadvantages for the poorest including increased levels of mental distress and ill health. While therapy on its own cannot compensate for the disadvantages of poverty, I find CAT can provide a useful framework to help families overcome some of the repeated interactional patterns experienced by powerless parents.

The mental health observatory

I asked a patient who suffered from an eating disorder to describe the house where he grew up and where the family had meals. He replied that when they were hungry they ate a bag of crisps or chips from the local fish and chips shop, nobody cooked, and the kitchen was the place where they stored their bikes. Occasionally, his mother would ask neighbouring mothers to share the food they had left in their cupboards. A loaf of bread and a tin of baked beans or spam had to feed several children while the mothers went hungry. They only had one cooked meal a week at their grandmother's house. The image the patient passed on to me was powerful and overwhelmingly sad. The centrality of deprivation and poverty as a causal factor for his eating disorder appeared to be overwhelming.

Working in NHS services and in private practice with distressed parents, they often express an intense fear of passing on to their children some of their own long-standing difficulties. Their concerns relate both to their mental health symptoms and to the complex interplay between different causal factors, with past traumatic events and depriving environments the most powerful determinants. They might accept the idea their emotional responses to terrible events and to the experience of emotional and material deprivation were natural and even useful at the time and that shock and denial are typical, but what parents really struggle to come to terms with are the longer-term effects of their early experiences, which include unpredictable emotions, flashbacks, strained relationships, addictive coping strategies and physical symptoms of various degrees of severity.

Men and women who struggle with keeping their anger under control experience intense feelings of guilt and powerlessness when they realise that their children have recurrent outbursts of anger or withdraw and isolate themselves from peers. Some find it difficult to help them when they are bullied at school, to comfort them when they have nightmares or to support them when they experience difficulties in their relationships. Their children become a constant reminder of aspects of themselves that they dislike and find difficult to change. Others become overprotective and distrusting of anyone who meets their children. They may wish to provide their children with everything they were deprived of and, in the process, reassure themselves that the cycle of deprivation can be broken, and that they are better parents than their own were. Their sense of responsibility includes preoccupation about the role they play within their communities and society and an under- or overestimation of the power that they ought to gain in order to play an active role in social and political change.

The emphasis in psychotherapy on personal trauma from growing up in depriving environments is problematic because many forms of violence, abuse and neglect can be understood as structural or implicit and so may remain hidden in individual accounts. A young man who was sexually abused, treated as a slave, beaten and forced by his relatives to work long hours in a remote rural area of a West African country, where he was left alone and at risk of becoming prey for wild animals, felt intensely ashamed of the way this had affected him since he described his childhood experiences as not uncommon in his country. As psychotherapists (in the NHS), we are expected to quickly 'fix' people and send them back to work. Generally, we are not encouraged to understand individual events as part of larger historical, social and political dynamics, which have profound effects for both individuals and communities. There have even been suggestions this would be unorthodox, alien to our discipline, a clumsy attempt at resolving the contradictions inherent in our ever-changing role by moving away from psychotherapy into the field of sociology or politics.

Nevertheless, there have been interesting and significant developments in trying to de-medicalise human suffering by taking a critical position with regard to diagnosing and prescribing medication (Moncrief, 2008; Rapley et al., 2011; Szasz, 1961/2010). Critical psychologists have extended their critique to the marketing of psychological therapies and to the ways in which the professions of clinical psychology and psychotherapy have adopted the powerful discourse of medicine (Hagan & Smail, 1997; McGrath et al., 2016; Newnes, 2014; Rahim, 2014; Rogers & Pilgrim, 2003, 2013; Smail, 1993, 2002). This retraumatises patients and 'tell[s] stories about the nature of suffering that advance the profession and not the patient' (Kerr, 2012). This leads to increasing pressure to gather outcome data to prove the effectiveness of one model of therapy against another and to offer only short-term treatment rather than longer-term interventions. These vested interest attempts to embrace the political and financial agendas that are promoted by neoliberal political groups and to protect our positions through the marketing of one model against the other and through the competing agendas of one training program against the other, almost inevitably transfer on to our patients a pressure to prove themselves and get better soon. We end up setting the stage for the re-enactment with the therapist of the damaging roles that our patients feel compelled to take on in their lives.

Recently, the UK campaign group Psychologists Against Austerity (PAA) has criticised the preliminary reports published on 12 December 2016 on the 'Origins of Happiness', a project conducted by a group of researchers led by Richard Layard at the London School of Economics. The study claimed that effective treatments for the most common mental health problems, such as anxiety and depression, would be a cheap and more effective way to reduce misery by 20%, while eliminating poverty would be more difficult and it would only reduce unhappiness by 5%.

Layard's work has previously contributed to David Cameron's adoption of national well-being statistics. This proved to be particularly controversial because it established return to work as an outcome of successful psychological treatment, which critics said may not be a suitable or even desirable outcome for many patients. However, the adoption of such criteria to monitor the effectiveness of a treatment model encouraged a policy of forcing people into work and professionals into roles that are outside the remit of therapy and contrary to the values of most clinicians. Layard was also a driving force behind the adoption of the Improving Access to Psychological Therapies (IAPT) program to increase access to 'talking therapies' on the NHS (predominantly very short-term CBT). A response published on the PAA website said that the researchers had not considered the complexity of the relationship between poverty and mental health.

The historical background

The first study concerning the trans-generational transmission of trauma was published in 1966 about survivors of the Holocaust (Rakoff et al., 1966). The author was a researcher at the Jewish General Hospital in Montreal, a city where thousands of Holocaust survivors had settled. Other psychiatrists and psychologists had published case reports proposing that the psychiatric disorders of these patients were the result of a 'survivor syndrome' passed on from one generation to the other. Since then, several hundred articles on intergenerational transmission – mainly limited to clinical cases and anecdotal reports – have been published, raising criticisms about the initial lack of systematic empirical studies, partially due to a lack of consensus about what was being transmitted. The clinical studies described a wide range of symptoms transmitted over generations including impaired parental function and ever-present fear of danger and distrust of the world. The idea that a parental traumatic experience could reach the second generation soon gained currency. Developing an attachment style that is deeply affected by the way the traumatised parent relates to their children may be one way the intergenerational transmission of trauma occurs.

Research by Yehuda (2015) on Holocaust exposure suggested the intergenerational impact of trauma could be passed down in epigenetic changes induced by severe environmental stress. Children of mothers who had experienced trauma often had a higher incidence of PTSD-related symptoms. However, Yehuda (2015) also found adults who had experienced abusive and neglectful childhoods but who had been able to process this trauma, were more resilient. Opportunities in later life to experience secure and nurturing relationships were found to be a particularly important aspect of developing resilience in adult life. Yehuda (2015) shows that epigenetic changes may be made throughout life, not just in childhood and these include positive transformations that increase resilience as well as negative changes associated with increased vulnerability.

In clinical practice, patients with parents who have never been able to mourn the losses that they experienced in childhood often describe anxious parents who are emotionally unavailable. Parental problems such as traumatic reliving, emotional numbing and dissociative phenomena, restrict children's capacity to develop a reasonable sense of safety and predictability in the world. These parents might be unresponsive during usual developmental crises, unable to help or make the world more comprehensible to their children. Such parents also experience difficulties with modelling a healthy sense of identity and autonomy, a capacity for self-soothing mechanisms and affect regulation, and maintaining a constructive perspective when life challenges arise. Instead, they model catastrophic or inappropriately numbed and disassociated responses and their high levels of anxiety can significantly interfere with the child's developmental progress. Children are also affected by the image they have of their parents. Parents' success in coping, achieving and being resilient influences whether the child can feel proud, ashamed or confused about their parents.

A number of studies (e.g. Danieli et al., 2016; Fromm, 2012) focused on the multigenerational transmission of trauma including the effects of war-related trauma, the psychological long-term effects of genocide, repressive regimes, migration, domestic violence and the effects of infectious and life-threatening diseases. However, researchers into the long-term effects of the multigenerational transmission of trauma acknowledge the constraints implicit in adopting trauma-focused models to address other political and social causes of suffering that are transmitted inter-generationally.

Often one child within a family or one member of a group is nominated to both carry and communicate the grief of their predecessors. The chosen child is charged with the task of keeping the family heritage, of becoming a 'holding environment'.

The task is 'something life defining and deeply intimate' (Fromm, 2012), the child speaks what his parents could not and carries their injuries into the future. At times, an individual must bear the painful process of separation from a self-sacrificing mother, from a depressed, unemployed father filled with humiliation and self-hatred or from a persecuted and stigmatised ethnic or religious group whose culture and guiding principles have informed the child's development and sense of identity.

Deprivation, trauma and human resilience

Social and psychological dimensions of material deprivation are gaining greater recognition in international literature on poverty. However, these studies have not yet sufficiently informed our clinical understanding of how poverty and poor mental health interact. Levels of poor mental health in communities are still predominantly understood and measured in terms of a number of individual pathologies. Psychobiological research (e.g. Wilkinson & Pickett, 2009) provides evidence of how chronic stress affects the physical health of individuals and groups. Wilkinson and Pickett (2009) also describe the poorer mental health of the 26% of the population living on a low income and subject to multiple deprivations and the significant impact on an individual's capacity for self-care, ability to establish intimate relationships and take care of their children.

Cohesive groups and closer-knit communities provide containing and protective factors to help people develop resilience to cope with adversities and inequality. Difference in local cohesion may explain why one poor neighbourhood has lower mortality rates than other equally deprived areas although all poorer communities still tend to have higher mortality rates than affluent areas. These influences are more complex when considering the experience of refugees and migrants from established communities in their countries of origin, who usually maintain their relationships with extended families who they have left behind or who have been displaced to neighbouring countries. They can experience acute feelings of guilt for having escaped and feelings of responsibility for those they left behind, especially when they live in areas at high risk from war or persecution.

Children and families at risk

Families with young children are at the highest risk of being adversely affected by increased levels of inequality in our society (Belfield et al., 2016; Department for Communities and Local Government, 2015; Elliott, 2016; Children Society, 2016; UNICEF Office of Research, 2013). In the UK we have sometimes been desensitised to the suffering of our children, as the adversities they experience at home, at school and in their communities seem less severe than the tragedies of refugee children who have been reaching the coasts and borders of European countries in increasingly larger numbers over the past years.

Children living in poverty usually have poorer physical and mental health and are less likely to achieve their potential academic or occupation level. Additionally, clear gender differences in young people's well-being are evident with girls less likely to enjoy the same quality of life or level of well-being as boys. It would be interesting to explore the correlation between the data reported and the historical views and expectations regarding the role and responsibilities of girls in households where the working day for fathers and mothers is becoming longer and longer. Research carried out by the Children's Society, Department of Education and a number of universities for over 20 years indicates poor care by parents and carers is most often a major factor affecting the life of teenagers who experience physical and mental health difficulties, including running away, taking risks, alienation from parents and social isolation.

Children of parents with a severe and enduring mental illness are more likely to be living in poverty than the rest of the population, experiencing raised levels of insecurity and anxiety. They may be bullied at school because of their parents' difficulties or their poverty. Children are often reluctant to ask for help fearing they will be removed from their parents. They may become carers for their parents, missing social and educational opportunities. Estimates suggest that 175,000 young carers in the UK are caring for a parent or other family member with mental health problems. Although many parents experiencing mental health difficulties can offer adequate parenting to their children, in some cases children are exposed to neglect or abuse.

The clinical use of CAT in therapeutic work with families affected by intergenerational disadvantages

Parents can find CAT useful as it provides an accessible structure to develop self-reflective activities, especially when they are struggling to make sense of traumatic experiences. A particularly valuable aspect of a CAT reformulation is that it can enable parents to see that the problems they are struggling with arose in circumstances they had no control over and often before they or even their own parents were born. Being able to contextualise their experience, validated in therapy, can be empowering by reducing self-blaming and self-recrimination; which otherwise would exacerbate reciprocal role procedures (RRPs) that are damaging to themselves and their children. A collaboratively constructed SDR (or map), of these relationships also encourages parents as they start seeing that changing how they relate to themselves and their children repairs some of the harm and institutes fresh, life-enhancing relational patterns in their family, increasing their children's opportunities for more rewarding relationships in their adult lives. I sometimes tell parents about the brain's 'plasticity' and how positive neurological changes can occur and 'traumatic symptoms' reduce when a child's relational environment changes.

Many referrals of parents for CAT come from Family Courts. However, parents referred by the courts, unlike self-referrals, often do not regard themselves as having psychological difficulties and may resent having to undergo therapy as a condition for seeing or being allowed to care for their children. This requires particular skills and sensitivity from the clinician. There is often conflict with the other parent and/or social services with the parties being locked into different and opposing narratives about what has gone wrong and who is to blame. Enabling parents to find a way through these tangled narratives to reach a place where they can accept different points of view, including those of their children, is arguably one of the most important clinical tasks with far-reaching consequences for families. I have found that engaging parents in a collaborative CAT-informed narrative of their concerns, including the historical antecedents, can stimulate their curiosity about their own responses and behaviour and enable them to see the need for change without feeling blamed.

Case example and discussion

The following is a case that was used to develop a Consultation Service for professionals working in an NHS mental health Trust who were confronted with many of the complex difficulties I described earlier, especially the intergenerational transmission of inequalities. I used CAT concepts as a structure for an exploration of the cultural, social and political context within which the patient, her partner, their children and all professionals involved experienced their difficulties.

Mary (the patient's name and narrative have been disguised to prevent her being identified) was referred to the Community Mental Health Team (CMHT) as she was profoundly despairing and feeling suicidal. She had lost hope in her capacity to protect herself and her four children, for her, the most intolerable of all losses, and expressed a wish to die. However, she said that she could not act on this death wish because of the trauma it would cause her children. She refused to be admitted into hospital and agreed to work with the local CMHT and be visited at home twice daily by the Crisis, Assessment and Home Treatment Team.

Her children were referred to the Children and Family Social Services and put on a Care Protection Plan. Mary perceived this as a punitive measure, but attended regular appointments with all professionals involved in her care and all the parenting classes offered by Children and Family Social Services. Mary was referred for psychological therapy and reluctantly engaged with an extended period of assessment and subsequently 24 sessions of CAT. She was afraid that the Children Services would take her children away and therefore she complied with all their recommendations, hoping to have the children taken off the Care Protection Plan.

Mary slowly established a trusting relationship with her care team and gradually disclosed information that she had never previously shared. She described having been sexually abused by her father at the age of 4. He had penetrative sex with her until her maternal grandmother noticed signs of infection and psychological distress and reported him to Social Services. Mary's parents then divorced and she was never allowed any further contact with her father. Mary's mother blamed her for the dissolution of the marriage and for the financial difficulties that they experienced. She subjected Mary to emotional and physical abuse including putting her cigarettes out on Mary's arms to punish her.

When Mary was 10, her mother remarried. Two years later her stepfather started repeatedly raping her with her mother's complicity and Mary became pregnant. Her grandmother, the only positive and caring presence in Mary's life, felt unable to report her own daughter and stopped all contact with the family and not long after this she died. Mary felt that there was no one to protect her. She gave birth to a baby boy when she was 13. He was registered in her stepfather's and her mother's name. Not only was Mary forced to raise her son/brother, but she had to witness her mother subjecting him to the same level of abuse that she continued to subject her to when her husband was not at home.

When Mary was 15 she ran away from home, living on the streets, working as a prostitute, abusing alcohol and drugs and self-harming until she came to the attention of a charity for homeless young people. They helped her to break this self-destructive cycle and housed her in a council flat where she met a neighbour who she later married. However, he controlled every aspect of her life, never allowing her money or social contact and was very demanding sexually. Mary longed for a stable family life and had tried her best to meet his needs although she felt that she was not heterosexual. When she told her husband that she identified as a lesbian he increased his sexual demands.

Eventually Mary could no longer tolerate this situation and left to live with another woman and her two children who attended the same school as Mary's children. When the head of the school attended by all children came to know of the relationship between the two women she called for a joint meeting with all parents. The meeting ended up in a fight and the headmistress called the police and Mary was charged with assault. Mary was banned from entering the school and the children's every word and action was put under close scrutiny. The headmistress kept a 'chronology' recording every detail observed that could be used as evidence of the couple's bad parenting skills.

When her children visited their father, Mary felt she had to spend nights there to reassure herself that the children were cared for and safe. During one of these nights her husband raped her. She reported him to the police and the children were put on the At-Risk Register to protect them against 'their emotionally abusive mothers' even though every professional working with the children had made statements on how well the children had been looked after by their mothers. The alleged rape was investigated and brought to court but all charges against Mary's husband were dropped. After listening to the ruling delivered by the court Mary wandered the streets feeling crushed and hopeless and considered suicide.

The professionals in the CMHT who worked with the family asked me for consultation, as I had developed a consultation service for colleagues working with patients at high risk within the local NHS Trust. The team complained of a general sense of 'feeling stuck'. We acknowledged that if Mary was to develop a level of resilience and capability to rebuild her life she needed emotional and social support, recognition for her strengths and help with developing social skills to increase her sense of competence and self-efficacy. We used Hagan and Smail's (1997) approach to power mapping to try and quantify the power Mary had in different areas of her life, such as home and family life, social life, personal resources and material resources. The aim was not to try and instill a sense of power in Mary, as an internal psychological attribute, but to help Mary to *obtain* power.

Inevitably, when the needs of individuals are so complex and damage so severe, the care provided struggles to meet not only the expectations of the person cared for, but also of the professionals who are expected to provide care. Mary loved her children and had their best interests at heart, but she often felt overwhelmed by intense feelings of powerlessness and anger that she directed against herself and others. She behaved in chaotic, inconsistent ways, restricted her diet, self-harmed and had suicidal thoughts when she felt unable to break the barriers preventing her from providing her children with the security, continuity, warmth and structure that she intuitively understood to be indispensable factors to develop their resilience and break the intergenerational pattern of destitution and marginalisation.

The continued collaborative use of diagrams in therapy helped Mary painfully come to terms with the fact that not only had she played the powerfully dominant and abusive parental roles described at the top end of her diagram against herself when she ran away from her family, self-harmed, restricted her diet and experienced suicidal thoughts, but she had also in some ways re-enacted the same roles with her children. Over time, she recognised how her children might have felt rejected, powerless, scared and unsafe when she abandoned them and responded to challenging situations in a chaotic and impulsive way. It was a devastating, but also a motivating experience for Mary to recognise that, despite her best efforts, her mental health and material instability were depriving her children of the possibility to develop and thrive.

As professionals attending the consultation meeting gained an understanding of Mary's difficulties, as described in her SDR, they moved from a position of hopelessness, of 'feeling stuck' to an active exploration of the intergenerational dynamics of oppression in Mary's life and in the life of her children. They reflected on how a child living in poverty might be viewed with sympathy, while an adult like Mary who grew up in poverty had been the object of great hostility and discrimination by professionals. Mary's poverty was finally understood in its tragic dimension as a long-term situation experienced across generations within her family. Understanding the impact that the intergenerational transmission of inequalities and resulting severe mental health difficulties had on Mary's life and on the life of her children was crucial for effective care planning to address difficulties, such as lack of opportunities and choice, lack of aspiration, inability to participate or feel included in society.

Figure 6.1 illustrates Mary's difficulties in diagrammatic format, how they developed in her relationship with her primary caregivers and the unhelpful strategies that she developed in order to cope with unmanageable relational experiences.

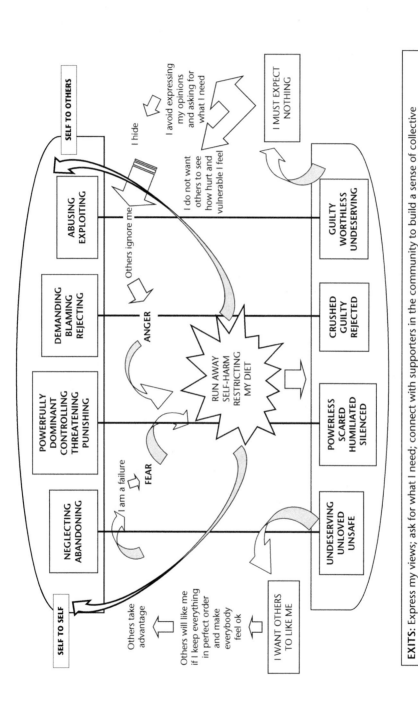

SELF TO OTHERS

I hide

I avoid expressing my opinions and asking for what I need

I do not want others to see how hurt and vulnerable I feel

I MUST EXPECT NOTHING

ABUSING EXPLOITING

Others ignore me

DEMANDING BLAMING REJECTING

ANGER

POWERFULLY DOMINANT CONTROLLING THREATENING PUNISHING

RUN AWAY SELF-HARM RESTRICTING MY DIET

I am a failure

FEAR

NEGLECTING ABANDONING

GUILTY WORTHLESS UNDESERVING

CRUSHED GUILTY REJECTED

POWERLESS SCARED HUMILIATED SILENCED

UNDESERVING UNLOVED UNSAFE

Others take advantage

Others will like me if I keep everything in perfect order and make everybody feel ok

I WANT OTHERS TO LIKE ME

SELF TO SELF

EXITS: Express my views; ask for what I need; connect with supporters in the community to build a sense of collective power – LGBT groups, friends, pressure groups; take care of my physical health, do not miss hospital appointments.

FIGURE 6.1 What life had shown Mary.

The process of developing a diagrammatic contextual reformulation reflected the team's experience of Mary's traumatic lack of power over her own life but also the staff team's experience of working with the Trust, with the NHS and within the public sector at a very difficult time. We realised that the repetitive patterns of reciprocation influencing the limited choices that Mary had were useful to describe the lack of power the staff experienced in the NHS and in relation to the social and political structures providing protocols and procedures for their work.

Figure 6.2 describes the patterns of reciprocation and the unhelpful coping strategies most often adopted by the professionals who attended the consultation meetings. The process of developing a contextual diagrammatic reformulation helped participants to understand how they could help Mary's children by helping Mary to recognise how her traumatic experiences were influencing the choices that she allowed herself as a person and as a mother (Bernardy-Arbuz, 2017). They became aware of the patterns of reciprocation they were drawn into when trying to help two generations of suffering human beings, but also and more generally, when they were trying to maintain a level of coherence and effectiveness in performing their roles in an ever changing and severely under resourced public sector.

They realised that in their relationships with managers, the NHS Trust they worked with and the 'higher powers' influencing the NHS policies and protocols they tended to enter patterns of reciprocation similar to those that Mary adopted when confronted with a challenge that was experienced as unmanageable. They recognised the power of the horizontal transmission of traumatic deprivation and the intensity of the feelings that they experienced as a result of this. They acknowledged that the unhelpful coping strategies they adopted seemed to mirror Mary's desperate attempts at escaping a pain that was too intense for her to endure. They shared with their patient an experience of lost identity, as the nature of their professional roles, the way they understood them, had been subverted. This had exacerbated a general experience of job insecurity and life instability.

Conclusion

In this chapter I have discussed how an unequal distribution of economic and social resources has a profound adverse influence on mental health and how this can be passed down from one generation to the next. The importance of the social and psychological dimensions of material deprivation is now gaining greater recognition in the international literature on mental health. This has informed research projects, which focus on developing indicators that capture the previously missing dimension of poverty.

There is a consensus in the studies that I have referred to on how the chronic stress of struggling with material disadvantage is intensified to a very considerable degree in more unequal societies. We have an extensive body of research that confirms the relationship between inequality and poorer outcomes – a relationship that is manifest at every position on the social hierarchy. The emotional, cognitive and physical effects of high levels of differentiation in social status are profound and

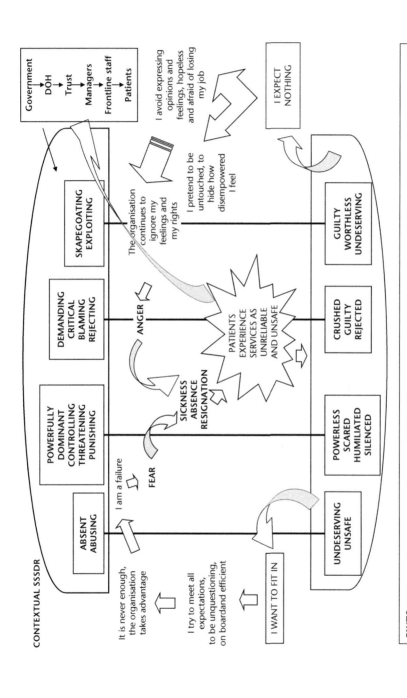

CONTEXTUAL SSSDR

Government
↓
DOH
↓
Trust
↓
Managers
↓
Frontline staff
↓
Patients

ABSENT
ABUSING

POWERFULLY
DOMINANT
CONTROLLING
THREATENING
PUNISHING

DEMANDING
CRITICAL
BLAMING
REJECTING

SKAPEGOATING
EXPLOITING

I am a failure

FEAR

SICKNESS
ABSENCE
RESIGNATION

ANGER

The organisation
continues to
ignore my
feelings and
my rights

I pretend to be
untouched, to
hide how
disempowered
I feel

I avoid expressing
opinions and
feelings, hopeless
and afraid of losing
my job

I EXPECT
NOTHING

It is never enough,
the organisation
takes advantage

I try to meet all
expectations,
to be unquestioning,
on boardand efficient

I WANT TO FIT IN

PATIENTS
EXPERIENCE
SERVICES AS
UNRELIABLE
AND UNSAFE

UNDESERVING
UNSAFE

POWERLESS
SCARED
HUMILIATED
SILENCED

CRUSHED
GUILTY
REJECTED

GUILTY
WORTHLESS
UNDESERVING

EXITS: Connect with patients and colleagues to build a sense of collective powers; Speak up and play an active role; take care of my physical and mental health; seek opportunities for personal and professional development to restore self-respect and social identity.

FIGURE 6.2   A sarcastic view of the pathologies affecting the public sector developed by a professional attending the consultation meetings.

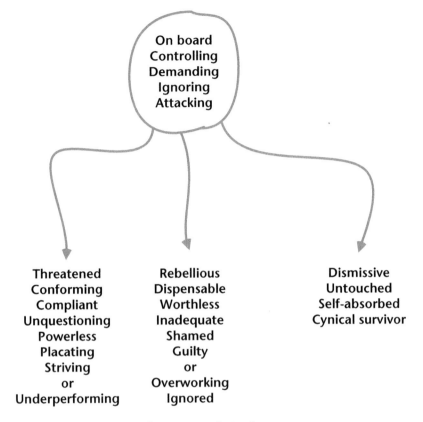

On board
Controlling
Demanding
Ignoring
Attacking

Threatened
Conforming
Compliant
Unquestioning
Powerless
Placating
Striving
or
Underperforming

Rebellious
Dispensable
Worthless
Inadequate
Shamed
Guilty
or
Overworking
Ignored

Dismissive
Untouched
Self-absorbed
Cynical survivor

FIGURE 6.3 What the system does to its professionals.

far-reaching. Parents who come to therapy often carry a heavy burden of shame and anger when their children are teased at school because they are not wearing 'cool' clothes, exhibiting the latest gadgets or engaging in popular activities, in addition to experiencing poor housing conditions and deprivation of basic necessities. They fear that they are losing control over their children because they are not at home to look after them, support them and to keep an eye on the people their children associate with. Recent cases involving child grooming have come to the attention of the public through media reports and have contributed to the intensity of some parents' feelings of failure and fear for the safety of their children.

A significant difference between poverty now and in the past is that employment is no longer a guaranteed route out of poverty; zero-hours contracts, stagnating wages and the increasing costs of housing mean that many families with two or more people in work live below the poverty line. Lack of job security has also contributed to many more people being vulnerable to falling into poverty. These changes are having a significant impact on family relationships, on the expectations that parents have of themselves and that children have of their parents. The structure of the intergenerational transmission of inequality makes it harder for an individual to overcome disadvantage as it blights children's development and jeopardises their future life chances.

As professionals living with the reality of the planned collapse of the NHS in favour of private consortiums, we are confronted with the ethical and political imperative to engage with these themes and with the disturbing vision that they offer of the mindlessness of our rulers. We can no longer sit comfortably with the present, private re-experiencing of historical trauma and fail to acknowledge that these experiences are tied to real injustices. These ties must set the direction for the transformative processes involved in our work, the guiding principles that make it possible for us not to succumb to arbitrary internal or external forces and to refuse to become the psychological army of oppressive powers.

Bibliography

Belfield, C., Cribb, J., Hood, A. & Joyce, R. (2016). *Living standards, poverty and inequality in the UK: 2016*. London: Institute for Fiscal Studies. www.ifs.org.uk/publications/8371.

Bernardy-Arbuz, M. A. (2017). If I work with the mother will the child get better? *International Journal of Cognitive Analytic Therapy & Relational Mental Health*. 1(1), March.

The Children Society (2013). *Briefing on child poverty*. www.childrenssociety.org.uk/sites/default/files/tcs/2013_child_poverty_briefing_1.pdf.

The Children Society (2016). *The good childhood report 2016*. www.childrenssociety.org.uk/sites/default/files/pcr090_mainreport_web.pdf.

Danieli, Y., Norris, F. H. & Engdahl, B. (2016). Multigenerational legacies of trauma: Modeling the what and how of transmission. *American Journal of Orthopsychiatry*, 86(6), 639–651.

Department for Communities and Local Government (2015). *The English indices of deprivation 2015: Research report*. London: Department for Communities and Local Government.

Elliott, I. (2016). *Poverty and mental health: A review to inform the Joseph Rowntree Foundation's Anti-Poverty Strategy*. London: Mental Health Foundation.

End Child Poverty News (2017). 4 million children now living in poverty in the UK, 16 March. www.endchildpoverty.org.uk/4-million-children-now-living-in-poverty-in-the-uk.

Fonagy, P., Steele, M., Steele, H., Leigh, T., Kennedy, R., Mattoon, G. & Target, M. (1995). Attachment, the reflective self, and borderline states. In S. Goldberg, R. Muir & J. Kerr (eds), *Attachment theory: Social, developmental and clinical perspectives*. London: Analytic Press.

Fromm, M. G. (2012). *Lost in transmission: Studies of trauma across generations*. London: Karnac Books.

Hagan, T. & Smail, D. (1997). Power-mapping I: Background and basic methodology. *Journal of Community and Applied Social Psychology*, 7, 257–267.

Kerr, L. K. (2012). When psychiatry retraumatises. www.laurakerr.com/2012/04/15/psychiatry-retraumatizes.

Layard, R. & Clark, D. M. (2014). *Thrive: The power of evidence-based psychological therapies*. London: Penguin.

McGrath, L., Walker, C. & Jones, C. (2016). Psychologists against austerity: Mobilising psychology for social change. *Critical and Radical Social Work*, 4(3), 409–413.

Moncrieff, J. (2008). *The myth of the chemical cure: A critique of psychiatric drug treatment*. London, Palgrave.

Newnes, C. (2014). *Clinical psychology: A critical examination*. PCCS Books.

Pickett, K. E. & Wilkinson, R. G. (2010). Inequality: An underacknowledged source of mental illness and distress. *British Journal of Psychiatry*, 197(6), 426–428.

Rahim, M. (2014). On trying to do therapy when your patient has no food or money. https://masumarahim.wordpress.com/2014/03/01/on-trying-to-do-therapy-when-your-patient-has-no-food-or-money.

Rakoff, V., Sigal, J. J. & Epstein, N. B. (1966). Children and families of concentration camp survivors. *Canada's Mental Health*, 14, 24–26.

Rapley, M., Moncrieff, J. & Dillon, J. (eds) (2011). *De-medicalising misery: Psychiatry, psychology and the human condition*. London: Palgrave Macmillan.

Rogers, A. & Pilgrim, D. (2003). *Mental health and inequality*. London: Palgrave Macmillan.

Rogers, A. & Pilgrim, D. (2013). *A sociology of mental health and illness* (5th ed.). Maidenhead, UK: Open University Press.

Smail, D. (1993). *The origins of unhappiness: A new understanding of personal distress*. London: HarperCollins.

Smail, D. (2002). Psychology and power: Understanding human action. *Journal of Critical Psychology, Counselling and Psychotherapy*, 2, 1–10.

Szasz, T. S. (1961/2010). *The myth of mental illness: Foundation of a theory of personal conduct*. New York: Harper Perennial.

UNICEF Office of Research (2013). *Child well-being in rich countries: A comparative overview* (Innocenti Report Card 11). Florence: UNICEF Office of Research.

Wilkinson R. & Pickett, K. (2007). The problems of relative deprivation: Why some societies do better than others. *Social Science & Medicine*, 65(9), 1965–1978.

Wilkinson R. & Pickett K. (2009). *The spirit level: Why more equal societies almost always do better*. London: Allen Lane.

Yehuda, R. (2015). How trauma and resilience cross generations. https://onbeing.org.programs/rachel-yehuda-how-trauma-and-resilience-cross-generations.

7

USING CAT TO BRIDGE THE GAP

Attending to the ultimate and the intimate

Emily Handley, Beth Greenhill and Kieron Beard

In this chapter we invite the reader to join us as we reflect on how CAT-informed thinking challenges and yet sustains us in our practice as psychological therapists, specialising in the mental health/psychological well-being of people with learning disabilities (LD). This chapter will be of interest to CAT therapists working in different areas as well as other health and social care professionals working with people with learning disabilities. We hope that it also has wider appeal and will be of interest to anyone working in the helping professions with an interest in equality, advocacy, social justice and human rights: Colleagues who may find themselves increasingly considering the political context of our work, and how we shape, and in turn are shaped by this context with direct consequences for both our own lives and the lives of the people we aim to support.

One thing we have all commented on, when reflecting on our teams and colleagues working with people with learning disabilities is that working with this community tends to attract people who have a strong interest in social justice, bringing the associated values to bear in their work. Probably related to this, many of us appear to identify with a particular minority group or have experienced oppression and societal shame and stigma related to an aspect of our identity. People with learning disabilities have a long history of exclusion, marginalisation and breaches of their fundamental human rights. Throughout history, this is reflected in the language used to describe this group of people being hijacked by society to become stigmatising labels used in the general population (Sinason, 1992). In addition to this their mental health needs have all too often gone unrecognised and they have been ignored by the therapy professions (Bender, 1993). Effective work in this area requires practitioners to also engage in advocacy and can put the practitioner in touch with painful feelings of exclusion and powerlessness. All of the above is currently being perpetuated by the present government's policy of austerity with a threat of a return to the days of institutionalisation.

We will describe how the concept of LD grew at a particular time, to serve a particular need of the industrial age. We will then consider how a CAT understanding and its associated radical social model of development of self and society challenges some of the commonly held assumptions that underpin the concept of learning disabilities and associated concept of intelligence upon which it is based – assumptions that tend to serve the status quo. We will consider how CAT can not only help us in our direct work with clients but also in our work at systems, organisational, community and political levels. We will also explore how CAT can help us understand our roles in this context and sustain our practice in an ethical way within this current challenging political context.

What's in a name? Defining people with learning disabilities

When we talk of people with learning disabilities, who do we actually mean? There are various definitions, however, they all currently have three components: a significant impairment in intellectual functioning, a significant impairment in adaptive functioning and for these to be manifest before the age of 18 (British Psychological Society, 2015). Definitions and associated criteria have changed over time. The existence of various definitions depending on the context says something about the social construction of the concept of learning disabilities, the difficulties in defining its precise boundaries and the various social functions such a label serves. The Department of Health (2001) estimates that there are approximately 1.2 million adults with mild-moderate learning disabilities living in the UK and 145,000 adults with severe or profound learning disabilities. However, a lack of data on this makes accurate estimates challenging, with some commentators stressing it is not currently possible to provide robust estimates but warning current quoted figures could be a serious underestimation (Emerson & Hatton, 2008). People with more severe learning disabilities come from a range of socio-economic backgrounds and their classification is usually more definite and associated with bio-medical conditions. However, it is not unusual for the number of those classified as mild to remain unknown. A disproportionate number of this group comes from disadvantaged socio-economic backgrounds (Hatton, 2012).

There are differing labels used, but the term 'people with learning disabilities' tends to be used in services in the UK. Internationally and for research purposes the term 'intellectual disabilities' (ID) is used. However, the official diagnostic term used in the ICD-10 continues to be 'mental retardation' (WHO, 1992). To add further confusion, most self-advocacy groups in the UK tend to prefer the term 'learning difficulties', with this meaning something else for professionals working within learning disability services (i.e. specific learning difficulties such as dyslexia and dyspraxia). The fact that the preferred term by the people who are assigned this label is not the predominant term used also communicates something about who holds the power to label. Throughout this chapter we will use the terms learning disability/difficulty interchangeably.

The history (creation) of learning disability and IQ

Throughout history the labels used to describe people with LD have been many. How differing societies have tended to relate to this group of people has also varied considerably. In Ancient Greece, people with learning disabilities were considered to have a deleterious effect on society and therefore needed to be eradicated (Plato 427–347 BC, in Lee, 1987). In the Mexican Olmec tribes (1500 BC–300 AD), Stratford and Gunn (1996) found that people with what would now be considered Down's syndrome (a genetic condition that includes the presence of learning disabilities) were depicted as god–human hybrids and concluded that people with Down's syndrome were probably worshipped by the tribe and held in high regard.

Although there is some mention of people who may be considered to have learning disabilities throughout ancient history, it was not until the Industrial Revolution of the eighteenth and nineteenth century that people came to be defined by their ability to cope with the technological and industrial advances of the age (Race, 2002). At a similar time, eugenics, the science of improving inborn human qualities through selective breeding (Galton, 1883) resurfaced as a social and political philosophy. The challenges posed by people with learning disabilities to contribute to 'profit-making' in a market system driven by greed and the, sometimes costly, need for care and support marked them for interest by the eugenicists. This led to the mass institutionalisation of people with learning disabilities, mass genocide in Nazi Germany (Burleigh, 1994), a selective immigration programme in the United States and a sterilisation programme within the UK (Brock Report, 1934).

We will now turn to briefly explore how intelligence testing developed simultaneously to the development of the eugenics movement and acted as a powerful tool to serve the vested interests of the privileged few. The first modern intelligence test was developed in 1904 by Alfred Binet and Theodore Simon to distinguish 'mentally retarded' children from 'normal intelligent, but lazy' children for the French ministry of education. The English statistician Francis Galton developed the first standardised test of intelligence. By 1915 these tests were being used to screen immigrants to the United States with federal law stating that anyone who failed the tests be turned away. It is important to bear in mind that these tests were highly Eurocentric and therefore many non-Europeans were turned away on the basis of failing these tests due cultural bias in the testing. Until the Education Act (1970) was introduced in the UK, people with severe learning disabilities were denied access to an education, being deemed uneducable. As we will explore later, a relational view of intelligence challenges the commonly head view of intelligence as being internal to the person and fixed over time.

Civil rights and de-institutionalisation

The civil rights movement of the 1960s and 1970s led to many advances in the rights of traditionally marginalised and oppressed groups. This also marked the beginning of change for people with learning disabilities and/or mental health needs with the publication of Goffman's (1961) critique of institutions. A decade later this was followed by Wolfensberger's (1972) principle of normalisation in human services. This principle was about appearing 'normal' and although progressive in some ways was also restrictive. For example, whereas this principle advocated that people with learning disabilities had the same opportunities as the rest of society, it also constrained the right of people to appear different or to behave in non-conventional ways. Later, as a result of these criticisms, Wolfensberger changed this principle to 'social valorisation'. By 1990, the UK government of the time passed the National Health Service and Community Care Act, which framed the legislative backdrop for the closure of the large-scale institutions and the move to care in the community. Although largely viewed as a positive move for people with learning disabilities, disagreement exists as to whether supporting the rights of people with learning disabilities was the primary motivator or whether cost-efficiency was hidden within this.

The move to community care models and de-institutionalisation was accompanied by a strong narrative of rights, inclusion, choice and independence. However, these have never really replaced the old narratives of paternalism, protectionism and segregation. There are fears that the current language of choice and independence is being used to enforce a programme of austerity and reduction in social care-funded support packages (Fyson & Cromby, 2013). Exploring these issues through a CAT lens leads to questioning of how 'independent' any member of society really is when we are all interdependent for our survival and this currently equating to 'loneliness' in many of the lives of people with learning disabilities. All of us support the provision of best quality services for the people we support and all work in specialist LD settings. However, as we will present later, a contextual reformulation also led us to question how our working within specialist services may also inadvertently contribute to the continuing segregation and exclusion of people with learning disabilities within society.

Learning disability through a CAT lens: theory and practice

Current understandings of learning disability remain anchored in two main theoretical approaches; namely the 'medical' and 'social' models of learning disability. Each of these models can risk lapsing into positions of biological reductionism (Lewontin et al., 1990; Read & Harré, 2009), or social determinism (Shakespeare & Watson, 2002) respectively. CAT has the potential to articulate a socially radical and more nuanced model of learning disability (Crowley et al., 2014; Potter & Lloyd, 2014), rooted in a dialectical and materialist biology, offering an 'exit' from this theoretical dilemma of whether the term 'learning disability' is a scientific or a political label (Greenhill, 2011; Varela, 2014).

Medical and social models of learning disability

Although the bio-medical model of (learning) disability originated in the nineteenth and twentieth centuries (Bury, 2001), it has recently enjoyed a resurgence due to the apparent promise of the 'New Genetics' (Ellison et al., 2013; Hare, 2016) and specifically of 'behavioural phenotypes' (Nyhan, 1972). The medical model views the conditions leading to severe and profound learning disability as having identifiable pathologies, including genetic disorders (Muir, 2000). Proponents of behavioural phenotypes argue that identifying specific genetic causes of learning disability (e.g. single-gene conditions and subtle chromosomal rearrangements) allows mapping of associated 'behavioural phenotypes'; the expression of these genetic changes at physiological and behavioural level (Dykens et al., 2000; Muir, 2000), including their distinctive social, linguistic, cognitive and motor profile (O'Brien et al., 2002, 2006). So, for example, a person with a label of Down's syndrome, defined by such authors as a genetic condition related to an additional copy of chromosome 21, may be at increased risk of developing the specific behavioural and physiological changes associated with dementia at a young age. This

> knowledge of behavioural phenotypes can help others to understand how a person interacts with their environment and how to adapt the environment to suit their needs, and it can help researchers track the path from causal underpinnings through to the difficulty the person is currently experiencing.
> *(Waite et al., 2014, p. 469)*

Diagnosis is argued to result in greater understanding and perceived control by providing prognosis, facilitating access to services and through more targeted care (Costain et al., 2012; Trottier et al., 2013).

In contrast, 'the big idea' of the British disability movement (Hasler, 1993), the social model of disability, was developed in the 1970s by activists in the Union of the Physically Impaired Against Segregation (UPIAS; Shakespeare & Watson, 2002) as a tool for action (Slorach, 2016). It emerged as a critique of the medical, individualised model (see Barnes, 1991; Finkelstein, 1980, 1981; Oliver, 1990, 1996), noting the tendency of the medical model to imply a 'personal tragedy model' of disability and impairment (Goodley, 2001) and its location of the 'problem' of disability within the individual (Oliver, 1990) and its propensity to see the causes of this 'problem' as stemming from the functional limitations or psychological losses assumed to arise from disability (Oliver, 1990). The central tenets of the social model are that the impairments that people have and the oppression that they experience are distinct. Disabled people, including people with learning disabilities, are an oppressed social group, with 'disability' being defined as the social oppression, not the form of impairment. In contrast to the medical model's emphasis on diagnosis and rehabilitation, the social model leads to a political strategy of removing barriers, collective action and, latterly, civil rights, rather than a focus on individual rehabilitation.

There are difficulties with both the medical and social models of learning disability. Many of the social model's historical criticisms of earlier incarnations of the medical model apply as readily to the current emphasis on behavioural phenotypes. Added to this, medical models of learning disability tend to express the doctrine of 'central dogma'. Central dogma is the idea that there is a causal relationship in biology running from our genes to the ribonucleic acid (RNA) and proteins they code for, to their eventual expression in our bodies and behaviour. This reductionist approach has been challenged by the 'dialectical biologists' (Lewontin et al., 1990) and also by the emerging science of epigenetics (Holliday, 2006), who both suggest that genes are altered by the environment and that this is not a 'one-way street'. The social model too is not without its difficulties. First, there is no impermeable membrane between the biological and the social: 'impairment' is often also social, for example caused by poverty and factors associated with lower socio-economic status (Slorach, 2016). Shakespeare and Watson (2002) argue in particular that the success of the social model created a 'sacred cow' for the disability movement, often avoiding or excluding the issue of impairment, emphasising a binary distinction between impairment and disability (similar to sex and gender) and, perhaps more importantly, note that many people with a disability resist the notion of owning an 'identity' as disabled (see also Beart et al., 2005). As a result, they argue, the social model often risks a crude social determinism. It is perhaps this social determinism that has created the space for biology to largely be left to the biological reductionists (Cromby et al., 2012) in disability theory.

Reformulating learning disability

Ryle's distinctive integration of object relations theory and Vygotskian approaches offers a unique platform from which to reformulate learning disability. CAT is generally understood 'as an alternative to . . . interventions based on diagnostic clusters linked to a neurobiological understanding of mental illness' (Ryle et al., 2014), and an alternative approach can equally be applied to the 'diagnostic cluster' of learning disability. This reformulation can be applied to our understanding of what is meant by cognitive or intellectual impairment, to our understanding of 'learning disability' and to our understanding of the rich dialogical interplay between them.

CAT has a distinctive perspective on our biology but in contrast to the emphasis on 'central dogma' in the medical model, insists that our biology is understood within its socio-cultural context. Drawing on Vygotsky's ideas, CAT views human beings as complex biological organisms who have evolved to collaborate socially through the use of speech and for whom both social co-operation and psychological attachment are key to our survival (Ryle, 2001). Ryle and Kerr (2002) argue that we are 'people whose nature it was to be formed by nurture' (p. 23). Ryle quotes Eisenberg, who states that '[m]ajor brain pathways are specified by the genome; detailed connections are fashioned by, and consequently reflect, socially mediated experience' (p. 23).

Attachment and language are socially and culturally situated expressions of our biology, enabled by our genetic make-up. As Aitken and Trevarthen (1997) state, 'the dependence of the child on co-operative understanding and cultural learning is part of human genetic inheritance . . . firmly grounded in the developmental neurobiology of the infant' (p. 664).

A relational view of intelligence

'Impairment' in the context of learning disability is an impairment of intelligence. Within neo-liberal Western society, intellect is assessed through 'subtests' of cognitive performance, with deficits attributed solely to the mind and functioning of the tested person. This intimate definition of cognition is a very specific cultural and historical definition (Gould, 1981). The Industrial Revolution created both the need for a skilled workforce and for testing to establish each person's capacity to develop through education. Thus, capitalism gave birth to our contemporary conception of IQ as a fixed and innate quality of individuals (Lewontin et al., 1990).

CAT has a profoundly different view of intelligence as *a socially mediated ability* (Varela, 2014, p. 78; see also Potter & Lloyd, 2014), drawing on the ideas of Vygotsky (1930–1933/1978, 1934/1986). Vygotsky was influenced by the radicalism of the Russian revolution, developing many of his most influential ideas through the study of children with 'special educational needs'. Vygotsky rejected 'the arithmetical conception of the handicapped condition' arguing instead that intelligence is relational and exists *between* people. One of Vygotsky's key theories, the Zone of Proximal Development (ZPD) describes how learning takes place when pitched in 'the gap between what a child is able to do alone and what he or she could learn to do with the provision of appropriate help' (Ryle, 2002, p. 41). When appropriate learning opportunities are provided within a child's ZPD, what is learned through interpersonal experience becomes part of the self and therefore part of the child's internal dialogue. This involves the creation and use of mediating signs conveying meaning and transforms the psychological structures that mediate it. Experience is internalised, such that, in Vygotsky's well-known phrase, 'What the child does with an adult today she will do on her own tomorrow' (1934/1986, p. 188). Here, learning is a process of enculturation, taking into account our historical and social being, in which emotion and cognition are deeply intertwined. Potter and Lloyd (2014) develop these ideas to describe a multifaceted model of relational intelligence. Here, intelligence lies in our ability to orchestrate various intelligences, including 'social intelligence', to function in the world. Potter and Lloyd's concept of relational intelligence implies that *all* of us share in the intellectual disability that we experience, rather than it being a property of one person in the presence of others who do not possess it. In CAT, 'The origins of intelligence are relational. The use of intelligence is relational. The sources of intelligence are relational . . . The problems with intelligence are relational' (Potter & Lloyd, 2014, p. 87).

A relational view of disability

For those of us whose biology or whose early childhood experience has led to difficulties in our use of speech or in our cognitive skills, learning is often then further disabled by the internalisation of social stigma and stereotypes, which shape the relational context of the care giver. As Ryle and colleagues (2014, p. 260) state:

A person's repertoire is derived from the interaction in infancy between their genetically determined temperament and the attitudes/actions of their caretakers and siblings. As well as shaping relationships with others, they are internalised as patterns of self-care, self-management and self-judgement, and may be manifest in internal dialogue.

In CAT, we become a person through other people and so stigma, social attitudes and stereotypes have a powerful impact on the experience of being a person in a world that places such huge value upon individual cognitive ability. Moreover, biological reductionist accounts of difference may contribute directly to this process of stigmatisation, at least in relation to mental health difficulties (Read & Harré, 2009).

Decades of research supports the idea that there is deep social stigma attached to 'having a learning disability' (Beart et al., 2005; Jahoda et al., 1988; Scior & Werner, 2016; Sinason, 1992), perhaps due to Sinason's three taboos of 'disability/ dependence', 'mortality' and 'sexuality', so that LD is often not acknowledged by others due to fear and shame (Sinason, 1992). Niedecken (2003) argues that people with learning disabilities can be damaged by the negative messages parents receive when they are born. These are then transferred to the infant by the parents in early socialisation. Shame is then internalised by the person: 'Overall, Each family will respond differently to discovering their child has an intellectual disability on account of their cultural beliefs about disability, ethnicity, religious beliefs socioeconomic status and broader social attitudes to disability' (Fletcher et al., 2016, p. 42).

Although there is a debate about the relationship between CAT and attachment theory, the literature concerning early attachment and learning disability is helpful, suggesting a number of mechanisms through which parents respond to negative social understandings of cognitive impairment (Fletcher et al., 2016). Grieving the 'loss of the healthy child' (Goldberg et al., 1995) may leave parents unable to internally represent their actual child (Atkinson et al., 1999), with unresolved grief potentially leading to rigid relationships (Goldberg et al., 1995) and difficulties with attunement, 'evidence suggests that grief and loss can have a wide-ranging impact, affecting mothers' emotional wellbeing, their ability to offer sensitive caregiving, the development of secure attachment relationships with their children and enjoyment in being a parent' (Fletcher et al., 2016, p. 52). Children with a learning disability are at increased risk of internalising a deep sense of shame that they have caused their parents to feel loss and disappointment; parents may be trying to protect their child in addition to managing their own feelings of loss and guilt, possibly about causing the disability or having been unable to prevent this (Lloyd & Dallos, 2006). Further, children with a learning disability may face additional disability-related barriers in expressing their attachment signals, leading to greater difficulty for their parents in responding appropriately (Schuengel & Janssen, 2006). CAT allows detailed mapping of the internalisation of these social processes as they emerge interpersonally in the lives of people with LD.

As well as being stigmatising, labels like that of learning disability, attract stereotypes: 'Labels have the power to oppress by stealing a person's individuality and then a collective stereotype replaces the personal consideration' (Lovett, 1996, p. 6, cited in Varela, 2014, p. 69).

In CAT terms, as Psaila and Crowley (2005) note, people with learning disability seem to have fewer reciprocal roles than many other social groups; stereotypes in our relationships to people with learning disabilities seem to restrict the roles that are available to them. Stereotyping through infantilisation may particularly restrict the reciprocal roles of a person with LD (King, 2005). Stereotyping may also be compounded by increased dependence leading to a less robust sense of a person's own identity and the increased likelihood of trauma for people with learning disabilities (Wigham & Emerson, 2015; Wright, 2013), which may in turn impact on attachment (van IJzendoorn et al., 1992), and may also restrict the available repertoire of reciprocal roles (Ryle, 1997).

Stereotyping may contribute not only to a person's sense of being defined by their disability but also directly to *actual* performance on tests of cognitive ability. Fine (2010) notes the impact that gender stereotypes have on tests of cognitive performance that are associated with socially desirable attributes for men and women. Given that subtle messages about gender congruence of tasks can have such a powerful impact on the performance of men and women, it seems highly likely that the blunt, negative messages society often conveys about learning disability are likely to impact on assessment of cognitive ability. Possibly the most limiting and constraining force on people with learning disability, therefore, is the societal and relational constriction of their roles, behaviours and voice, rather than any 'natural' individual ability.

Although as a society we do not give permission for people with learning disabilities to occupy the full breadth of the relational spaces, which might ameliorate any 'organic' difficulty, increasingly there is space to celebrate those who occupy the 'rebel role' (Fisher & Harding, 2009) to break through restrictions. At a local community awards ceremony, one of us was recently honoured to witness the recognition of a young woman who happened to have a learning disability through achieving the title of 'sports personality of the year'. Shauna Elise Hogan had been told at school that she would not be allowed to swim as she presented a 'health and safety risk'. Confounding her critics and the limited expectations of others, she has gone on to win hundreds of medals, including bronze and silver through competing internationally in the Special Olympics.

Practice and activism: both/and not either/or

What follows from this analysis is the need to work with both Ryle's 'ultimate and intimate' levels in our practice with people who have a learning disability (see also Maloney, 2013). Work at different levels of influence (Bronfenbrenner, 1986) can include direct CAT therapy, indirect contextual reformulation with a person's systems and work at the organisational and societal levels through activism and political engagement. CAT is also well placed to bridge work across these different levels – all are needed.

A politically informed approach to therapy with people with learning disabilities aims to ensure that disability is part of the reformulation, but not the only focus. It strives to ensure that people with LD are offered Bender's (1993) 'unoffered chair', with reasonable adjustments to make the intimacy of therapy accessible to all (Lloyd & Clayton, 2014). It also resists the notion that behavioural approaches are the only means of intervention, so that we can do therapy *with* people with LD, not just do behavioural interventions *to* them. CAT also offers multiple means for facilitating indirect work within the systems of people with LD (Lloyd & Clayton, 2014). Supporting staff teams, families, carers and partners to map their enactments towards the person labelled with LD can help to reduce the impacts of stereotyping and interpersonal friction and restriction. At the organisational level, CAT can help us to reflect on the interpersonal impacts of the commodification of care in the NHS (Welch, 2012)

More broadly, if to experience learning disability is to experience the wounds caused by social oppression, then as practitioners seeking to reduce distress, challenging these 'ultimate causes' is also part of our role. Celebrating diversity, championing role models who resist stereotypes of LD, problematising individualised definitions of IQ and the medical model, questioning derogatory language, fighting to create relational spaces in which to truly connect, supporting people with LD to learn about and claim their rights; these are all acts of solidarity, as important for our humanity as practitioners as they are to people who are labelled with LD. People with LD and other disabilities have been at the forefront of challenging the impact of welfare 'reform', through the activism of Disabled People Against the Cuts (DPAC) and other organisations. As staff, we have much to learn from the courage, organisation and conviction shown by the contemporary Disability Rights Movement. Sedgwick (1982) argues that such solidarity between staff and 'service users' is vital for effective change.

CAT also provides a powerful set of tools to facilitate our own reflexivity and to acknowledge our own positions within the system. In short, to support us to recognise when we are part of the problem. Positioning ourselves as critiquing may reinforce a sense of being judged in those we would seek to question (Greenhill et al., 2013; Handley et al., 2014). The 'rescuing to rescued' procedures so often found in practitioners who are passionately committed to developing services for people with LD can inadvertently reinforce disempowerment. The remainder of this chapter seeks to provide an example of how CAT can be used to map the system and intervene reflectively in it.

Dying too soon: reformulation at a systems level

What follows is a description of our experience of using a CAT framework to develop a systems level reformulation of a deeply concerning problem, namely the propensity for many people with learning disabilities to encounter marginalisation and neglect in the NHS, leading to premature and often preventable deaths, dying 13–20 years younger than the general population (Heslop et al., 2013). In addition to providing a psychological perspective on the factors perpetuating this known phenomenon, we also hope to demonstrate the value of CAT in supporting consideration of the complexities of relational functioning to inform endeavours to improve health or social care services.

Our work in this area involved the development of a diagrammatic reformulation of the problem and a reformulation letter addressed to the NHS. We began from a painful emotional state, as we found ourselves distressed and despairing when connecting with the pain of the inequalities faced by the people with learning disabilities who we encountered in our professional roles as specialist learning disability clinical psychologists. One author had recently lost her brother Richard Handley to constipation at the age of 33 (see the dedication to this volume), a wholly preventable death wherein Richard's physical health needs were overlooked and his difficulties attributed to his mental health and learning disability. Richard was a man with a lively sense of humour who loved Mr Bean, his theatre group and tickling the toes of the people he liked. Severe constipation is not uncommon among people with learning disabilities and, quite shockingly, Richard is not the only person with learning disabilities to have lost his life to constipation (a supposedly 'never event') in the UK in recent years. Indeed, another woman with learning disabilities died from constipation at the same hospital only six months after Richard, leaving us concerned and curious about obstacles to timely learning and service improvement.

Struck by personal grief and an increasing recognition of the lengths that many families have to resort to in order to 'fight' for good-enough health care, we also found ourselves feeling tired and hopeless as we recognised the limited impact that our battles to advocate for individual clients has had at a societal level in reducing inequality. We found ourselves wondering why 40 years of awareness of this 'target problem' had not led to significant change and what was preventing 'lessons learnt' from so-called 'never events' being translated into meaningful changes in practice. We also wondered what would be needed at a human level to overcome this repeating pattern and what we could do in our professional lives to resist 'joining the dance' and instead identify 'exits' to contribute towards social change.

We were encouraged to consider this impasse using a CAT perspective and found ourselves reflecting, with curiosity, on the likely feelings, aims and motivations of our compatriots within mainstream health services, who we often found ourselves battling with in pursuit of fair access and treatment for our clients with learning disabilities.

We undertook a review of the literature, attending to the language and themes utilised to describe the subject area. We entered into dialogue with colleagues from both mainstream and specialist learning disability services within the NHS as well as staff from learning disability charities. We also attended closely to the '@JusticeforLB' (or 'laughing boy') social media campaign led by the family of Connor Sparrowhawk, a much loved 18-year-old man with learning disabilities and autism who drowned while unsupervised in a bath following an epileptic seizure, in an NHS mental health assessment and treatment unit. Connor was a fit and healthy young man who loved buses, London, Eddie Stobart and speaking his mind. His death too was entirely preventable, but this was only recognised by services following tireless campaigning by his family (see Ryan, 2017).

We engaged in a process of mapping, using the language and concepts of CAT to translate our observations from the aforementioned sources into reciprocal roles, feeling states and patterns of relating. At the outset, we expected to encounter contrasting states when considering the feelings and experience of different parties, namely those of people with learning disabilities, their families, mainstream NHS staff and specialist learning disability professionals. However, we were instead struck by parallels, shared experiences and a range of observations that, when considered in therapeutic terms, can be summarised in terms of identifying elicited and personal counter-transferences. We realised that complex relational dynamics were at play between these different parties and that, as such, attention to elicited and reciprocating responses could offer insights into the factors seemingly perpetuating the identified inequalities.

We reflected on the core pain that is likely associated with the lived experience of the many inequalities faced by people with learning disabilities. We noted that family carers and professionals may at times connect emotionally with or identify with this core pain while, at times be paralysed by it. We then noted the different responses that can be elicited by this, either through prompting a championing and advocating response or through disengagement and inactivity. We realised that championing may overwhelm those we are attempting to engage, thus inadvertently perpetuating inequality. Furthermore, disengagement may serve as a defence, blinding NHS staff to the presenting needs of this vulnerable client group.

Prior to taking the time to explicitly consider these relationships at a systems level, we had not recognised the complexities of these relational dynamics. It struck us therefore how unlikely it would be that NHS staff working under pressure without psychotherapeutic expertise would recognise and overcome these manifestations and enactments.

What follows is the reformulation letter and diagrammatic reformulation in full. This is an example of the 'system' positioned as the 'client' within a CAT framework wherein the target problem for the 'system' is the propensity for people with learning disabilities to face health inequalities and premature mortality.

> Dear NHS colleagues,
>
> We are writing to you as fellow employees of our National Health Service (NHS) to begin a conversation about the experience of people with learning disabilities using the NHS. We hope that by lending our voice to this emotive subject this letter will encourage us all to welcome the voice and acknowledge the needs of this often unheard and unseen client group.
>
> We are clinical psychologists specialising in NHS learning disability services and we have noticed a striking divide between specialist and mainstream

services; we fear that this perpetuates the struggles faced by our clients in accessing the full range of NHS services.

It is widely documented that people with learning disabilities face health inequalities and that this directly results in an alarming rate of premature and preventable deaths in this population; people with learning disabilities are dying with illnesses that are easily treatable. While this is acknowledged in policy and many causal factors have been identified, the supposed 'lessons learnt' have not been translated into changed practice; consequentially the death toll continues to rise.

So-called 'lessons learnt' from the confidential inquiry into premature deaths in people with learning disabilities include the misinterpretation of policies such as the Mental Capacity Act (2005) and the Equalities Act (2010). This leads to dangerous assumptions, where patients are considered to 'opt out' of certain procedures. Opportunities are then missed to make decisions in people's best interests or to make procedures acceptable via reasonable adjustments.

There is a long history of people with learning disabilities having a very raw deal from society. We don't have to cast our minds back far to recall an accepted culture of institutionalisation and societal exclusion. A lot of progress has since been made and the right to meaningful community participation has been recognised; however, it is our sense that society has a long way to go before fully accepting those whose needs may exceed their economic contributions.

The NHS can feel like a powerful and impenetrable organisation to people with learning disabilities and their families. Too often in our work we meet those who feel utterly powerless, worthless and despairing in their attempts to access NHS services, as reasonable adjustments and flexibility are not forthcoming.

We recognise that we perhaps have idealised hopes for 'perfect care' for people with learning disabilities and it is important for us to appreciate that the NHS is not an infinite resource for any group. However, the ongoing failure of our NHS to address what has been termed by Mencap as 'Death by Indifference' leaves us identifying with the experience of our clients in feeling powerlessness and despairing.

Many people with learning disabilities have communication difficulties, making it difficult for them to make demands, complain or advocate for their rights to NHS treatment. People are either left without advocacy or it falls to family carers, support staff and specialist professionals to attempt this on their behalf. Our frustration within the learning disability field has inevitably led us, along with our colleagues in Mencap, to an assertive and championing position, striving to 'educate' staff in mainstream NHS services. You have no doubt experienced us as demanding, critical and without empathy towards your position. While our intentions were good, we realise on reflection that we may have inadvertently contributed to the impasse!

As NHS employees ourselves, we recognise that we all have a difficult task, as we strive to provide 'good health care for all' in an increasingly challenging system. As demand has increased, resources have decreased at an alarming rate. We find ourselves in a target-focused culture with increasing emphasis on throughput and statistics. We struggle to provide 'good enough' care while constrained by bureaucracy, waiting lists and an expectation that we will give more and do more for less. Most of us came into the NHS with values and ideals, compassion towards our patients and high hopes for providing good health care. Yet we risk burn out and our compassion towards our patients and each other may be threatened by this dehumanising culture.

We have been reflecting on the demands that we make on behalf of people with learning disabilities and thinking about your experience of these, in the context of the above pressures. You perhaps feel powerless in response to our demands and deskilled when faced with clients with communication difficulties, difficulties describing symptoms and difficulties understanding your questions and advice. Perhaps our championing demands maintain your sense of powerless uncertainty, undermining any hopes for change.

We find ourselves wondering if NHS staff in mainstream services are motivated to protect patients from pain and distress. Exposing patients to painful procedures may be additionally hard when they lack the capacity to consent; in these instances, you are required to explicitly state that the painful procedure is 'in their best interests'. Perhaps you are reluctant to impose further suffering on patients already living with a disability and a quality of life you may perceive to be poor. These value judgements unwittingly leave people with learning disabilities neglected, excluded and dying. Yet we are struck by how dehumanising it is for well-meaning NHS staff to be accused of 'indifference' when 'misguided kindness' may be more fitting.

We never fail to be surprised in our work by the tendency of some of our clients with learning disabilities to acquiesce with us, giving us the answer they think we want to hear. Valerie Sinason termed this the 'handicapped smile', wherein people with learning disabilities minimise their emotional needs to 'protect' society from the pain of their disability. Where these dynamics are present when relating with NHS staff, illnesses and symptoms may remain unseen and NHS staff may be blissfully unaware of the need to act. Taking this one step further, we wonder if we wear a 'handicapped smile' of our own as NHS employees, colluding with bureaucratic constraints in the NHS that we know to be inadequate, overwhelmed by our own sense of powerlessness and despair.

In writing this letter we are offering a different perspective on the reality of health inequalities for people with learning disabilities. A cognitive analytic framework has enabled us to map out the lived experiences of all parties from a relational perspective, to reflect on the development of the problem and to identify the beliefs, motivations and aims that may inadvertently maintain it. We hope that this perspective and acknowledgement of our reciprocal contributions offers a non-blaming stance, which might liberate us all towards a more constructive, collaborative and compassionate response.

In writing this letter, we are hoping to mobilise a sense of shared ownership between learning disability specialists and mainstream NHS staff and to encourage the co-creation of solutions or 'exits'.

We recognise that in working together towards these aims, there is a possibility that, at times, we might revert back to unhelpful relational dynamics. In championing this cause, we may too be perceived as critical and demanding, ultimately adding to the sense of overwhelm. Our hopes may be idealised, and we are reminded of a need to strive for 'good enough' care. Given the current NHS climate and lack of resources it may be important for us to remain alert to feelings of powerlessness; creative and collaborative thinking could be useful in identifying exits.

This is a sensitive and distressing subject and in trying to protect people with learning disabilities, there may be a danger that we exclude their voice from the process. It will be important for us to monitor the extent to which our motivation to protect may inadvertently lead to exclusion.

We hope that this letter may be the start of an ongoing conversation.
Best Wishes,
Emily Handley, Kieron Beard and Beth Greenhill

Our experience of undertaking this work was beneficial in a number of ways. We became more self-aware and better able to contemplate our own potential, as learning disability specialists, to unintentionally and unconsciously perpetuate the impasse and challenges. An increased awareness of our own elicited and identifying countertransference responses gave us helpful insights into the likely feeling states of other parties. This enabled us to take a more compassionate and empathetic stance towards staff within mainstream services that we had previously experienced frustrations towards. Two of the authors developed a programme of training for NHS staff in mainstream services, recognising the need to validate any anxieties or concerns that attendees might arrive with and focusing on the development of confidence and motivation rather than skills alone. This training was delivered over a number of years; it received consistently good feedback, self-reported increases in confidence, motivation and skills among attendees and a reduced reluctance for staff among mainstream services to work with people with learning disabilities. Earlier versions of this training had focused instead on the legislation that commands mainstream services to provide equitable access, which likely risked overwhelming or disengaging the staff whose need it was designed to meet.

As CAT therapists, clinical psychologists and NHS employees, our job roles require us to connect with high levels of emotional pain and distress. Working with people with learning disabilities often requires us to relate with people experiencing significant levels of oppression and inequality. The emotionality of this

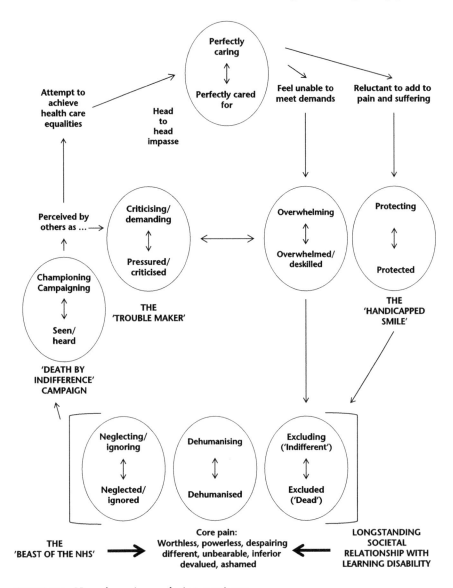

FIGURE 7.1 How damaging exclusion continues.

work can elicit passionate drive among some but also a sense of overwhelm among others and efforts are required to ensure that service improvements are approached not only strategically but also compassionately, meeting all parties where they currently are and attending to the ultimate as well as the intimate causes of distress. We believe that it is our duty to extend our therapeutic and theoretical insights to our work at a political and systems level as well as our work with individual clients. This should help us to reduce our areas of ignorance and move past the current impasse, which we may be at risk of inadvertently perpetuating.

Bibliography

Aitken, K. J. & Trevarthen, C. (1997). Self/other organisation in human psychological development. *Development and Psychopathology*, 9, 653–677.

Atkinson, L., Chisholm, V. C., Scott, B., Goldberg, S., Vaughn, B. E., Blackwell, J. Dickens, S. & Tam, F. (1999). Atypical attachment in infancy and early childhood among children at developmental risk: Maternal sensitivity, child functional level, and attachment in Down's syndrome. *Monographs of the Society for Research in Child Development*, 64, 45–66.

Barnes, C. (1991). *Disabled people in Britain and discrimination: A case for anti-discrimination legislation.* London: Hurst & Co in association with the British Council of Organisations of Disabled People.

Beart, S., Hardy, G. & Buchan, L. (2005). How people with intellectual disabilities view their social identity: A review of the literature. *Journal of Applied Research in Intellectual Disabilities*, 18, 47–56. doi:10.1111/j.1468-3148.2004.00218.x.

Bender, M. (1993). The unoffered chair: The history of therapeutic distain towards people with a learning difficulty. *Clinical Psychology Forum*, 54, 7–12.

British Psychological Society. (2015). *Guidance on the assessment and diagnosis of intellectual disabilities in adulthood: A document compiled by a working group of the British Psychological Society's Division of Clinical Psychology, Faculty for People with Intellectual Disabilities.* Leicester, UK: British Psychological Society.

Burleigh, M. (1994). *Death and deliverance: Euthanasia in Germany c.1900–1945.* Cambridge: Cambridge University Press.

Bury, M. (2001). Illness narratives: Fact or fiction, *Sociology of Health and Illness*, 23, 3, 263–285.

Brock Report (1934). n. 22, 60–74; Appendix IX, 131–134.

Bronfenbrenner, U. (1986). Ecology of the family as a context for human development: Research perspectives. *Developmental Psychology*, 22(6), 723–742.

Costain, G., Chow, E. W., Ray, P. N. & Bassett, A. S. (2012). Caregiver and adult patient perspectives on the importance of a diagnosis of 22q11.2 deletion syndrome. *Journal of Intellectual Disability Research*, 56, 641–651.

Cromby, J., Diamond, B., Kelly, P., Moloney, P., Priest, P., Smail, D. & Soffe-Caswell, J. (2012). Draft manifesto for a social materialist psychology of distress. *Journal of Critical Psychology, Counselling and Psychotherapy*, 12(2), 93–107.

Crowley, V., Field, B., Lloyd, J., Morrison, P. & Varela, J. (2014). When the therapist is disabled. *Reformulation*, Summer, 6–9.

Department of Health. (2001). *Valuing people: A new strategy for learning disability for the 21st century.* London: Stationery Office.

Dykens, E., Hodapp, R. & Finucane, B. (2000). *Genetics and mental retardation syndromes: A new look at behaviour and interventions.* Baltimore, MD: Brookes.

Education (Handicapped Children) Act (1970). Available at: www.legislation.gov.uk/ukpga/1970/52/enacted.

Ellison, J. W., Rosenfeld, J. A. & Shaffer, L. G. (2013). Genetic basis of intellectual disability. *Annual Review of Medicine*, 64, 441–450. https://doi.org/10.1146/annurev-med-042711-140053

Emerson, E. & Hatton, C. (2008). *People with learning disabilities in England: Centre for Disability research report.* London: Mencap and Learning Disability Coalition.

Fine, C. (2010). *Delusions of gender: The real science behind sex differences.* London: Icon.

Finkelstein, V. (1980). *Attitudes and disabled people.* New York: World Rehabilitation Fund.

Finkelstein, V. (1981). To deny or not to deny disability. In A. Brechin et al. (eds) *Handicap in a social world.* London: Hodder & Stoughton.

Fisher, C. & Harding, C. (2009). Thoughts on the rebel role: Its application to challenging behaviour in learning disability services. *Reformulation, Journal of the Association of Cognitive Analytic Therapy*, Winter, 4–5.

Fletcher, H. K., Flood, A. & Hare, D. J. (2016). *Attachment in intellectual and developmental disability: A clinician's guide to practice and research*. Chichester, UK: Wiley.

Fyson, R. & Cromby, J. (2013). Human rights and intellectual disabilities in an era of 'choice'. *Journal of Intellectual Disability Research*, 57(12), 1164–1172.

Galton, F. (1883). *Inquiries into human faculty and its development*. London: Macmillan.

Goffman, E. (1961). *Asylums: Essays on the social situation of mental patients and other inmates*. Garden City, NY: Anchor Books, Doubleday & Co.

Goldberg, D., Magrill, L., Hale, J., Damaskinidou, K., Paul, J. & Tham, S. (1995). Protection and loss: Working with learning disabled adults and their families. *Journal of Family Therapy*, 17, 263–280.

Goodley, D. (2001). 'Learning difficulties', the social model of disability and impairment: Challenging epistemologies. *Disability & Society*, 16(2), 207–231. doi: https://doi.org/10.1080/09687590120035816.

Gould, S. J. (1981). *Mismeasure of man*. New York: Norton & Company.

Greenhill, B. (2011). 'They have behaviour, we have relationships?' *Reformulation, Journal of the Association of Cognitive Analytic Therapy*, Winter, 10–15.

Greenhill, B., Roberts, A. & Swarbrick, R. (2013). We need decent people as well as decent laws. *Reformulation, Journal of the Association of Cognitive Analytic Therapy Winter*, Summer, 18–25.

Handley, E., Beard, K. & Greenhill, B. (2014). Death by indifference: A letter to the NHS. *Reformulation, Journal of the Association of Cognitive Analytic Therapy*, Winter, 42, 45–46.

Hare, D. J. (2016). Beyond IQ: The case for a new conceptualisation of intellectual disabilities. *Bulletin of the Faculty for People with Intellectual Disabilities*, 14(3), 12–19.

Hasler, F. (1993). Developments in the disabled people's movement. In J. Swain et al. (eds), *Disabling barriers, enabling environments*. London: Sage.

Hatton, C. (2012). Intellectual disabilities: Classification, epidemiology and causes. In E. Emerson, C. Hatton, J. Bromley & A. Caine (eds) *Clinical psychology and people with intellectual disabilities*. Chichester, UK: Wiley.

Heslop, P., Blair, P., Fleming, P., Hoghton, M., Marriott, A. & Russ, L. (2013). *Confidential inquiry into premature deaths of people with learning disabilities (CIPOLD) Final Report*. Bristol: Norah Fry Research Centre.

Holliday, R. (2006). Epigenetics: A historical overview. *Epigenetics*, 1(2), 76–80.

Jahoda, A., Markova, I. & Cattermole, M. (1988). Stigma and the self-concept of people with a mild mental handicap. *Journal of Mental Deficiency Research*, 32(2), 103–115.

King, R. (2005). CAT, the therapeutic relationship and working with people with learning disability. *Reformulation, Journal of the Association of Cognitive Analytic Therapy*, Winter, Spring, 10–14.

Lee, D. (1987). *Plato: The republic*. London: Penguin.

Lewontin, R., Rose, S. & Kamin, L. (1990). *Not in our genes: Biology, ideology and human nature*. London: Penguin Books.

Lloyd, H. & Dallos, R. (2006). Solution-focused brief therapy with families who have a child with intellectual disabilities: A description of the content of initial sessions and the processes. *Clinical Child Psychology and Psychiatry*, 11(3), 367–386. https://doi.org/10.1177/1359104506064982.

Lloyd, J. & Clayton, P. (eds) (2014). *Cognitive analytic therapy for people with learning disabilities and their carers*. London: Jessica Kingsley Publishers.

Lovett, H. (1996). *Learning to listen: Positive approaches and people with difficult behaviours.* London: Jessica Kingsley Publishers.

Maloney, P. (2013). *The therapy industry: The irresistible rise of the talking cure, and why it doesn't work.* London: Pluto Press.

Muir, W. J. (2000). Genetics advances and learning disability. *British Journal of Psychiatry,* 176(1) 12–18. doi: 10.1192/bjp.176.1.12.

National Health Service and Community Care Act (1990). Available at: www.legislation. gov.uk/ukpga/1990/19/contents.

Niedecken, D. (2003). *Nameless: Understanding learning disability.* Brunner-Routledge: New York.

Nyhan, W. L. (1972). Behavioral phenotypes in organic genetic diseases: Presidential address to the Society for Pediatric Research. *Paediatric Research,* 6, 1–9.

O'Brien, G. (ed.) (2002). *Behavioural phenotypes in clinical practice.* Cambridge: Cambridge University Press.

O'Brien G. (2006). Behavioural phenotypes: Causes and clinical implications. *Advances in Psychiatric Treatment,* 12, 338–348.

Oliver, M. (1990). *The politics of disablement.* Basingstoke, UK: Macmillan.

Oliver, M. (1996). *Understanding disability: from theory to practice.* Basingstoke, UK: Macmillan.

Potter, S. & Lloyd, J. (2014). In J. Lloyd & P. Clayton (eds), *Cognitive analytic therapy for people with learning disabilities and their carers.* London: Jessica Kingsley.

Psaila, C. & Crowley, V. (2005). CAT in PLD: An investigation into the common RRs found within this client group. *Mental Health and Learning Disabilities Research,* 2, 96–108.

Race, D. (2002). *Learning disability: A social approach.* London: Routledge.

Read, J. & Harré, N. (2009). The role of biological and genetic causal beliefs in the stigmatisation of 'mental patients'. *Journal of Mental Health,* 10(2), 223–235.

Ryan, S. (2017). *Justice for laughing boy: Connor Sparrowhawk – A death by indifference.* London: Jessica Kingsley Publishers.

Ryle, A. (1990). *Cognitive analytic therapy: Active participation in change.* Chichester, UK: Wiley.

Ryle, A. (1997). *Cognitive analytical therapy and borderline personality disorder: The model and the method.* Chichester, UK: Wiley.

Ryle, A. (2001). CAT's dialogic perspective on the self. *ACAT News, Journal of the Association of Cognitive Analytic Therapy,* Autumn.

Ryle, A. (2010). The political sources of reciprocal role procedures. *Reformulation, Journal of the Association of Cognitive Analytic Therapy,* Summer, 6–7.

Ryle, A. & Kerr, I. (2002). *Introducing cognitive analytic therapy: Principles and practice.* Chichester, UK: Wiley.

Ryle, A., Kellett, S., Hepple, J. & Calvert, R. (2014). Cognitive analytic therapy at 30. *Advances in Psychiatric Treatment,* 20(4), 258–268. doi: 10.1192/apt.bp.113.011817.

Schuengel, C., & Janssen, C. G. C. (2006). People with mental retardation and psychopathology: Stress, affect regulation and attachment. A review. *International Review of Research in Mental Retardation,* 32, 229–260. doi: 10.1016/S0074-7750(06)32008-3.

Scior, K. & Werner, S. (2016). (eds). *Intellectual disability and stigma: Stepping out from the margins.* Basingstoke, UK: Palgrave Macmillan.

Sedgwick, P. (1982). *Psychopolitics.* London: Pluto Press.

Shakespeare, T. & Watson, N. (2002). The social model of disability: an outdated ideology? *Research in Social Science and Disability,* 2, 9–28.

Sinason, V. (1992). *Mental handicap and the human condition: New approaches from the Tavistock.* London: Free Association Books.

Slorach, R. (2016). *A very capitalist condition: A history and politics of disability*. London: Bookmarks Publications.

Stern, D. N. (1985). *The interpersonal world of the infant: A view from psychoanalysis and developmental psychology*. New York: Basic Books.

Stratford, B. and Gunn, I. (1996). Historical aspects: In the beginning. In B. Stratford & I. Gunn (eds), *New approaches to Downs syndrome*. London: Cassell

Trottier, M., Roberts, W., Drmic, I., Scherer, S. W., Weksberg, R., Cytrynbaum, C., Chitayat, D., Shuman, C. & Miller, F. A. (2013). Parents' perspectives on participating in genetic research in autism. *Journal of Autism and Developmental Disorders*, 43, 556–568.

Van Ijzendoorn, M. H., Goldberg, S., Kroonenberg, P. M. & Frenkel, O. J. (1992). The relative effects of maternal and child problems on the quality of attachment: A meta-analysis of attachment in clinical samples. *Child Development*, 63, 840–858.

Varela, J. (2014). Formulating and working therapeutically with the concept of intellectual disability model in cognitive analytic therapy. In J. Lloyd & P. Clayton (eds), *Cognitive analytic therapy for people with learning disabilities and their carers*. London: Jessica Kingsley Publishers.

Vygotsky, L. S. (1930–1933/1978). *Mind in society: The development of higher psychological process*. Cambridge, MA: Harvard University Press.

Vygotsky, L. S. (1934/1986). *Thought and language*. Cambridge, MA: MIT Press.

Waite, J., Heald, M., Wilde, L., Woodcock, K., Wedham, A., Adams, D. & Oliver, C. (2014). The importance of understanding the behavioural phenotypes of genetic syndromes associated with intellectual disability. *Paediatrics and Child Health*, 24(10), 468–472.

Welch, L. (2012). Reciprocal roles in the NHS. *Reformulation, Journal of the Association of Cognitive Analytic Therapy*, Winter, 39, 14–18

Wigham, S. & Emerson, E. (2015). Trauma and life events in adults with intellectual disability. *Current Developmental Disorders Reports*, 2(2), 93–99.

Winnicott, D. W. (1971). *Playing and reality*. London: Tavistock.

Wolfensberger, W. (1972). *The principle of normalization in human services*. Toronto, ON: National Institute on Mental Retardation.

World Health Organization (1992). *The ICD-10 classification of mental and behavioural disorders: Clinical descriptions and diagnostic guidelines*. Geneva, Switzerland: World Health Organization.

Wright, S. (2013). How do we prevent another Winterbourne? A literature review. *Advances in Mental Health and Intellectual Disabilities*, 7(6), 365–371. https://doi.org/10.1108/AMHID-02-2013-0013.

8

FROM DEVIANCE AND SIN TO UNMET NEEDS

A CAT conceptualisation of challenging behaviour

Jo Varela

Introduction: the historical background to behaviour that challenges

This chapter offers a description of the cultural, historical and social underpinnings of our responses to being challenged by the behaviour of another within health and social care settings. We take a Western and predominantly British perspective. This is owing to the perspective and viewpoints of the authors, but also reflects the development and context of the growth of cognitive analytic therapy as a model and the political and social climate from which the model grew. The chapter explores what happens when we are challenged by the presentation or behaviour of those we care for, and how our responses may not be those of the caring professional we strive to be.

What is challenging behaviour?

The Association for the Severely Handicapped coined the term 'challenging behaviour' in an attempt to reframe 'problem' behaviour more humanely. This challenges carers to take a curious stance to understanding and supporting people. Such reframing was intended to transfer the burden and responsibility for change from those who struggled to carers. The definition of challenging behaviour is relational (Varela, 2014), in that in order to be 'challenging' there must be another who is challenged.

From behaviour that challenges to challenging behaviour and back again

Behaviours described as challenging may include aggression, self-harm, disengagement or any behaviour that limits social inclusion or is 'culturally abnormal'

(Emerson, 2001). In shortening the term 'behaviour that challenges' to 'challenging behaviour', this ethos has lost its power to invite relational reflection. Although it invites curiosity about the challenger, responses and feelings that are hard to speak about – rage, fear, loss of control and harm on the part of the challenged – remain unseen and unresolved.

People who challenge though their behaviour have always experienced an uneasy relationship with those who provide care. Despite the humane intent of those attempting to care, the derogatory words used to describe people illustrate tensions, fear, frustration and 'otherness' and inevitably expose a history of ruptured relationships. This chapter postulates that despite a development in understanding of the causes of challenging behaviour (as expressions of unmet needs, pain and trauma), enactments of historical responses to being challenged still dominate the care of people who challenge us today.

Challenging whom?

Humans are fundamentally social creatures. We have a finely constructed set of social rules and norms to co-exist. Individuals whose behaviour undermines this order are perceived to be highly threatening. We may construe this behaviour as criminal, a wilful breaking of social order for personal gain. We understand humanity to be sinful and flawed, amenable to change through redemption, and justice to be achievable though reparation or punishment.

However, what of those whose behaviour breaks social norms for reasons that are hard to comprehend, or who cannot give a good account of their motivations? Crudely put, we have understood that if people are not 'bad', they must be 'mad', and as such do not have the capacity for regulating their behaviour. This group of people challenge our perceptions of the world as safe and predictable. Their disruption of order challenges our sense of power, control and agency. We may feel dominated by their chaos and misrule and seek to control and assert ourselves to establish equilibrium. People who challenge often evoke a multitude of complex feelings including disgust, fear, pity, confusion and anger. The person who challenges becomes the 'other' to us; feared, objectified, diminished and excluded. They may challenge us further if they do not respond 'normally' to social controls such as punishment. We are confused and remain fearful, unable to understand and respond in ways that resolve the problem.

The history of challenging behaviour

The history of understanding and working with challenging behaviour can be told in single words. Predecessors to the term 'challenging' include wicked, degenerate, disorderly, indecent, obscene, insubordinate, amoral, defective, difficult, antisocial, disordered, non-compliant, non-concordant, attention-seeking, aberrant, dangerous and undesirable. These words were used not just to describe behaviour but to summarise people: the 'undesirables', the 'wicked', the 'aberrant' and the 'degenerate'.

The current paradigm for conceptualising challenging behaviour evolved in the middle of the last century: medical understandings of mental health and brain function, and psychological and social models of behaviour, development and socialisation. Prior to this, the understanding of those whose behaviour challenged social order was superficial (uncomplicated notions of 'bad from birth') or spiritual (possessed or cursed). Those with (now recognisable) mental health problems were 'lumped' with others who broke social rules: the unwed mother, the irreligious, the 'crippled' and those 'seized by grief or anger' who lost their reason (and with it, knowledge of the Bible and salvation). Those who professed to cure were also 'magical' prophets healing those tormented by spirits, perpetuating a myth that only the all-powerful divine had nothing to fear. 'Cure' consisted of forcibly casting out devils through corporeal subjugation, 'working' the idle to find a Godly life through discipline or exclusion, and confinement (see Scull, 2016, for further discussion.)

Relationships to those who challenged social order could thus be understood from a CAT perspective as shown in Figure 8.1.

We remain challenged to know what to do with those whose behaviour challenges us. From believing in challenging behaviour as a product of evil or bedevilment, we have progressed to more benevolent explanatory models such as the medical model that seeks to locate disorder and deficit within the person and simultaneously models that stress the influences of society and the environment.

If the patient is unable to change their behaviour, the Mental Health Act (DOH, 1983) gives trained individuals the power to detain in order to treat. Less well acknowledged is the use of this power to control, exclude and force; a method of social control that may be unconscious echoes of the relational responses outlined above. Unless we view challenging behaviour as a social and reciprocal phenomenon, old responses to challenging behaviour risk being repurposed and repackaged within the medical and behavioural model. Whether we use medicine or a behavioural approach, unless we are careful – even now – we may re-enact similar responses of exclusion, rejection, control and forcible cure without insight or humanity and provide superficial explanations and interventions such as 'doing it for attention so just ignore them', 'take away their privileges so they learn that their behaviour is not acceptable' or use technical behavioural language such as 'time out' to mask exclusion.

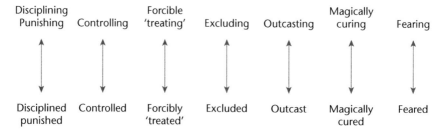

FIGURE 8.1 Seen as socially deviant.

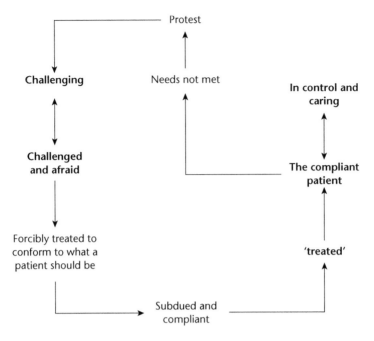

FIGURE 8.2 Responding to being 'done to'.

To find ways of addressing the actual needs of people whose behaviour we find challenging, we must find new ways of formulating their difficulties and our responses to them. To be excluded and forcibly 'cured' challenges people we care for by re-traumatising them. In being challenged, invalidated and excluded, it is understandable that they may behave in ways that are seen as challenging and the vicious circle is complete (see Figure 8.2).

These 'care' responses in turn challenge our ideas about what it is to be an equal human and a professional carer. If people who challenge are no longer considered to be part of society then they are seen to be less of a human being, powerless and 'done to'. To be excluded from formative and restorative mutual relationships leaves people dehumanised; their needs and selves are not valued, validated or met.

What is challenging behaviour? A socio-political approach

Challenging behaviour, people and society

Challenging behaviour is a socially constructed concept. We now understand it to have a communicative function. The behaviour may be the person's only way of attempting to gain temporary agency in their world.

> Behaviour that is challenging results in a response from others and is a way of gaining a sort of control. For an individual's behaviour to be viewed as challenging, a judgement is being made that this behaviour is dangerous,

frightening, distressing or annoying and that these feelings, invoked in others, are in some way intolerable or overwhelming.

(Learning Disabilities Professional Senate, 2016, p. 8)

Construing challenging behaviour as social and relational allows the opportunity to re-formulate 'deviance in the individual' as relational trauma, mutually reinforced and therefore relationally resolvable. In broad terms challenging behaviour may be seen to be a reciprocal enactment of establishing personal agency in order to manage an intolerable situation.

Challenging behaviour, inequality and social power

A relational rethink of the whole area of mental health has been suggested by Pūras (2017). Pūras (2017) suggested that the current paradigm 'contributes to exclusion, neglect and coercion and abuse of people [. . .] who deviate from prevailing cultural, social and political norms' (p. 4) (i.e. those who challenge). To resolve this, Pūras suggests we address 'power imbalances rather than chemical imbalances' (p. 19), which involves relating to individuals and acknowledging the social influences on their expressed distress and our role in it.

Social class can be seen as influencing perceptions of challenging behaviour. Those who have little power and influence are more likely to be perceived as intolerably challenging by others and to receive more punitive responses such as exclusion, detention or punishment than those with higher social status. For example, from the data published on control and restraint in NHS settings (NHS Digital, 2017) black people are more than three times as likely to be restrained than white people, and women more than men. Similar patterns emerge in statistics of those who are arrested, detained under the Mental Health Act and imprisoned.

In discussing the use of punishment for challenging behaviour in schools, Dix (2017) also discusses power. He notes a social class issue in terms of responses to challenging behaviour with punishment: 'Punishment is specifically targeted at children in poverty [. . .] it seems that few parents want to pay for their children to be bullied into submission for poor behaviour [. . .] the poor have sanction-based systems or exclusion imposed on them' (p. 109). An invitation to view the care of people through the lens of social, political and power relationships opens the area for a reformulation using the CAT model.

Challenging behaviour and politics

For Lovett (1996) the dangers of labelling behaviour as 'challenging' are political ones, saying that 'we reduce people to their behaviours and our ability to control them and fail to consider the political context in which they live, their poverty and political powerlessness' (p. 31). Governments exist to maintain a well-functioning society and good order. Threats to this order are seen as dangerous. The challenge to individuals is therefore also to society and government. A large degree of social policy and law is concerned with its social regulation. Regulating behaviour depends on the political norms of the day. This can be seen by the change in how we see homosexuality, slavery, or the freedom of women to express themselves, all of which historically conformed to definitions of challenging behaviour as aberrant or socially unacceptable. Our view of behaviour as being challenging impacts upon the extent to which we judge that 'challenging' people be allowed freedoms or rights, and the extent to which the State meets the needs of those who they judge to be vulnerable or need care rather than control or punishment. In understanding challenging behaviour to be a social construct, and political policy to be an attempt to manage social challenge, we can see that explanatory clinical models (such as CAT) are of vital importance in supporting the shaping of policy development.

Challenging to challenged: a reciprocal political stance

The Learning Disabilities Professional Senate (2016) expresses the link between challenging behaviour and social control thus: 'behaviour should also be regarded as challenging when responses that are neglectful, socially and morally unacceptable, abusive or restrictive are being used to manage or contain it, particularly when basic human rights are being contravened' (p. 8). This definition of challenging behaviour as conceptualised by the actions of others and the State places challenging behaviour firmly in the political and relational arena. In this social context, the construct invites clinicians to in turn challenge the system if they see that political decisions about service design and finances are driving decision-making about how to relate to and care for people who challenge.

The politics of challenging behaviour

Politics is concerned with the enactment of political ideals for the social good. This definition of social good may vary over time with prevailing culture and reaction to national events. Political parties promote their ideology and express to the voting public how this ideology can be practically realised. Inevitably, this ideology is expressed in absolute terms, for example health services strive for excellence and compassion and the criminal justice system (CJS) for reparation, redemption and punishment for those who offend. There was a much greater emphasis on redemption, particularly with younger offenders in the 1970s but the system has become more punitive from the 1980s onwards. The State positions its stance as offering the possibility of 'perfect care' through its political ideology.

How then does the political world cope with messy issues such as dealing with those who are challenging and do not conform, those for whom cure is not evidenced as effective, or those who are not deemed to be responsible and aware of the impact of their behaviour? Politics is concerned with that which is behavioural. Difficult thoughts or feelings can exist (albeit uncomfortably at times) in a democratic society, but difficult behaviour cannot. An individual's thoughts cannot be governed or regulated by the State, but their behaviour can be. In conceptualising the problematic other as reduced to their behaviour, the State understands the solutions to be, also, behavioural. This may lead to simplistic behavioural interventions or social control.

Challenging behaviour and social control: enactments of old reciprocal roles

The State empowers care services and professionals to segregate and exclude until the person who challenges can change, through legal frameworks that deprive an individual of their liberty (through the Mental Health Act or Deprivation of Liberty Safeguards). There is an implicit message therefore that the person who challenges cannot belong in society until they conform, and professionals may become 'the most dangerous type of protector oppressor' (Lovett, 1996, p. 12). Professional carers acting on behalf of the State enact and justify historical responses (punishment, exclusion and forcible treatment) in modern unassailable concepts such as 'care' or scientific and technical behavioural language. Health and social care professionals 'help' and 'treatment' unwittingly becomes an 'instrument of oppression' and, in 'dehumanising' the other by labelling them or simplifying their experience as a product of their disorder, 'we fail to meet their needs' (Lovett, 1996, p. 10) and are at risk of enacting the State-sanctioned abuse and neglect found in countless inquiries into the death and mistreatment of the vulnerable (Mandelstam, 2011).

Political guidance professes to deliver care in health services, but rarely does it explicitly name the need to 'manage' or control people who are challenging. As a result, there is little acknowledgement of health care responses as a form of social control under the guise of treatment. The Mental Health Act (DOH, 1983) gives us powers beyond treatment. It gives mental health professionals the power to restrain, segregate and seclude. None of these interventions are treatments. They have no evidence base that they lead to mental well-being. Indeed, quite the opposite (Agenda, 2017; Mind, 2015). The seclusion room provides physical and psychological separation from the person whose behaviour is challenging, creating the illusion of safety in the 'now-purified wider community' (Stowell-Smith, 2006, p. 74). The Mental Health Act (DOH, 1983) reflects the political uncertainty about what to do with people who challenge but it is couched in a values base of care and treatment of the vulnerable, making it harder to acknowledge and validate the experiences of many that detention can be abusive or punitive, and may be exercised as a social control measure in the absence of treatment. If we are unable to acknowledge this function of the Mental Health Act, we unconsciously repeat patterns of the past, invalidate and confuse and, in not acknowledging the experience of being challenged, struggle to form healing and collaborative relationships with those we 'care' for. We deny vulnerable individuals their rights, full citizenship, autonomy and dignity to the extent of evoking Article 3 of the European Convention on Human Rights (1953) regarding inhumane treatment (Mental Health Alliance, 2017).

Reformulating responses to challenging behaviour as social control as well as care supports us in acknowledging the unhelpful procedures that may accompany the functions of 'carers'. Early research in the area includes Haney et al.'s classic study (1972, 1973), in which they selected emotionally stable participants and randomly assigned them to the role of prison guard or prisoner. These roles and accompanying procedures were adopted and polarised so quickly that after six days of the planned two-week experiment, it had to be aborted due to the levels of control, abuse and distress that were enacted. It would appear frighteningly easy to adopt roles and procedures that are not necessarily part of our personal repertoire in relation to those who challenge, but are part of a collective, 'archetypal' and damaging social repertoire. CAT allows us to acknowledge roles and procedures within care settings that aim to make people conform and comply. The model makes it possible to reflect in ways that invite compassionate change.

Reformulation of unhelpful dynamics in relation to challenge

CAT may be able to illuminate the politics of the social control of challenging behaviour in the context of the relationships we make, and to support the generation of a collaborative narrative emphasising splits as an idealised 'valuing to valued/ treating to treated', a dreaded 'challenged and fearful and at risk/challenging unpredictable' and a chronically endured 'controlling/controlled' or 'restricting/restricted' (see Figure 8.3). Instead of dehumanising and infantilising the person, understanding them from a relational perspective creates a narrative in which the person and others' experiences can be validated and held rather than split and repressed.

When we control others, and believe ourselves to be caring for them, we deny them the possibility of collaborative care, autonomy and choice. The Mental Health Alliance (2017) found that 49% of respondents to their survey felt that they were not treated with dignity under the Mental Health Act and 50% felt that their human rights would not be protected.

Saints and sinners: reformulating organisational splitting as a response to challenging behaviour

Failures in the care system have led governments of all political persuasions to commission guidance such as *Transforming Care* (DOH, 2012) and *Building the Right Support* (NHS England, 2015) (see Chapter 13 of this volume). Absent from these idealised reports and guidance is an acknowledgement of the 'messy'. Carers are either saints, who at best need training in 'skills for care', or sinners, who are sacked or prosecuted. There is little said within these documents about supporting carers with the difficult feelings and reactions evoked by being challenged. This is an area that can be powerfully supported through CAT case supervision and management models.

Political ideology leads to idealised guidance being issued by government. Reading this guidance, it is easy to fantasise that it will be prioritised and followed,

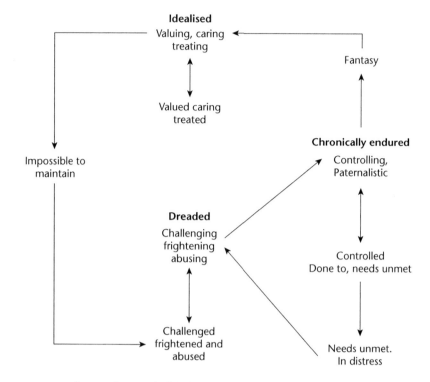

FIGURE 8.3 The social control of challenging behaviour.

and all will soon be well. Care will be 'transformed'; care will be 'high quality for all' (DOH, 2008). Commissioning decisions are based on this guidance (but with limited resources, which limits its impact). Services are expected to conform to this guidance perfectly, with little acknowledgement that they are facing an impossible task.

We can see this idealised splitting in recent inquiries and guidance around failings in learning disability mental health services. The Ely inquiry (1969) found inappropriate restraints, untrained staff, poor reporting, ineffective monitoring, weak leadership, cruel ill-treatment of patients by members of staff and a lack of care. This has been echoed by repeated investigations into abuse in services (Francis, 2013) and notably, more recently, the inquiry into abuse at Winterbourne View. These service failings have led to legal sanctions against professionals who fail, and yet the guidance has done little to acknowledge systems necessary to support staff to cope with being challenged by behaviours that evoke fear, helplessness, rejection, disgust and trauma.

Ballatt and Campling (2011) suggest that policies to promote the social inclusion of people from vulnerable groups tend to underestimate the degree to which the urge to hurt and eject those who overwhelm us with difficult feelings (due to the nature of their needs) is operating and that this can lead to the very abuse, scapegoating and institutionalisation noted in various inquiries. Dartington (cited in Obholzer & Zega Roberts, 1994), suggests that in order to cope, staff avoid attachment and being overwhelmed by emotional demands that threaten competence, and are deprived of the gratification of helping when they are challenged by a patient's condition. They keep the patient at a safe distance and so are not attuned to their needs. They then superficially see only 'a behaviour' that needs 'treatment'.

CAT reformulation is a tool that has been used to explore societal and organisational processes as well of enactments of individuals and those caring for them (Dunn & Parry, 1997). CAT reformulation can be used to support organisations to be more aware of relational care processes such as splitting and the interplay of dynamics at all levels between the State, services, staff and clients (Ryle & Kerr, 2002; Walsh, 1996) through the medium of an SDR referred to as a 'contextual reformulation' (Carradice, 2004; Ryle & Kerr, 2002).

Working with behaviour that challenges

The modern paradigm for understanding the challenges posed by those whose behaviour evokes strong emotion or breaks social norms, is one of health and social 'care'. The words 'care' or 'treatment' pervade our description of the acts we complete on behalf of those who we seek to help. As professional carers, we are so wedded to this model of interaction, and so concerned that we might not be caring, that we may fail to see when our actions cease to be caring. We continue to label actions as 'caring' when they are clearly not and are actually challenging to the individual. This can be seen in the use of language such as 'poor care', 'failing care', 'inadequate care' (which are clearly not care at all but acts of abuse or neglect). It leads us to name actions as 'care' or 'treatment' when they are in fact designed to control and exclude, for example, restraint, seclusion or long-term segregation.

The current conceptualisation of challenging behaviour as being a communication of unmet need is, on the face of it, intuitively acceptable. It implies that if we work hard to understand the communication and meet the need, the problem behaviour is no longer functional to the individual and is extinguished through the lack of reinforcement. However, this conceptualisation of behaviour, despite the inference that it challenges 'us', does not lead to models of intervention that explicitly address the impact of the challenge (strong feelings of fear, rejection and disgust) before focusing on the intervention (to do something different). We know that there is a human impact on carers through looking at helping behaviours and attributions (Hastings, 1997; Hill & Dagnan, 2002; Markham & Trower, 2003) but this is often not worked with within clinical models of challenging behaviour. The currently popular 'Positive Behaviour Support' model is one such model of challenging behaviour. It acknowledges the human emotions and responses in the 'other' who challenges but does not offer a way for the individual family or staff member who is challenged to manage their difficult feelings within the plan of care. The 'challenged' carer is expected to transcend these feelings and perfectly meet the other's needs. A CAT understanding provides the possibility of acknowledging that the challenge is mutual and allowing discussion of the consequent impact on both carer and cared for. This can lead to the possibility of exits from a cycle of blame and unmet need (to be cared for and care perfectly or face the consequences).

Health care professionals usually express their choice to serve others as a wish to care for, give to, help or develop others. It is terrifying to acknowledge that they (we) are frightened and do not understand a situation and do not know what to do.

Dartington (cited in Obholzer & Zega Roberts, 1994) describes this as the pain of helplessness and failed idealism. Professionally, it is difficult to acknowledge our response to being in a situation that is beyond our expert knowledge or superhuman ability to contain through good will alone. The expert professional is idealised and expected to be all knowing and benevolently powerful, imbued with godlike or magical powers of cure. This is certainly what is professed and reinforced in much NHS marketing. This invitation is seductive. It allows concerned public, service users and carers to devolve responsibility to these professionals and bolsters gratifying fantasies of those who dedicate themselves to care.

Staff are invited to 'raise concerns' about poor or dangerous services. We know from the Francis Report (2013) that 'whistle-blowers' are in a vulnerable position. Politically, it is dangerous to acknowledge that services commissioned by the State act in ways that are abusive, neglectful or ostracising. Indeed, it has proven so difficult that the duty to be candid about failures in care needed to be made a legal requirement. It is easier for staff to deny knowledge and responsibility than be ostracised themselves or suffer the emotional and mental pain of being knowingly complicit in dehumanising control, abuse or neglect in the name of the organisation they represent.

Why do good people do bad things when they are trying to care for people who challenge?

The dominant model for supporting people whose behaviour challenges others is Positive Behaviour Support (DOH, 2014; NICE, 2015). This model is a synthesis of applied behaviour analysis and a human rights and person-centred values base to guide work with a client group who may not be able to speak for themselves.

It would be difficult to find a service that did not purport to hold such a value base, yet controlling ineffective and inadequate care is relatively frequent, and abuse and neglect of people and their rights is not uncommon (DOH, 2009, 2012; NHS England, 2015). It would seem logical that if one holds the right set of values, it is hard to act in ways that are restrictive, controlling, neglectful or abusive. However, bad things continue to be done by good people.

This failure to respond helpfully may be understood if reformulated as a human response to challenge (see Figure 8.4).

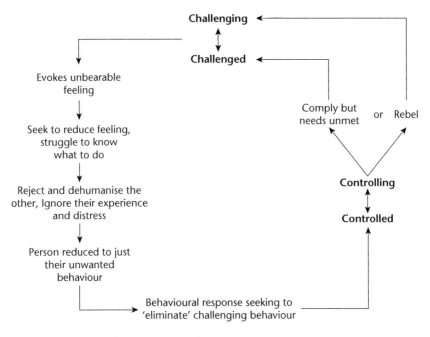

FIGURE 8.4 Why good people end up doing bad things.

Values are principles, a standard to strive for and an intent to do good. Values-based constructs are complex. They require higher-order cognitive processes to define, articulate, execute and monitor in terms of whether our actions are congruent with our intentions. As described earlier, when others are stressed and challenging in their expression of a need, we as carers are challenged and stressed, our ability to access higher-order cognitive processes such as reflection and proactive planning become compromised. We struggle to access our value base in the moment (or reflect on whether our behaviours are congruent with it) and become reactive, relying on developmentally immature responses such as fight, flight and freeze and enactments of primitive role procedures such as excluding, dominating, forcibly curing and punishing.

We know that our cognitive systems function differently under threat (see Kahneman, 2011). When challenged, we perceive the need to 'react', This relies on 'fast-thinking' processes that are characterised by instinct, emotion and primitive understandings and stereotypes (such as those outlined at the start of this chapter) When threat is less immediate, such as in supervision, we may be more able to enact valuing and respectful role procedures with our clients. This requires 'slow-thinking' skills that are more effortful, calculating, logical and able to cope with complexity.

As a result, we are inconsistent. We may be 'in two minds' or 'states' about how to respond (nurture or punishment) to the challenge of being drawn into split roles (fearful and challenged while trying to maintain valuing and caring roles). This split may be enacted within individual staff or in the team.

Psychoanalytic theory suggests that the patient–carer dichotomy may be maintained as a means of projecting unwanted aspects of the ideal carer into the denigrated patient. The patient becomes a container into which are projected hated, disavowed parts of the carer self.

In CAT, cognitive and analytic understandings can be integrated (see Figure 8.5).

A CAT reformulation allows us to acknowledge authentically that we are human, recognise and process splits in the self or team, and understand that we may both (staff and client) be mutually reinforcing agents in a difficult situation (see Figure 8.6).

We may feel 'forced' by the client to act in ways that are not congruent with our values, leading to cognitive dissonance. This is a process by which a 'split' is maintained, through the cognitive process of trying to formulate our actions as care, in order to manage unbearable feelings. It may lead to processes such as 'scapegoating' and 'group think' in order to protect the team in an impossible situation. An example of this dissonance is when staff who entered a profession in

What is challenged?
Our ability to integrate?

FIGURE 8.5 What splitting looks like.

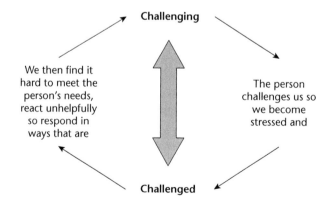

FIGURE 8.6 How we unwittingly maintain challenging behaviour.

order to care, find themselves acting in ways that are inconsistent with their values, for example, restraint and forcible medication. In hearing accounts of incidents, they maintain their caring values and may justify restraint as enacting care, even if the service user's experience is one of trauma. This formulation of these powerful interpersonal dynamics and the procedures that maintain them may be further illuminated by the findings of classic social psychology studies of social conformity and authority. For example, Milgram (1976) demonstrated that participants were very distressed by acting in ways that did not match their values (participants were asked to punish subjects for failure to learn, using increasingly dangerous, but fake, electric shocks). He found that participants coped by (i) focusing on the task or 'routine-ising' what they did; (ii) transferring moral responsibility to a higher authority; (iii) developing a belief that they were acting for a 'higher purpose'; and (iv) devaluing the subject of their acts (see Figure 8.7). All of these processes may be seen as an attempt to cope with the strain of cognitive dissonance, i.e. on the one hand trying to enact procedures of care and striving for a caring-to-cared-for position, while on the other hand enacting restrictive procedures to cope with distress and challenge.

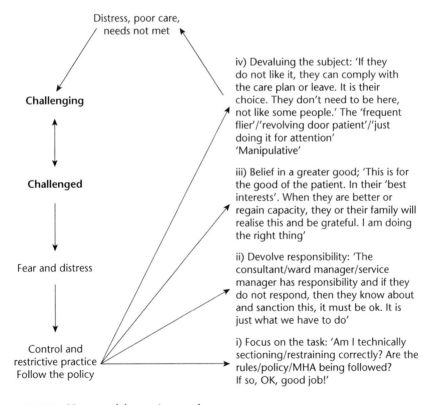

FIGURE 8.7 How we dehumanise people.

Conclusion

Applying a CAT perspective allows us to think relationally about challenging behaviour. In doing so we can move away from a locus within the person to a reformulation within a mutual social model of distress in the social environment. Within the CAT model, behaviour is not located within the individual as something that requires change to conform with social norms. Rather, behaviour and the challenge exist between people who can then make conscious decisions that do not mutually reinforce each other's distress. This conceptual shift mirrors that of B. F. Skinner in which he postulated that behaviour was not a result of 'indwelling agents' but of the influence of the world upon people, and that if we design better (social) environments, we will better support people and 'create cultures in which there are less aversionary controls [to social behaviour] such as the threat of punishment, and more positive ones that people freely agree to' (Butler-Brown, 2007, p. 270). In using CAT to develop understanding of social challenge, we may be able to use the model to inform not only individual and team level but also to inform policy on the wider social stage, for example to emphasise the need for 'care for carers'.

Bibliography

Agenda: Alliance for Women and Girls at Risk (2017). Agenda briefing on the use of restraint against women and girls. https://weareagenda.org/wp-content/uploads/2017/03/Restraint-FOI-research-briefing-FINAL1.pdf (Accessed 21/03/17).

Ballatt, J. & Campling, P. (2011). *Intelligent kindness: Reforming the culture of healthcare.* London: Royal College of Psychiatry.

Butler-Brown, T. (2007) *50 psychology classics: Who we are, how we think, what we do. Insight and inspiration from 50 key books.* London: Nicholas Brealey.

Carradice, A. (2004). Applying cognitive analytic therapy to guide indirect working. *Reformulation Journal of the Association of Cognitive Analytic Therapy,* Autumn, 18–23.

Department of Health (1983, amended 2008). *The Mental Health Act.* London, HMSO.

Department of Health (2009). Valuing people now: A three-year strategy for people with learning disabilities. http://webarchive.nationalarchives.gov.uk/20130105064234/www.dh.gov.uk/prod_consum_dh/groups/dh_digitalassets/documents/digitalasset/dh_093375.pdf (Accessed 07/12/17).

Department of Health (2012). *Transforming care: A national response to Winterbourne View Hospital: Department of Health review final report.* www.gov.uk/government/uploads/system/uploads/attachment_data/file/213215/final-report.pdf (Accessed 07/12/17).

Department of Health (2014). Positive and proactive care: Reducing the need for restrictive interventions. www.gov.uk/government/uploads/system/uploads/attachment_data/file/300293/JRA_DoH_Guidance_on_RP_web_accessible.pdf (Accessed 07/12/17).

Department of Health and Social Care (2008). *High-quality care for all.* NHS next stage review final report- full text. www.gov.uk/government/uploads/system/uploads/attachment_data/file/228836/7432.pdf (Accessed 07/12/17).

Department of Health and Social Security (1969). *Report of the Committee of Inquiry into Allegations of Ill-Treatment of Patients and Other Irregularities at the Ely Hospital.* Cardiff: Department of Health and Social Security.

Dix, Paul (2017). *When adults change, everything changes: Seismic shifts in school behaviour.* Carmarthan, UK: Independent Thinking Press.

Doyle, D. (2009). The differences between sex offending and challenging behaviour in people with an intellectual disability. *Journal of Intellectual and Developmental Disability,* 29(2), 107–118. doi: 10.1080/13668250410001709467

Dunn, M. & Parry, G. (1997). A formulated care plan approach to caring for people with borderline personality disorder in a community mental health service setting. *Clinical Psychology Forum,* 104, 19–22.

Emerson, E. (2001). *Challenging behaviour: Analysis and intervention in people with learning disabilities* (2nd ed.). Cambridge: Cambridge University Press.

Francis, R. (2013). *Report of the Mid Staffordshire NHS Foundation Trust public inquiry executive summary* (1st ed.) [ebook]. London: Stationary Office. Available at: http://webarchive.nationalarchives.gov.uk/20150407084003/www.midstaffspublicinquiry.com/sites/default/files/report/Executive%20summary.pdf.

Haney, C., Banks, W. C. & Zimbardo, P. G. (1972). Interpersonal dynamics in a simulated prison. *International Journal of Criminology and Penology,* 1, 69–97.

Haney, C., Banks, W. C. & Zimbardo, P. G. (1973). Study of prisoners and guards in a simulated prison, *Naval Research Reviews,* 9, 1–17.

Hastings, R. P. (1997). Staff beliefs about the challenging behaviours of children and adults with mental retardation. *Clinical Psychology Review,* 17, 75–90.

Hill, C. & Dagnan, D. (2002). Helping attributions, emotions and coping style in response to people with learning disabilities and challenging behaviour. *Journal of Learning Disabilities,* 6(4), 363–372.

Jaques, E. (1955). Social systems as a defence against persecutory and depressive anxiety. In M. Klein, P. Heinman & R. E. Money-Kyrle (eds), *New directions in psychoanalysis.* London: Tavistock.

Kahneman, D. (2011). *Thinking, fast and slow.* New York: Farrar, Straus & Giroux.

Learning Disability Professional Senate (2016). *Challenging behaviour: A unified approach – update clinical and service guidelines for supporting children, young people and adults with intellectual disabilities who are at risk of receiving abusive or restrictive practices.* Report from the Faculties of Intellectual Disability of the Royal College of Psychiatrists and the British Psychological Society on behalf of the Learning Disabilities Professional Senate. London: British Psychological Society.

Lovett, H. (1996). *Learning to listen: Positive approaches and people with difficult behaviour.* London: Jessica Kingsley Publishers.

Mandelstam, M. (2011). *How we treat the sick: Neglect and abuse in our health services.* London. Jessica Kingsley Publishers.

Markham, D. & Trower, P. (2003). The effects of the psychiatric label 'borderline personality disorder' on nursing staff's perceptions and causal attributions for challenging behaviours. *British Journal of Clinical Psychology,* 42(3), 243–256.

Mental Health Alliance. (2017). A Mental Health Act fit for tomorrow: The case for change. *Rethink Mental Illness.* www.rethink.org/get-involved/policy/mental-health-act-survey (Accessed 06/12/17).

Milgram S. (1976). *Obedience to authority: An experimental view.* London: Harper & Row.

Mind (2015). Restraint in mental health services: What the guidance says. Produced in partnership with the National Survivor User Network. www.mind.org.uk/media/3352178/restraintguidanceweb.pdf (Accessed 06/12/17).

NHS digital (2017). http://digital.nhs.uk/catalogue/PUB30160 (Accessed 06/12/17).

NHS England (2015). Building the right support: A national plan to develop community services and close inpatient facilities for people with a learning disability and/or autism who display behaviour that challenges, including those with a mental health condition. www.england.nhs.uk/wp-content/uploads/2015/10/ld-nat-imp-plan-oct15.pdf (Accessed 07/12/17).

NICE. The National Institute for Clinical Excellence (2015). *Violence and aggression: Short-term management in mental health, health and community settings*. www.nice.org.uk/guidance/ng10 (Accessed 06/12/17).

Obholzer, A. & Zega Roberts, V. (1994) *The unconscious at work: Individual and organisational stress in the human services.* London: Routledge.

Pūras, D. (2017) *United Nations report of the Special Rapporteur on the right of everyone to the enjoyment of the highest attainable standard of physical and mental health.* Human rights council 35th session, 6–23 June, A/HCR/35/21.

Royal College of Psychiatrists (2007). *Challenging behaviour: A unified approach. Clinical and service guidelines for supporting people who are at risk of receiving abusive or restrictive practices. College Report CR144.* London: Royal College of Psychiatrists.

Ryle, A. & Kerr, I. (2002). *Introducing cognitive analytic therapy: Principles and practice.* Chichester, UK: Wiley.

Scull, A. (2016). *Madness in civilization: A cultural history of insanity from the Bible to Freud, from the madhouse to modern medicine.* London: Thames & Hudson.

Varela, J. (2014). Cognitive analytic therapy and behaviour that challenges. In J. Lloyd & P. Clayton (eds), *Cognitive analytic therapy for people with intellectual disabilities and their carers.* London: Jessica Kingsley Publishers.

Walsh, S. (1996) Adapting cognitive analytic therapy to make sense of psychologically harmful work environments. *British Journal of Medical Psychology*, 69, 3–20.

9

RESPONDING NOT REACTING TO CHALLENGING BEHAVIOUR

A reformulation approach

Jo Varela and Lianne Franks

Introduction

In this chapter we aim to bring together the concepts outlined in the previous chapter. By using a series of case studies and sequential diagrammatic reformulations (SDRs) we illustrate how CAT can be used to understand and respond, rather than react, to challenging behaviour. In so doing we outline a human rights-based approach to care in mental health settings.

Understanding stress-related procedures in response to behaviour that challenges

Challenging behaviour is *challenging*. It challenges us to know what to feel, think and do and how to respond (Hastings, 1997a, 1997b; Hill & Dagnan, 2002; Markham & Trower, 2003; Wanless & Jahoda, 2002). In chronic stress situations where an individual or a team is subject to chronic challenge with little useful support, this reactive and threat-based response may become cemented into custom and practice. Staff may 'fight' – coping by adopting more punitive and controlling measures (which may breach human rights); 'flee', literally, leading to high staff turnover or sick leave; or 'switch off' by becoming emotionally absent. In enacting a freeze response, staff may be paralysed and helpless, subjected to assault, or collude with poor treatment by mutely witnessing and not knowing what to do. They may also 'become assimilated' to the situation and, worryingly, become accustomed to challenge and unconcerned by distress and poor practice (see Figure 9.1). Understood in this way, the staff and team response to chronic stress can be seen as a parallel process to a patient's trauma history.

In situations of chronic challenge, assimilated to a new normal, we fight to justify actions needed to stay in control (restraint and restriction or punishment) as

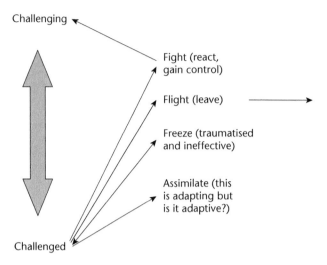

FIGURE 9.1   The stress response.

being 'care' ('seclusion is part of the treatment plan'), or become immune (we are no longer challenged by the behaviour). In both these scenarios, abuse and neglect become normal and 'justified'.

Additionally, professing 'excellent, expert care' sets up a dynamic whereby it is not acceptable to admit to 'fumbling along' with your patient, attempting to 'get it right' but making mistakes, or becoming mutually angry and frightened by each other along the way. In professing to care 'excellently', it denies both patient and carer the possibility to suggest otherwise in a way that we can hear.

In this situation, we become deaf to the meaning of the behaviour. We are no longer relating to a human being in distress; we no longer see that they have needs or that their behaviour is anything other than something to be 'trained' out of the individual by ignoring or punishing it. We find ourselves 'out of dialogue' with the person. This results in our no longer being able to meet the person's needs, thereby perpetuating the initial reason for the behaviour (distress) and adding new reinforcers and antecedents (challenging as protest against inhumane treatment).

Using the CAT model to respond to individuals who challenge us

In formulating our responses to an individual relationally and emotionally using the CAT model, we can explore openly our clinical rationale and intent towards the person who challenges us. The CAT model gives us permission to validate our response and the impact of our actions on the individual in a compassionate and non-blaming way. The SDR is often seen as a reflection of the client's internalised reciprocal role procedures and therefore may enable staff to respond therapeutically rather than simply react to such clients (Ryle & Kerr, 2002). This minimises the likelihood of staff adopting defensive, abusive care practices in response to behaviour that challenges us all. Shannon et al. (2017, p. 8) show this in their use of an organisational formulation for Kenny (all names used in the chapter are pseudonyms), where in recognising feelings of shock and disgust, 'the reformulation helped staff to acknowledge their feelings of anxiety, frustration, anger, resentment and stress when they felt de-skilled and inept in finding ways to work successfully with Kenny and 'sidestep enactments' to form good relationships with him'.

Behaviour that challenges our caring identity

If we understand and acknowledge that we are challenged and distressed by another, and do not respond to our need to maintain the pretence that we are expert and in control, we can start to attune to our feelings and responses in helpful ways.

Case study: 'But we have to . . .' – the unbearable dilemma of forcible treatment

Jenny has a history of trauma and harm. She is sectioned and brought to the inpatient unit using force by the police. She is inconsolable and fearful. She is struggling with dissociation and is frightened by beliefs that she is being poisoned and by hearing violent voices. Staff try to reason with her, but she cannot process their words. With her recent experience of force and confusing mental experiences, she cannot yet form a valid, trusting relationship with staff. They are an unknown threat. Staff find that she is 'acutely psychotic' and find it intolerable to witness her distress. They are doubly challenged by her distress, her frightening and incomprehensible behaviour and their impotence to relate and act with care. They are caught in a dilemma of *either* impotently witnessing her distress and being challenged by her unpredictable reactions to them, *or* forcibly 'treating' using rapid tranquilisation. They justify forcible treatment as the only 'care' that they can offer. Jenny is traumatised by being forcibly treated by the more powerful staff, even so, the staff also feel traumatised by feeling as if they had no choice. Communication and relationships break down, and staff and patient are caught in a trap of fear and mistrust and compulsion to act to protect themselves. Jenny copes by protecting herself at all costs by fighting and withdrawing, and the staff cope by – despite accusations of abuse by the patient – 'cutting off', reassuring themselves that in restraining, medicating and secluding her, they are caring for Jenny, and by labelling her with 'personality disorder' they are explaining the difficulties in engagement (see Figure 9.2).

A reciprocal pattern emerges whereby in feeling forced to act in restrictive and controlling ways, the client 'forces' us and we force the client. Both the person and the carer feel forced to do something highly aversive that neither wanted; positions

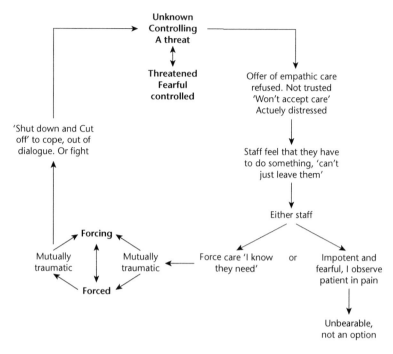

FIGURE 9.2 Seeking protection by cutting off.

are entrenched, leading to a dyad out of tune with each other's intentions, needs and good will. We cannot reflect on whether our response was the least restrictive; we took the only course of action available, we try to account for our actions as caring as that is what we set out to do. We justify unilateral actions in terms that take power away from the person using the reasonable sounding language of the Mental Health Act (DOH, 1983), best-interest decisions and capacity assessments. This results in infantilising the person, recasting them as the 'holy fool' who 'knows not what they do'. This formulation is more bearable than an ugly situation, which, although authentically human, reflects poorly on both. We are working 'at the edges of kinship' (Ballatt & Campling, 2011, p. 101) where 'goodwill and rejection compete'. In our mutually experienced trauma of violence, we demonise the other and retreat from models of care and treatment into primitive understandings of 'madness' and exertions of power, painfully cut off and allowing the 'myth' of care to continue.

In acknowledging the above dynamic, we have the freedom to articulate truly the experience of being challenged, and instead of *reacting* to the situation, try instead to *respond* to the person.

Supporting challenged teams

Research exploring how CAT consultations influenced staff teams' understanding of patients' behaviours within a high-secure hospital suggested that there are a number of factors that affect staff teams' experiences and their understanding (Franks et al., 2015). When the consultations were accessible and available, they appeared to be genuinely valued. This appeared to lead to mirrored enlightenment for the staff, patients and the system, which in turn creates therapeutic relationships and environments and enables positive changes to patient care and staff experiences. This included a deeper understanding of how past life experiences have led to current unhelpful behaviours, which include staff–patient dynamics and risk issues.

Case study: the 'experts' in challenging behaviour – 'We can cope with anything'

A residential home for people with learning disabilities made a number of referrals for challenging behaviour but did not engage with the psychologist employing a Positive Behaviour Support (PBS) approach. Visits to the service by the psychologist were met with a chaotic response, with no record of the appointment, no notes or incident monitoring and, frequently, no staff to talk to about the presenting problems (and alarming descriptions of restraint and control). The psychologist was met with anger and frustration from the staff, who were aggrieved at being expected to set time aside to meet them while the problem of the challenging residents was unsolved. The psychologist arranged to attend handover meetings to map some of the organisational issues that were preventing progress with residents (using the diagram shown in Figure 9.3), and find a way of articulating problematic organisational procedures to management to facilitate systems change.

The parallel challenges between patients, the team and the wider system

CAT coherently conceptualises the parallel processes occurring between staff and organisations in relation to the patient through the SDR, which is referred to as a 'contextual reformulation' (Kerr et al., 2007; Ryle & Kerr, 2002). In understanding the importance of setting and context, staff find it easier to recognise risks that a client may pose and will be in a better position to respond (Reid & Thorne, 2007, p. 8).

Sharing or collaboratively developing reformulations with staff teams helps them understand the person in context and provide a more consistent and coherent understanding (Aitken & McDonnell, 2006). It allows staff and patients to make sense of previously challenging and confusing behaviours (Walsh, 1996) by making explicit the complex staff processes involved in perpetuating and exacerbating an individual's issues (Carradice, 2004). This facilitates staff and teams to respond in more adaptive, helpful ways, predict transference enactments (Dunn & Parry, 1997) and contain staff anxieties about future behaviours (Kerr, 1999; Ryle & Kerr, 2002). It can protect against 'splitting' and fragmentation of the team (Mitzman, 2010; Ryle & Kerr, 2002) and against staff burnout, serious incidents, demoralisation, communication problems and staff sickness (Kerr et al., 2007).

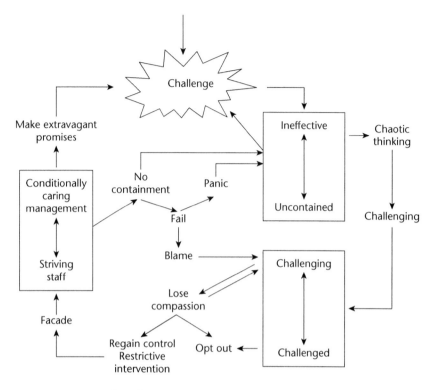

FIGURE 9.3 SDR to show how a service was inviting and maintaining challenge and then 'cutting off' from distress to 'contain the chaos'.

Case study: the seclusion illusion

We used CAT principles in consultation with a staff team within a medium-secure unit for female adults with learning disabilities. Although set up as a five-bed female ward, there were six service users living on the ward as one service user was in long-term segregation in the high-dependency unit. All service users had histories of abuse, trauma or neglect, and had been in contact with the criminal justice system for offences related to violence. On the ward, the service users were presenting with emotional dysregulation and behaviours that challenge such as cutting, damaging the ward environment and being verbally or physically abusive to staff or other service users. There were a high number of restrictive practices including long-term segregation, seclusions, restraints and rapid tranquilisations and a high number of staff injuries, low staff morale and an increasing risk of staff burnout. Additionally, high expressed emotion abounded across the institution owing to a difficult Care Quality Commission (CQC) visit with another inspection planned. These anxieties were further compounded by rumours that the hospital would close or that it would be merging with another NHS Trust. The psychologist working in to the ward was feeling stuck but also felt compelled to 'fix' things. As staff often walked away feeling powerless and not knowing what to do, the psychologist developed a contextual reformulation to understand the multiple processes that were occurring daily. Observing in many forums on the ward – community meetings, ward rounds, 'sitting duck' in the nurses' station and many kitchen conversations – the psychologist could see how mutually challenging some of the reactions between the staff and service users were. There were parallel processes with the service users, the staff team and the wider institution and, on reflection, the political context of the NHS nationally. The service users' collective history of neglect, abandonment and control were being re-enacted on the ward by service users in their relationships to themselves, between service users and staff but also within the staff team and the wider institution. The staff felt there was a perceived expectation from the Trust and service users about provision of idealised care and that although the staff team felt they were trying their best to achieve this, they also felt they were failing.

The constraints of a medium-secure unit left service users feeling powerless and controlled, which evoked intolerable feelings that they were unable to articulate. In response, service users would aim to regain some power and control by refusing to do things, often referred to in mental health services as 'non-compliance to treatment'. After trying various strategies in order to care and protect, staff would feel overwhelmed and helpless at not being able to offer care aligned to their values. Staff were left feeling stuck and would *either* back off, which the service users would experience as abandoning, *or* would enter a power 'tug of war' by putting in more rules or conditions, for example, 'You can't go to that session unless you've taken your medication'. Service users would express protest through challenging behaviour, which for a short period would place them back in a more preferable powerful position. This dynamic often escalated to physical violence and staff responding with restraint and seclusion. Parallel to this process, other service users felt envious of the time taken by staff being drawn into these enactments that created the illusion of 'care'; this was understandable given the neglectful and abusive histories that service users had experienced and also the consistent messages that staff in hospitals are there to care for them. In seclusion or segregation service users were given one-to-one observations at all times so the threat of staff support or care being taken away was reduced. As this relational pattern was repeated, seclusion became the 'idealised care' for service users so the demand was high. Subsequently, both staff and service users became more overwhelmed and burnt out and their ability to respond – to their own and other's needs – diminished. Staff and service users could end up in a state of paralysis, which reinforced feelings of abandonment; the service users feeling abandoned by nursing staff and the staff feeling abandoned and let down by managers and senior managers (see Figure 9.4).

The SDR was shared with senior ward staff in the first instance, and then developed in group clinical supervision and ward rounds. We used it to inform systemic 'exits' creating healthier reciprocal roles, replacing feeling contained

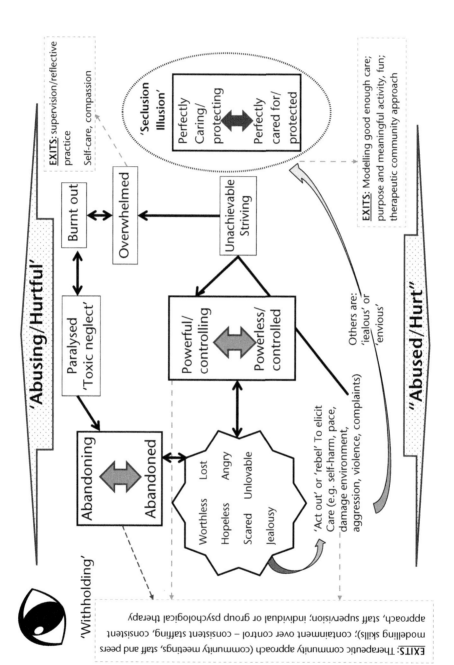

FIGURE 9.4 Contextual reformulation of a female medium-secure unit in a forensic learning disability service.

'Abusing/Hurtful'

EXITS: supervision/reflective practice

Self-care, compassion

'Seclusion Illusion'

Perfectly Caring/ protecting ⟷ Perfectly cared for/ protected

EXITS: Modelling good enough care; purpose and meaningful activity, fun; therapeutic community approach

Burnt out

Overwhelmed

Unachievable Striving

Paralysed 'Toxic neglect'

Powerful/ controlling ⟷ Powerless/ controlled

Others are: 'jealous' or 'envious'

Abandoning ⟷ Abandoned

Worthless   Lost
Hopeless   Angry
Scared   Unlovable
Jealousy

'Act out' or 'rebel' To elicit Care (e.g. self-harm, pace, damage environment, aggression, violence, complaints)

"Abused/Hurt"

'Withholding'

EXITS: Therapeutic community approach (community meetings, staff and peers modelling skills); containment over control – consistent staffing, consistent approach, staff supervision; individual or group psychological therapy and safe instead of controlled and powerless. Over a six-month period, group clinical supervision sessions were protected and became a consistent and well-attended resource for the staff team. Within this the SDR became the framework for discussion and education, and training around attachment theory, trauma and mindfulness followed. Community meetings on the ward developed a more relational focus where the staff team held in mind the SDR. The SDR was used to reflect on incidents, forecast risk potential and help develop risk management strategies for the ward while also making some of the 'exits' more person-centred. This was reflected in individual service users' care plans and 'positive behavioural support' (PBS) plans.

Feedback from the team highlighted how the SDR enabled them to think about the ward's complex dynamics. The 'exits' equipped them with opportunities to respond rather than react to service users. The contextual reformulation and systemic approach to reducing seclusion episodes was acknowledged in the CQC inspection report – ironically, the inspection that people were feeling powerless about. In addition, data showed that restrictive practices were reduced by more than half over a period of approximately nine months following the introduction of the SDR and the exits (see Figure 9.5). Peaks in the data could be accounted for by the readmission of one service user who was immediately placed in long-term segregation. The largest peak was the month following the much anticipated CQC inspection, when staff sickness was at the highest across the hospital. Low staffing meant that regular staff for this ward were deployed to other ward areas and agency staff were covering some areas so regular staff were not available to

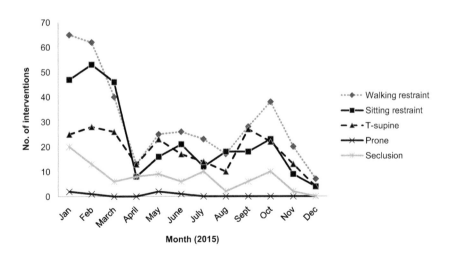

FIGURE 9.5 The number of restrictive practices before, during and after the sharing of contextual reformulation.

implement the exits. We wondered whether having a high number of unfamiliar staff on the ward also made service users feel scared and unsafe, resulting in them trying to elicit care in ways that others experience as more challenging, and thus enacting some of the patterns described in the SDR.

The challenging organisation: who is challenging whom?

CAT can be an effective collaborative model in which to unpick difficult dynamics, develop client and staff and derive exits that meet the needs of both. However, there are few examples of applications of clinical models to understanding how a *distressed service* affects clients' feelings and behaviour and how an organisation's distress can be enacted with the service user. This is despite a growing acknowledgement that services do enact their distress and that service users do suffer as a consequence (Ballatt & Campling, 2011; Obholzer & Zega Roberts, 1994), particularly in challenging times of austerity. Service users may suffer doubly if services frame distressed behaviour as internal, stable and specific to the patient (Hastings, 1997a, 1997b; Hill & Dagnan, 2002) and respond in punitive or restrictive ways. For example, Obholzer and Zega Roberts (1994, pp. 129–138) write about the 'troublesome' individual in stressed institutions and explain how a person enacting the troubles of an institution may be scapegoated and ejected, fulfilling a fantasy that once they are 'got rid of', all will be well.

There are a small number of interventions such as Schwartz rounds (Schwartz Centre, 2017) aimed at supporting staff in dealing with challenges by providing a forum for staff to discuss emotional and social aspects of working in health care. However, these interventions do not involve clients. In understanding challenge as reciprocal or a shared problem of unmet needs and difficulties in communication and helping behaviour, CAT offers an opportunity to co-formulate issues and derive exits that benefit both client and service.

Challenged organisations: the struggle to care

Organisational challenges include recruitment, retention, finances, organisational change and parity of esteem, which lead to stress responses and coping strategies including raising referral criteria, reducing interventions to below optimum 'dose', and labelling clients who speak out as 'difficult' or rejecting them as 'unfit for treatment'. Any of these responses are additionally challenging to a distressed client.

If we understand that challenging behaviour is a reciprocal cycle and originates in unmet needs, it opens up the possibility of increasing our awareness of when the service is unwittingly causing the problem.

Austerity and transactional models of care (i.e. care reduced to component tasks) are causal in reducing the importance of 'the relational' concepts of care, leading to reductionist 'othering' of people who challenge as we struggle to engage. Poverty of resource invites efficiency and care pathway mapping, which may reduce care to itemised tasks, limiting the emphasis on care as a relational construct.

What is care?

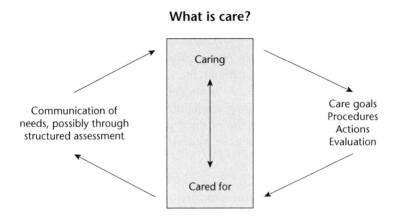

FIGURE 9.6   Care in CAT terms, as a relationship and procedures (tasks).

When viewed as care procedures performed under pressure, uncoupled from a caring reciprocal role, it is easy to see why compassion falters and repeated abuse occurs, such as that at Mid Staffordshire Hospitals (Francis, 2013). The 'caring' organisation acts without relational attunement and challenges the patient to survive its enactment of so-called 'care' (see Figure 9.6).

A man referred for 'challenging behaviour' and an assessment of dementia. On assessment his challenging behaviour involved 'wandering' at night then becoming angry and aggressive with staff. An analysis showed no particular pattern to the behaviour except that it was nearly every night between 9pm and midnight. Aggression was triggered by the man being told to go back to bed. A history of the behaviour was taken and found that the 'wandering' was not recent. What had changed was a new assistive technology that 'increased the person's independence' by 'reducing dependence on paid support' and alerting staff when the person 'needed support'. The technology was an alarm that alerted staff when someone left their room. As the man in question did not 'need anything' when he set the alarm off, and the service had reduced staffing as a result of the technology, the staff became frustrated at the interruption and had construed the behaviour as meaningless wandering rather than 'mooching about'. The change in service delivery away from relational support to one of meeting explicit needs through care tasks had reduced the value placed on 'being with' him and labelling his mooching as challenging.

By reformulating using the CAT model, we can see care given as both relationship *and* tasks. In doing so we can support services to value and support both care relationships (reciprocal roles) and tasks (procedures, such as giving medication). The challenge is in those services that focus on commodifying care in order to 'pay by results' and assume relational aspects of care (such as compassion) are innate and stable constructs within their staff group.

Services challenged by political ideology: the challenge of being perfect

In the late 1980s and early 1990s, state provision of health care 'free for all at the point of delivery' and run centrally by the Department of Health was revised. With increasing costs and need, the politics of health looked to the heavily marketed world of private business for a solution. With lean business practice came marketing. This and the extension of the expert health model in mental health care created a marketing challenge in which services that pronounced themselves as expert could not fail.

Case study: the challenging organisation – fear of failure getting in the way of care

A specialist 'complex needs' community team was commissioned as a local response to very public failings in care. It consisted of a highly experienced group of clinicians, who were recruited to the team on the basis of their skills and professed values towards those they cared for.

They set out their service using the latest evidence base and with consultation from a wide range of stakeholders including service users. In line with organisational values they were committed to excellence and quality of care. However, the team quickly became troubled, defensive, quarrelsome and ineffective, despite gaining national reputation. Commissioners and the host organisation made little attempt to acknowledge the difficulty of working in an area with little evidence base and high emotion. To gain and maintain a reputation of excellence and fulfil the promise of the service, mess and failures were suppressed or projected on to others – the 'rubbish team member' or the 'difficult family'. Unhelpful team processes developed and maintained splitting through 'expert' certainty without checking, blame of others, group think (Janis, 1972) and scapegoating. This harmed service users who were often discharged and blamed or consigned to residential or long-stay hospital care out of the city. A culture developed whereby if the team could not help them, despite their 'expert' efforts, service users were deemed to be beyond help or pejoratively labelled 'treatment resistant'. Restrictive interventions were defended by the team as the 'least restrictive option' despite the frequency of such actions being higher than before the team was set up. As suggested by Ballatt and Campling (2011), these actions not only removed 'difficult' people but also banished unpalatable and warded-off aspects of the team's experience of 'inexpert failure' and the resulting intolerable feelings (see Figure 9.7).

It was hard to empathise with the team. However, in reformulating using the CAT model, a narrative can be generated and owned by the team, all of whom had started out with good intentions, skills and values. In creating an SDR, it is possible to hold in mind and use the formulation to understand staff in relation to service user processes and also to generate organisational exits.

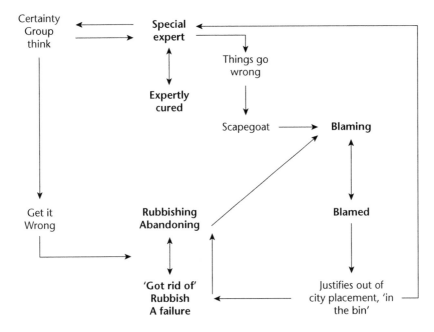

FIGURE 9.7   A contextual reformulation of a challenged complex needs team.

Exits

In formulating challenging behaviour relationally, as a shared problem of distress and unmet need, it is possible to create space to reflect and think rather than to react. It gives an essential opportunity to see the other's point of view and that the exit rests on their ability to attune, relate and acknowledge the awfulness of the experience. It enables us to see that there are other possible choices, such as questioning whether the only option is to forcibly treat. It frees us from practices of the past and allows us to be creative and advocate more powerfully for those whose challenging behaviour communicates their need for care (see Figure 9.8).

Conclusion

This chapter aims to offer the practitioner a way of reformulating situations when they and those they support are challenged. In all the case examples illustrated here there is a suffering patient who is often blamed for their suffering and/or how they cope with it and who may or may not be the origin of the challenge. Such ways of formulating patients' distress and behaviour leads to exclusion, rejection or punishment. Exits to these unhelpful and often damaging relational patterns are: recognition of the reciprocal nature of challenge, revision of relationships to enhance attunement and curiosity, compassion for and empowerment of the client, in short, a human rights-based approach.

Can 'good enough' care of an organisation be contagious?

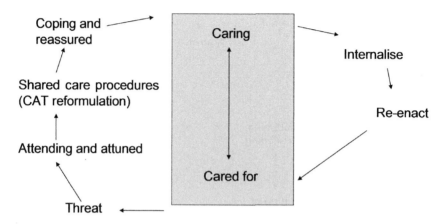

FIGURE 9.8 *Caring* in relation to *cared for* – for everyone.

Bibliography

Aitken, G. & McDonnell, K. (2006). The use of cognitive analytic therapy in women in secure settings. In P. H. Pollock, M. Stowell-Smith & M. Göpfert (eds), *Cognitive analytic therapy for offenders: A new approach to forensic psychotherapy* (pp. 121–137). London: Routledge.

Ballatt, J. & Campling, P. (2011). *Intelligent kindness: Reforming the culture of healthcare.* London: Royal College of Psychiatry publications.

Carradice, A. (2004). Applying cognitive analytic therapy to guide indirect working. *Reformulation: Journal of the Association of Cognitive Analytic Therapy*, Autumn, 18–23.

Carradice, A. (2012). 'Five-session CAT' consultancy: Using CAT to guide care planning with people diagnosed with personality disorder within community mental health teams. *Clinical Psychology & Psychotherapy*, 20, 359–367. doi: org/10.1002/cpp.1812

Department of Health (1983, amended 2008). *The Mental Health Act.* London, HMSO.

Dunn, M. & Parry, G. (1997). A formulated care plan approach to caring for people with borderline personality disorder in a community mental health service setting. *Clinical Psychology Forum*, 104, 19–22.

Francis, R. (2013). *Report of the Mid Staffordshire NHS Foundation Trust public inquiry executive summary* (1st ed.) [ebook]. London: Stationary Office. http://webarchive.nationalarchives. gov.uk/20150407084003/www.midstaffspublicinquiry.com/sites/default/fil.

Franks, L., Reilly, J., Hansen, L. & Petersen, T. (2015). Exploring multi-disciplinary team (MDT) experiences of cognitive analytic therapy (CAT) as a systemic consultation tool in an adult forensic service. Unpublished. Doctoral thesis. University of Liverpool.

Greenhill, B. (2011). 'They have behaviour, we have relationships?' *Reformulation, Theory and Practice in Cognitive Analytic Therapy*, 37 (Winter), 10–15.

Hastings, R. P. (1997a). Staff beliefs about the challenging behaviours of children and adults with mental retardation. *Clinical Psychology Review*, 17, 75–90.

Hastings, R. P. (1997b). Measuring staff perceptions of challenging behaviour: The challenging behaviour attributions scale (CHABA). *Journal of Intellectual Disability Research*, 41, 495–501.

Hill, C. & Dagnan, D. (2002). Helping attributions, emotions and coping style in response to people with learning disabilities and challenging behaviour. *Journal of Learning Disabilities*, 6(4), 363–372.

Janis, I. L. (1972). *Victims of group think: A psychological study of foreign policy decisions and fiascoes*. Boston, MA: Houghton Mifflin.

Kellett, S., Wilbram, M., Davis, C. & Hardy, G. (2014). Team consultancy using cognitive analytic therapy: A controlled study in assertive outreach. *Journal of Psychiatric and Mental Health Nursing*, 21(8), 687–697.

Kerr, I. B. (1999). Cognitive analytic therapy for borderline personality disorder in the context of a community mental health team: Individual and organisational psychodynamic implications. *British Journal of Psychotherapy*, 15, 425–437. doi: org/10.1111/j.1752-0118.1999. tb00473.x.

Kerr, I. B., Dent-Brown, K. & Parry. G. (2007). Psychotherapy and mental health teams. *International Review of Psychiatry*, 19, 63–80.

Lovett, H. (1996). *Learning to listen: Positive approaches and people with difficult behaviour*. London: Jessica Kingsley Publishers.

Markham, D. & Trower, P. (2003). The effects of the psychiatric label 'borderline personality disorder' on nursing staff's perceptions and causal attributions for challenging behaviours. *British Journal of Clinical Psychology*, 42(3), 243–256.

Mitzman, S. (2010). Cognitive analytic therapy and the role of brief assessment and contextual reformulation: The jigsaw puzzle of offending. *Reformulation*, Summer, 26–30. www.acat.me.uk/reformulation.php?issue_id=3&article_id=43.

Obholzer, A. & Zega Roberts, V. (1994). *The unconscious at work: Individual and organisational stress in the human services*. London: Routledge.

Reid, W. H. & Thorne, S. A. (2007). Personality disorders and violence potential. *Journal of Psychiatric Practice*, 13, 261–268. doi: org/10.1097/01.pra.0000281488.19570.f8.

Ryle, A. & Kerr, I. (2002). *Introducing cognitive analytic therapy: Principles and practice*. Chichester, UK: Wiley.

Schwartz Centre (2017). Schwartz rounds. www.theschwartzcenter.org/supporting-caregivers/ schwartz-center-rounds.

Shannon, K., Butler, S., Ellis, C., McLaine, J. & Riley, J. (2017). 'Seeing the unseen': Supporting organisational and team working at YMCA Liverpool with multiple complex clients. *Reformulation: Journal of the Association of Cognitive Analytic Therapy*, Summer, 5–15.

Stowell Smith, M. (2006). States and reciprocal roles in the wider understanding of forensic mental health. In P. H. Pollock, M. Stowell-Smith & M. Göpfert (eds), *Cognitive analytic therapy for offenders: A new approach to forensic psychotherapy*. London and New York: Routledge.

Varela, J. (2014). Cognitive analytic therapy and behaviour that challenges. In J. Lloyd & P. Clayton (eds), *Cognitive analytic therapy for people with intellectual disabilities and their carers*. London: Jessica Kingsley Publishers.

Walsh, S. (1996). Adapting cognitive analytic therapy to make sense of psychologically harmful work environments. *British Journal of Medical Psychology*, 69, 3–20.

Wanless, L. K. & Jahoda, A. (2002). Responses of staff towards people with mild to moderate intellectual disability who behave aggressively: A cognitive emotional analysis. *Journal of intellectual Disability Research*, 46(6), 507–516.

10

TRANSFORMING CARE IN ENGLAND FOR PEOPLE WHO HAVE INTELLECTUAL DISABILITIES AND FORENSIC FORMULATIONS

Philip Clayton

Transferring people with intellectual disabilities who have offended out of secure NHS hospitals into the community is being fast tracked. These strategic and clinical plans currently being rushed through are in response to institutional abuse and neglect, such as at Winterbourne View. The reports: *Building the Right Support* (NHS England, 2015), *Winterbourne View: Time for Change* (2014) and *Transforming Care: A National Response to Winterbourne View Hospital* (DOH, 2012), have encouraged a level of action that has gradually gathered momentum and includes considering for transfer people with complex needs and/or personality difficulties.

There is widespread agreement between most professional bodies, members of the public and families of people who have an intellectual disability that hospitals should not be used as campuses; one-stop places to house and 'hide' people. In line with the Department of Health report *Valuing People* (2001) and the *Mansell Report* (2007) (which aimed to support commissioners in developing local services for people whose behaviour presents a significant challenge), care should be provided near to the person's home, or in their home. Exceptions include people who have offended and been assessed by psychiatrists and psychologists in conjunction with the courts as requiring diversion from custodial placements in prisons, young offenders' institutions and sometimes hospital.

Forensic formulations

There are many difficulties when considering the needs of people who are referred to secure services for treatment within a defined period. Taylor et al. (2016) describe the complexities of assessment and treatment of individuals who have an intellectual disability and who have offended. Often a constellation of life experiences that caused or are associated with offending means that, as Taylor points out, appropriate assessment and treatment involves a high level of skill and resources to enable a person to find new ways of managing thoughts, feelings, emotions, behaviours and relationships. Such a programme requires expert planning, sufficient time and a highly skilled workforce.

As a socially responsible and 'inclusive' paradigm, the strategic NHS program 'Transforming Care' is aimed at non-offenders. 'Fast tracking' might have unintended and risky consequences with regard to people who have offended and the closure of hospitals that exist for managing and helping people who have offended could be seen as irresponsible: The policy is to transfer people out of hospitals despite considerable doubt as to how and whether services in the community would be able to manage the risk presented by the complex needs of these individuals within a serviceable infrastructure.

Support system

Working with offenders with complex needs requires people who are highly skilled within sufficient structures of support. This requires clinical expertise to supervise these teams with the capacity to offer reflective practice and training. Small community-based teams rarely have sufficient resources to manage these functionally essential activities, especially without the backup system or support such that is available in hospital settings. Community settings require more staff to provide sufficient backup than is needed in hospitals. However, many community teams have seen severe reductions to their staffing levels under the government's general policy of reducing NHS facilities and there are insufficient numbers of staff currently in place to staff and support these teams. Moreover, community team staff are usually not trained to deal with people with complex problems who are also offenders. The current system of self-funding on a student loan basis is a deterrent to staff undertaking further training. Staff retention is already a serious a problem, and staff who feel untrained and unsupported to deal with the risks of this client group will leave, leading to further weakening of the teams' capacities. Unless these issues are addressed, the 'reshaping' of therapeutic and mental health services will be a failure.

Managing risk

Multi agency working (MAPPA – multi-agency public protection arrangements) is the present framework in which the safety of the public and the effective use of therapeutic strategies are coordinated. This requires all the people who are involved in a person's care and treatment to understand the risks and to be cognisant of the legislation required to be applied to that individual. When assessing individuals for alternatives to hospital and prison and/or treatment the process needs to be more rigorous than when risk can be managed through secure institutions. If small, secure hospitals that have been dedicated and designed to assess, treat, manage and discharge or transfer individuals who are a risk to the public and/or themselves are closed then the capacity to perform these tasks in the community without more resources will be severely compromised. This is a particular concern for those people who may require supervision orders and if this fails, then custodial provision in prisons becomes the only option. However, their level of intellectual disability often makes them vulnerable to exploitation and people with an intellectual disability are already overrepresented in the prison population (Bradley Report, 2009). This requires training and knowledge retention. The withholding and non-resourcing of the high level of community service that would be required and non-communication of the level of risk is what might be seen as 'the neglecting system' (or 'the system neglected') (see Figure 10.1).

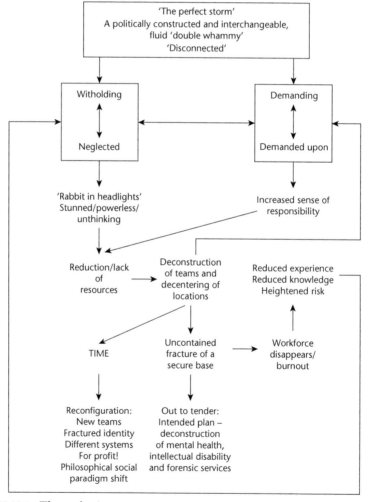

FIGURE 10.1 The neglecting system.

Consequences include burnt-out and neglected professionals seeking alternative employment. Figure 10.2 represents a system that perhaps reflects bygone times, but that depicts a model we aspire to work to.

As the transformation of care continues and NHS hospitals are closed, the private sector is expanding, and competing for contracts to care for, manage and treat people who have an intellectual disability and who have offended. It is difficult to understand why this transformation (fragmentation) is occurring given that the financial gains are unsustainable and limited to the sale of large plots of land in prime locations that bring a few million pounds into the treasury.

The long-term plan when reviewing the transformation of care documentation is not philosophically sound, particularly for those who have offended, as there is a need for asylum for both the person whose difficulties might not be adequately

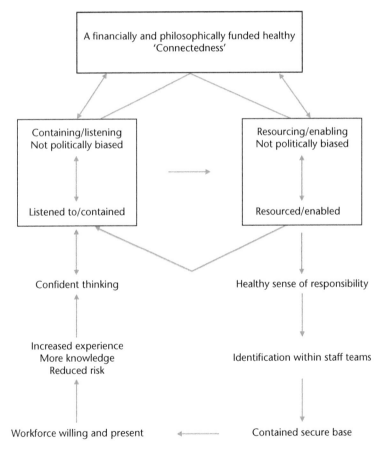

FIGURE 10.2 The OK system.

managed in a house in the community and for the public who might be exposed to unnecessary risk.

Conclusion

Can there be a non-dogmatic political approach that views NHS mental health/intellectual disability care systems as a service, and not as business opportunities, that is fit for purpose? Would better services develop if there were a referendum about transforming care, encouraging issues to be clearly described to the voting public? This might then give a mandate for an NHS as a health service for all, richer or poorer, healthy or not, safeguarding those who are less fortunate and protecting the public from those who for reasons outside their control puts the safety of themselves and others at risk.

Bibliography

Bradley report. (2009). www.rcpsych.ac.uk/pdf/Bradley%20Report11.pdf (Accessed 08/08/18).

The Bradley report five years on. (2014). www.centreformentalhealth.org.uk/Handlers/Download.ashx?IDMF=33874f52-53cb-4a40-b8a7-db8d34d7b583 (Accessed 12/03/18).

Department of Health. (2001). *Valuing people: A new strategy for learning disability for the 21st-century a white paper.* London: Stationery Office.

Department of Health. (2012). *Transforming care: A national response to Winterbourne View Hospital*: Department of Health Review Final Report. www.gov.uk/government/uploads/system/uploads/attachment_data/file/213215/final-report.pdf (Accessed 07/12/17).

Mansell report. (2007) Services for people with learning disability and challenging behaviour or mental health needs. http://webarchive.nationalarchives.gov.uk/+/http://www.dh.gov.uk/en/Publicationsandstatistics/Publications/PublicationsPolicyAndGuidance/DH_080129 (Accessed 07/12/17).

NHS England. (2015). Building the right support. www.england.nhs.uk/learning-disabilities/natplan (Accessed 12/03/18).

Taylor, J., McKinnon, I., Thorpe, I. & Gillmer, B. (2016). The impact of transforming care on the care and safety of patients with intellectual disabilities and forensic needs. *British Journal of Psychology Bulletin,* 41(4), 205–208, doi: 10.1192/pb.bp.116.055095.

Transforming Care and Commissioning Steering Group (2014). *Winterbourne View: Time for Change.* www.england.nhs.uk/wp-content/uploads/2014/11/transforming-commissioning-services.pdf.

11

UNEQUAL GROUND

Working with people affected by child sexual abuse

Julie Lloyd and Hilary Brown

Introduction

We did not know whether to write this chapter and having decided to do so we were unsure how open to be. The chapter deals with an area of practice in which the personal is most definitely political. Patients who have a history of sexual abuse in childhood will have had to navigate not only the original abuse, but the contradictory responses of those around them. Writing about these issues is difficult now, but 40 years ago there was very little recognition that child sexual abuse (CSA) occurred at all let alone that it mattered and, when disclosures surfaced, children were blamed, seen as deluded or made to feel complicit. Many younger therapists, operating in a post-Savile environment will have little awareness of the level of incredulity and stigma that followed any disclosure, or how the experience of sexual abuse in childhood reverberates across a person's whole lifetime. Older therapists may also find it helpful to think about how their own practice has changed to take on board wider and more supportive political and social attitudes.

People affected by a history of sexual abuse may be disadvantaged in therapy, so we make some suggestions about addressing this in the CAT community. CAT acknowledges how far the outside world permeates a person's inner dialogue but often fails to examine how this particularly haunts people abused in childhood. Their experiences will almost certainly have had to be concealed at some points and with some people, which creates a kind of inner duplicity hard to heal. Public discourse, while changing, remains fractured and contradictory; a dilemma at one end of minimising the impact of CSA while at the other burdening survivors with the message they can never 'get over it' or contribute helpfully from their experiences. These ambivalent attitudes to the victims of child sexual abuse affect and compound their original experiences, forcing them to stay silent, to lie, to share their stories in roundabout ways and to develop procedures that can easily be pathologised.

These issues take on added salience when you are also a therapist and as therapists who were, in different ways, and to different extents, sexually abused as children, we were caught in the horns of this dilemma in the writing of this chapter because:

1. We wanted to share our lived experiences and to show how these have enriched our work as therapists.
2. We did not know how to be open without undermining our own credibility, by seeming to be too 'wounded' as 'healers' who might seem to be too close to these 'raw' experiences and/or too damaged by them.
3. We were not sure if we would be seen as unassailable, powerful, 'smug' victims or as worthless 'trash'? We wondered whether readers might apply diagnostic categories to us as a way of responding to our accounts and this would occlude us and all the things we became after the events that we describe.
4. Given the prominence belatedly afforded to these issues, we wondered if we would be seen as jumping on a bandwagon, rather than taking part in a social movement.

We worked by writing our own accounts separately and then through collaborative conversation to tease out shared and different aspects of our experiences and responses. We are grateful to each other for the opportunity that joint working invites to develop creatively our understanding of how things have changed. As clinicians we do not usually disclose our own histories even when to do so might assist the therapeutic alliance and as academics we tend to write from a disembodied position, removing our own experience as if looking down on these 'other' victims through the wrong end of a telescope.

We noted that we sometimes write in the first person, sometimes in the third person as if observing our younger selves from a distant vantage point, sometimes we write as victims and at other times as therapists and by writing this chapter together we can take shelter behind each other. Thus, the chapter weaves together our different voices and self-states and we have not tried to paper over these cracks by repeated editing because these are all valid parts of our experience and our 'selves', each deserving to be heard. We are both experienced as writers and noted this pattern as being particular to this material, evidence perhaps of the fragmentation that occurs as a result of undisclosed abuse.

In the context of other work within the Association for Cognitive Analytic Therapy (ACAT) we arbitrarily discovered we have this experience in common, but we do not know of many other people in ACAT who have experiences of child sexual abuse because currently members don't talk about it beyond the confidential boundaries of their own therapy or inner circle. This has the effect of exaggerating the dilemma we have outlined above because it colludes with the fiction that either these experiences are so common they do not need to be mentioned or of creating a sense that they are so rare that no one could function well in their wake. So, we decided to swallow hard and write this chapter, resisting the assumption that we should be quiet within ACAT, and seeking to change this culture.

Challenges are occurring elsewhere too, such as in the Honest, Open, Proud project (Rhodes, 2017), which explores the stigma of owning any past difficulties as a mental health professional and the pressure many professionals feel to appear invulnerable so that they can position themselves firmly on the side of the helper and rarely alongside the helped. Anyone disclosing to their colleagues or employers would have to go through this kind of consideration of the costs and benefits of disclosing their lived experience and/or making it an explicit focus of their practice.

Keeping quiet colludes with a myth that child sexual abuse (CSA) does damage that cannot be repaired or lived with in constructive ways. But as CAT always tells us, the middle ground is safer. This position is taken up by Roxane Gay who, having been raped as a young teenager, says in her book, *Hunger*:

> I am marked, in so many ways, by what I went through. I survived it, but that isn't the whole of the story. Over the years I have learned the importance of survival and claiming the label of 'survivor' but I don't mind the label of 'victim'. I also don't think there is any shame in saying that when I was raped I became a victim, and to this day, while I am also many other things, I am still a victim.
>
> It took me a long time, but I prefer 'victim' to 'survivor' now. I don't want to diminish the gravity of what happened. I don't want to pretend I'm on some triumphant, uplifting journey. I don't want to pretend that everything is okay. I'm living with what happened, moving forward without forgetting, moving forward without pretending I am unscarred.
>
> *(Gay, 2017, p. 18)*

Both of us acknowledge having been profoundly affected by our experiences in ways that did not go away but bled into our other relationships and coloured our adult lives. But we also assert we have been able to turn this into useful knowledge for our clients and we hope, in this chapter, for our colleagues. Positioning ourselves specifically in this way allows us to acknowledge how our own experiences offer our clients a different observing-eye perspective, an 'outside view' achieved through our training, alongside the insider understanding and empathy that come from our shared experience and common humanity. This reflects Bakhtin's key idea of 'outsideness' that is 'my seeing, knowing and processing in relation to any other human being is founded in the uniqueness and irreplaceability of my place in the world' (Bakhtin, 1990, p. 23).

Pollock (2001), in his key text, *Cognitive Analytic Therapy for Adult Survivors of Childhood Abuse*, made no mention of the political climate in which disclosures were made or of the possibility that therapists might have been victims of childhood abuse themselves, so we hope to add to this important literature by urging change in two directions: first, to increase understanding of the wider social and political context influencing people affected by CSA and, second, by making it safer for therapists who are also survivors to talk about their own (hidden or disclosed) experiences and use this when helpful within their practice.

The trauma from child sexual abuse not only reflects what happened between the perpetrator(s) and the child, but also the way that this is, or is not acknowledged afterwards in the stances taken by immediate family members, authority figures and the prevailing political, judicial and societal culture. Sexual abuse affects people on a continuum that varies according to how pervasive and invasive the abuse was, whether it was perpetrated by, or condoned by, a parent or other family member, whether it was penetrative and whether it occurred over a long period of time. The younger a child was when they were abused, the more damaging it is because that child would have had fewer resources i.e., language and communications skills, to draw on or means of escape. But for each person affected, there are ripples in the lake of their emotional experience that wash over their subsequent relationships, changing the ecology around that lake. If survivors want to make some sense of what happened to them, and therapists are to help survivors thrive, both must track not only their personal journeys but also society's mixed, discordant and evolving reactions.

So, what are the contours of CSA and how are these complicated by the ways in which public discourse is conducted? We want to address this under the following headings:

- Fear and trauma
- Truth and lying
- The impact of CSA on sexual development
- Losing trust in other adults
- Deciding whether to disclose
- Blame and complicity
- Dealing with unstable states
- Professional changes
- Political and legal changes

Fear and trauma

A person can emerge from CSA with no visible scars, but it is important to start by reminding readers that being sexually abused is, at the time and in retrospect, terrifying. This is not only a subjective perception, as failed paedophile assaults are responsible for a significant proportion of child murders both within and outside the family. During an assault a child must 'read' their abuser from a position of inexperience and identify his or her intentions, submitting while they remain at risk and finding ways to escape if they can see a safe window of opportunity. They then must decide whether to 'own' the experience and if so who to tell, which demands more mind reading trying to anticipate how various members of one's family and community would respond.

> HB's experience was a one-off assault committed by a man who had lived next door but who then moved to another part of the country with his family. She was ostensibly visiting his children with whom she had been friendly.

> She remembers arriving at Paddington station after a long train journey to be met awkwardly by Mr C, going through the station and getting on to a crowded suburban train so that they had to stand in the corridor by one of the doors. She had no time to think when he started kissing her. They were standing in a public space and she hoped someone would walk through the corridor making him stop, but no one did. When they got to his station he took her to his large company car parked in the station car park and began the drive to his house. He stopped on the way by a wood and again began kissing and fondling her. She had no idea where she was and no money to get home independently.

There was no overt threat involved in HB's experience, other than that she had no option but to stay with him for the duration of the stay, but other children are explicitly threatened and pick up terrifying and contradictory messages that teach them to comply *at all costs* if they want to stay alive, and not to do anything that encourages others to hurt them, including when the adults in their world are behaving as if hurting children is their God-given right. Some children are sexually abused in the context of physical punishment and must deal with this as an extra layer of threat, vulnerability and complicity; after all what is meted out to them is 'their' fault and well deserved. Some children learn that they must put up with (disassociate), parts of themselves belonging to excited individuals and /or the 'laughing gangs' that, existing first in reality, find their way into a person's inner world.

If a child is being sexually abused by multiple people or if the one person abusing them shifts, a bit like Jekyll and Hyde, from one persona to another (known in CAT as a self-state), the child is likely to be given a multitude of conflicting statements about their role in causing the abuse to happen and their responsibility for covering it up. If they continue to live with the perpetrators and are subject to ongoing abuse they become watchful, focusing on the perpetrator's moods and movements, rather than on their own, attempting to anticipate and avoid further abuse. The predominant role they are taught is that there is nobody around to help; the very idea of being a person in their own right, or of approaching another safer adult in the expectation of rescue is closed off and/or does not occur to them. This seems to create another dilemma for survivors, that of being either invisible (as a victim) or exposed as a troublemaker.

Truth and lying

HB writes:

> My trip was supposed to be an exciting sightseeing tour and my mother had urged me to be polite, being more concerned about my table manners than about my safety. Mr C told me not to tell his wife or children and, being a conforming child, I did what I was supposed to do, I tried not to be alone with him again, but I knew that I could not avoid being driven to the station on the return trip. My anxiety about this coloured the whole stay.

Central to the experience was the need to lie. When clearing out her parents' house recently, she found three large postcards of Buckingham Palace, Big Ben and the Houses of Parliament with simple sentences in large handwriting on the back. There was no hint that anything was wrong, because she had already made the decision to act as if nothing had happened.

One of the things we have learned together by talking is how our experiences forced us into a problematic relationship with truth because the perpetrators were duplicitous to us, but also by concealing what had happened we were forced to be duplicitous to others. HB was told not to tell Mr C's family, but also *decided* not to tell her own, pretending instead that she had had a lovely time in London. This kept part of the world 'normal' while other parts of her were cut off. JL had to deal with the ongoing presence of lying adults in her life, so she had to be on alert about being lied to all the time. As a 10-year-old, in a library book JL came across a picture of a lie detector machine and decided she was going to get one . . . then she could press the button and up would pop 'lie' or 'truth' and she would know what was going on. Children who have been sexually abused are also being emotionally abused in that they are duped and lied to and then told to pretend. In our day, we were both pretty sure that if we did tell the truth we would be told we were liars, so this was a no-win position.

Lying may serve a person's self-interest but can also be altruistic when 'white lies' are told to spare the feelings of others. Some lies are 'paretic' protecting both the speaker and the hearer and lying in the aftermath of sexual abuse often falls into this category as it allows the hurt child to preserve some normality as well as to protect their parents from what has happened. It is moving to note that many individuals who delayed coming forward to report historical sexual abuse in schools and churches, waited to do so until their parents had died. The child held on to their pain to protect their parents from acknowledging how their decisions had, often unwittingly, contributed to the circumstances that had led to the abuse. Lying that is designed to exploit or mislead is rightly condemned or pathologised but in this context, lying to save the feelings of important people in your life may be a profoundly selfless act.

The impact of CSA on sexual development

Children's sexual feelings are normally reacted to differently from their other feelings. Whereas general emotional regulation arises out of the mirroring of affect by primary caregivers, children's sexual feelings are normally ignored by caregivers and more likely to be influenced by peers. As Fonagy (2008) points out, this often means that a child is left to explore her or his own sexuality, unless adults impose their own construction of the child's sensorimotor experiences or intrude with prohibitions or shaming.

The sensuality of children and their innocent reaching out for affection is distorted when adults view these qualities as signs of sexual desire that remain outside the child's Zone of Proximal Development (ZPD, Vygotsky, 1978) instead of responding to them as children. One of the reasons that HB did not tell her parents about the abuse was that she had already been embarrassed by a story her father told and retold about a photo of her as a toddler playing in a paddling pool in the garden with no clothes on. The picture shows her as an alive and determined girl, revelling in her separateness, but was overlaid by the narrative that a male friend of the family had come into the kitchen shortly after the picture had been taken and said, 'Your daughter is trying to seduce me'.

Such projection happens when adults do not have access to their own experiences of discovering and exploring their sexuality in childhood and/or when they cannot read the way that children move through different stages indicated by their being 'rude', shy or 'embarrassed'. As Miller (1984) states, 'Children are the mute receivers of our projections. Unable to defend themselves against them, unable to give them back to us or interpret them for us, they are only able to serve as their bearers' (p. 154). This leads to some abused children being prematurely sexualised, while remaining emotionally immature and isolated. Other children retreat from sex entirely. Their often-secret knowledge makes them vulnerable to older, more knowing adults who register that they are acting in either a more sexualised way or in an anti-sex way that does not fit with their chronological age and so they become a target for further abuse. This is defended on the grounds that they are 'asking for it' and seems to confirm that the primary abuse originated with them or was somehow their fault. Premature sexualisation also separates abused children from their peers and an abused child might come across as haughty and aloof because in important ways they no longer feel like a child. Neither of the authors could have known at the time that these extremes, of presenting a premature or misplaced sexual language or actions or a determined attempted refusal to have anything to do with sex are now considered reliable signals of abuse, rather than grounds for punitive and rejecting attitudes or self-doubt.

This is not the place to debate factors causing sexual offending other than to say that this represents an extreme alienation from one's own body and a failure of empathy. There is some evidence that some boys and some girls who are abused either physically or sexually have an increased risk of offending, *if they are not helped*, and that this should lend extra weight to the commitment to provide proper support to young people abused in childhood. However, current research indicates that around half of sexual offenders against children report they were not sexually abused in their own childhoods; some were abused physically but not sexually, so the routes from victim to perpetrator are not simple or inevitable. As Salter et al. (2003) points out, 'it is very difficult, however, to accurately determine this proportion and results from studies vary substantially' (p. 474). Figures in a range of studies (Hindman & Peters, 2001; Lee et al., 2002; Salter et al., 2003; Simons, 2007) vary between 29% to 58%, but offenders admitting to a history of being abused themselves may be seeking a justification or they may hide their own experiences of being violated out of shame. Role reversals do provide one model that can be used to think about abusive behaviour, that it represents a way of turning the tables away from the vulnerability of the abused child to the inviolability of the abusing adult, but it is not the only, nor the inevitable model.

Losing trust in other adults

Cognitive analytic therapy's focus on relational description posits that, in addition to the immediate '*doing to* in relation to *done to*' relational dyad, the child must manage complex and contradictory responses in their immediate circles and in the wider society, complicating what the child has met with in the abusive dyad. JL had to face the fact that her abuse was actively incited by her mother and ignored by her father. HB was permanently on guard in case her father turned out to be like this other man and switched between being provocative (that reflected her hidden knowledge of male sexuality) and acting like a 'prude' trying to shut up any talk of sex that made her feel uncomfortable.

> JL described how as a trainee psychologist (and protecting herself by keeping her childhood experiences secret), she was watching through a one-way mirror a foster family with a 13-year-old sexual abuse victim, together with a trainee psychiatrist. 'Did you see how flirtatious that girl is?' commented the psychiatrist. She hadn't noticed any flirtation and the ignorance of the trainee psychiatrist could have adversely affected their work with the victim who had even less power than the psychology trainee (JL hid in a loo weeping as she wondered if she had been flirtatious herself without knowing it).

This attitude extends to clinical formulation. A child who comes across as flirtatious may indeed be signaling they have been sexually abused, but in the past, this was often seen as the child being the cause of the original abuse. Children and young people with sexual knowledge that is outside their ZPD are often seen as 'inappropriate', experiencing further stress when they cannot be sure what signals they are giving off or what others read from their behaviour.

Taking a historical perspective, we can both see that those responsible for the child, whether as parents or relatives or as professionals or law enforcers, react to CSA in the force field of the social views that were prevalent at the time. A few individuals may have been able to hear and take on board a more child-centred and innovative position, becoming 'early adopters' of the newer imperatives to believe, support and protect children that gradually spread to become the new social norm. But in the period we lived through, disbelief was the default position so that children met with, or rightly feared that they would meet with, a wall of adults prepared to take the person accused of abuse's side, minimising or denying the veracity of their account. Hagan and Smail (1997) described group work using power mapping showing how the misuse of power, both past and present, is at the core of the difficulties that survivors experience. Those who are otherwise 'good, honest, kind citizens', 'know' that the accused must be innocent and defend the person publicly thereby undermining the child's direct but hidden knowledge. Recent cases involving celebrities in sport and entertainment have demonstrated this unwillingness to knock a person off their pedestal. JL described her rejection and shame in an incident when she was 10 years old:

I liked chatting to the school dinner ladies and some of the teachers on playground duty. I always made a beeline towards these kind grown-ups. One day I suddenly found myself describing how my mother would undress me and put me with men and also carry me from my own bed at night to put me in bed with them. I told the friendly teacher about one of the men, William Mayne, who had said to me as I sat on his lap when I was 6 years old that he knew I was a Laplander. When I had objected that I was English, he pointed out that he was right. 'That was a funny joke,' I said laughing. I also told her what my mother encouraged the men to do to me. For the next three days, the teachers refused to talk to me. I stood in the playground looking up at the staffroom window and saw a group of teachers standing staring at me silently. I felt I was being crushed as I realised to my horror that they were a part of 'it' too as they did not like me anymore because I had spilled the secret. This meant there were no grown-ups in the entire world for me. I heard the bell go for dinner and knew I would have to walk into the school where the teachers would not talk to me anymore. I told myself. 'Just one step . . . just one step' and taking one step at a time I walked back into school.

JL was being systematically and repeatedly sexually abused from the age of 6 (until she said 'no' when she was 14), with her mother's active collusion, initially by children's author William Mayne. As well as abusing her in her parents' house, she was sent to stay with him for three weeks most summers from when she was 8–14 years old. Forty years later she gave evidence in court where he was convicted and received a prison sentence. This had been part of a pattern of abuse at home wherein her sadistic, paedophile mother had also enticed half a dozen trainee teachers from a teaching training college to sexually abuse her. JL's mother was actively involved in this, giving instructions and watching as it unfolded. JL thought this was normal and had no vocabulary to describe it to anyone else. She thought everybody did it, although she also knew that people were not allowed to talk about it.

We both, in common with other victims of our era, found it impossible to tell anyone our experiences or trigger helping mechanisms, leaving us both open to further abuse and enforced self-reliance. NSPCC current figures suggest that 1 in 3 children who had been sexually abused by an adult at that time did not tell anyone (Radford et al., 2011); we hope that this figure is less today. Moreover, The National Association of People Abused in Childhood (2017) found that one-third of adults who suspected another adult had abused a child did nothing for fear that they were wrong. But what this does to a child is profound because what she or he knows, other adults do not understand, and this fundamentally erodes her or his trust. It takes away any sense that other adults could help her but it also either leaves her wondering why she knows so much more than these naïve people who cannot see what she so powerfully knows or makes her wonder if she knows anything at all as she wonders why other people are not bothered by what bothers her.

Not that becoming a 'grown-up' means sexual assaults disappear; the Crime Survey for England and Wales and police-recorded crime data (2018) show that 1 in 5 women (i.e. 3.4 million women) have been sexually assaulted since the age of 16. An estimated 646,000 men have also experienced sexual assault since they were 16. These figures are unchanged since 2005 and 80% did not report their experiences to the police.

Deciding whether to disclose

Abuse victims may be very worried that getting someone else to acknowledge trauma risks that the listener might disintegrate. It may also confront their own 'defences' by making an experience that has been dissociated seem very real. When, as therapists, we reflect a history of abuse back to a person through reading a CAT reformulation letter, our patients can be powerfully surprised when we show that we can hear and hold the abuse in mind and understand that the client might feel frightened or ashamed by the letter. Victims may also be afraid that listeners could be secretly sexually aroused, and question what the other person's agenda is, even if at face value a person is indicating that they are open to hearing the child's story because it will help them, the child victim, to share it. Some people seem to know but not know; they may recognise that a child, teenager or adult is in some way needy (without knowing their history) and will be generously kind towards them, while also assuming it is none of their business to ponder about why the individual elicits this response in them.

There has also been a gendered bias that assumes that sexual offenders are always male and victims always female. Boys and young men experiencing sexual abuse as children have sometimes experienced even more shame-inducing stigma than girls and young women, which, by silencing them, acts to reduce social awareness of the necessity to develop appropriate protective strategies across a range of institutions such as boarding schools, seminaries, churches, scouts and other youth organisations. It is as if the knowledge of same-sex acts was suppressed alongside the knowledge that some adults abuse children making a double barrier to overcome.

Other listeners are angry, reacting based on who the alleged perpetrator is, needing to affirm that 'decent people like us' would never abuse a child and batting away the child's account. Festinger's (1957) cognitive dissonance rules here; because to this kind of person the decent individual would never hurt a child, they believe that they themselves as decent people would never make friends with or be a member of a family alongside someone who is this monstrous or be a member of a family that has an 'evil monster' in its midst.

Festinger's findings have been replicated experimentally on numerous occasions confirming that an action, if it represents an anathema of someone's core beliefs, must be explained away. The 20% of sexually abused children who are abused by women, especially by mothers, face this extra layer of disbelief. CAT's multiple self-states model helps us to analyse the behaviour of perpetrators and their culpability and to explain how it is that perpetrators present such different faces to the world. But for the ashamed and unprotected survivor, this destructive, invalidating silencing can feel at times like a worse betrayal than the original abuse and has a deep and frightening impact on subsequent relationships.

The top half of Figure 11.1 describes the self-protective motivation of people who, coming across the likelihood that someone they know (either personally or by reputation) is sexually abusing children, decide to ignore it, and in the bottom half of this split egg, how this further confirms and perpetuates the victim's powerlessness.

Decent people know 'monsters' exist, but obviously as 'good judges' of character, no one they would ever consort with would fall into that category. Both of us faced this struggle to work out which 'group' other people belong to and can be more astute in retrospect in deciphering the way others acted. While some responses to disclosure are patient and kind, victims are also subjected to willfully blind, scary, cruel, furiously rejecting, embarrassed, confusing or publicly pitying

FIGURE 11.1 Seeking to ignore, dreading being powerless.

reflections. 'It has always been the case that it is not cruelty itself that arouses public indignation, but rather paying attention to the cruelty' (Miller, 1984, p. 190).

In cases of historic CSA these boundaries are sometimes breached in ways that are outside the person's control because a case comes out into the open following other disclosures or is reopened when further evidence becomes known. This may not be the adult/child's decision and if there is publicity about an impending court case that includes them, they may fear being exposed to people who 'know' them but do not 'know' about their experience. Younger victims of CSA face similar fears of being suddenly exposed in ways that they cannot control in that many are afraid that images of their abuse can be posted online and be seen by people in their network or neighbourhood. The press and the online community play a significant part in escalating this.

When the alleged perpetrator is someone powerful or admired these dynamics are magnified. Paedophiles know this and often operate by putting themselves into prominent roles in the community and by bolstering their credibility. Sometimes they step across the threshold by offering support to the families of their victims so that they co-opt the very people who should be taking a more challenging stance in support of the child. This was the case in relation to abuse within the church as reported by victims in Boston, many of whom could not disclose what had happened because the priest who had abused them had also wormed their way into the family and had come to be seen as a friend and supporter to other family members. In this way, the paedophile also 'messes with the head' of those who should be helping and allows his or her own disjointed states to muddle and paralyse those who should be taking responsibility as members of the child's protective network.

One of the main findings about why the sexual abuse of children in Rotherham, Bradford, Rochdale, Oxford and other towns in the UK went unchallenged by the police and social services for so long despite their knowledge of what was happening, was that there was an institutional fear of addressing anything that could upset the apple cart in relation to race and ethnicity. The idea that the risk of being seen as racist trumped the need to protect children shows how confused white people can be about their attitudes to others and about their right to call them out without abusing their privileged position in society at large. They feared being accused of racism as the abusers were Asian more than they feared failing to do their job by protecting girls and young women who were unable to challenge their abusers.

Furthermore, these girls were not the 'right type' of 'nice' middle-class victims and were disregarded, their abuse being rationalised away on the feeble grounds that they were making 'lifestyle choices' rather than being abused. The response of authorities placed the responsibility for first recognising and second for stopping organised paedophile gangs on the heads of confused and neglected girls and when their attempts to get redress failed, blamed the girls as if the behaviour of grown men had been their own choice or responsibility. It is no wonder that hearing about another person's experience of abuse elicits strong reactions. Hearing a child's experience may elicit visceral feelings, felt as sickening, tightness in the chest and gut and immediate feelings of wanting to detach or avoid, especially if the therapist wants to disavow knowledge about who the perpetrator was. As therapists, this powerful countertransference is very useful to tune into and use for the patient, but without restorative work on the issues, former victims may find it harder to hear accounts of other people's abuse if it chimes with their own experiences, because the words are too full of meaning.

Blame and complicity

Paedophiles, in common with other sex offenders, employ many rationalisations to persuade their victims to comply and to quieten any qualms they have about their own behavior (see Finkelhor & Araji, 1984). The notion that was promulgated by perpetrators and their enablers is that sexual contact between children and adults is not abuse, but instead liberating, progressive, harmless and fun with objections coming from outdated bourgeois conventions (a view that gave permission for rife child–adult sexual activities in schools and youth groups such as Odenwaldschule in Germany) and represented by organisations such as the Paedophile Information Exchange (PIE) and more recently by online apologists. PIE operated openly from 1974–1984 and was supported by the National Council for Civil Liberties (NCCL) claiming hostility to PIE would involve increasing censorship and damage to gay rights. In June 2015, documents emerged following a BBC Freedom of Information request that the then Conservative Home Secretary, Leon Brittan, had refused to support a bill designed to outlaw PIE. In March 2014 evidence emerged that PIE had received campaign grants totalling £70,000 from the Home Office in 1977 and 1980. Although this action by the government is *now* viewed at best as embarrassing and at worst appalling, it demonstrates how different attitudes and knowledge were so very recently.

Paedophiles argue with children and with their detractors in the following terms:

- They say that they really 'love' the child and that 'ours is really a special relationship in which I love you and know this is what you really want'.
- They blame the child, saying, 'I wouldn't do it myself, but you must have been seductive or have done something to encourage it'.
- They minimise the impact of the abuse by trivialising it or saying, 'You'll get over it'.
- They claim enlightened values to normalise the abuse saying that it is bourgeois, stuffy and old-fashioned to believe that adults and children should not have sex together. This way they make an argument that the child should even feel privileged and liberated to have sex with adults (a particularly 1960s mentality).
- They press on the child the enormity of disclosure in an attempt to secure their silence, 'You are utterly responsible for my well-being because if you tell anyone I shall be ruined, which will be all your fault'.
- They may, in order to threaten the child, disregard their feelings altogether, treating the child as a thing that they have a right to use in the pursuit of getting

high and intimidating them with hints that they will abandon or destroy the child if he or she resists.

- They may invoke others present or imagined, amplifying the noise surrounding the assaults that may later become lodged in the victim's internal dialogue.

These 'messages' align with what Pollock (2001) describes as a number of 'lessons learnt; by survivors', namely that, 'Being close is dangerous; anger must be hidden; I must keep the awful secret: I am guilty: I must endure the pain: others can't cope; and reality is false' (pp. 197–205). HB recalls: 'I did tell my father about the abuse when I was 35 and he said exactly what I thought he would say. He said, "You were always seductive"'. Perhaps it was that accurate reading of the mental state of an adult man that had also allowed her to read the man who abused her and to go along with his shifting states enough to survive as opposed to being abandoned in London or pushed out of the train. JL was also disbelieved and served up a version of her famous abuser (who was culturally admired) that undermined her own experience and perceptions. In a post on Liberal England blog regarding convicted paedophile and award-winning child author William Mayne one adult stated,

It seems to me challengingly important, because so challengingly dreadful, to propose that a genuinely lovely writer, a writer deeply worth reading, by children and adults, can at the same time be an abusive man who betrayed trust and responsibility.

*(Liberalengland.blogspot.com/2010/03/
death-of-william-mayne-html)*

Dealing with unstable states

So, the child picks up any or several messages. For some the message is they may be especially loved as sex is a special currency and/or they will have been told that they are powerfully seductive and responsible for making the perpetrator do what he did and subsequently responsible for his or her well-being and reputation. HB recounts that,

Sixty years on I don't remember what it felt like to be kissed by this large and relatively strange man, but I do remember feeling bewildered about the sudden shifts that saw him move from this assured and overbearing behaviour into a childlike state, crying and begging for forgiveness and urging me to keep his secret by not telling his wife or children. When I said I was looking forward to seeing them, he asserted that it was much nicer to 'be alone' and after that I said nothing.

The sexualised child becomes frightening/challenging to adults so that sometimes such children come away from abusive situations confused, not knowing if they have been powerless or powerful, especially when a pathetic paedophile, such as in the case of abusers who occupy powerful positions, plead with the child not to tell anyone for fear of being ruined. HB recounts how later, as a professional drawn to work in this field, she read first-person accounts of abuse by priests in which young children spoke of this same confusion. Typically, the priest would first overwhelm them with arguments about their sinfulness and with distorted spiritual ideas to get them to perform sexual acts with him, but then he would break down and beg the child not to expose him because it would end his life if they brought him down. He would thereby place the responsibility not only for causing the abuse but for the consequences of it, on the child's already narrow shoulders. This is a huge responsibility for a child to seemingly have this man's life in their small hands shortly after it had seemed the other way around.

This speaks to the heart of the experience of CSA, in that an inexperienced child must 'read' and manage the shifting states of more experienced and powerful adults. They are almost bound to dissociate their experiences because everywhere they look their attempts to disclose are turned back on them and they therefore develop splits and dissociated states in their own personalities. To name this in therapy can be supportive and a step towards greater integration, but this understanding of their internal fractures is often used against them or summed up in stigmatising, blanket diagnoses and disempowering labels. These can have the effect of creating a greater 'them and us' protective differentiation for 'helpers' who can further distance themselves from the disturbing accounts that they are being asked to validate. Every time they pathologise the child/adult they miss the opportunity to validate the child's response and to respect the adult's healthy drive to survive.

> JL recalled standing chatting in a car park with a group of her health and social care colleagues. They were talking about the clients they found hardest. One of them said that she could not stand people who had been sexually abused because those people insisted on describing what had happened. The others all agreed and vied with each other to describe how aversive they found survivors. 'They're all borderlines anyway; shouldn't take it seriously,' one replied trying to comfort the others. I stood there terrified in case any of them had guessed my secret.

Moreover, as HB set out in the beginning of the chapter, the sense victims have that they are not good or nice people to help, leads them to present in ways that elicit blame or that can legitimately be stigmatised, for example by acting promiscuously or by self-soothing with alcohol or drugs.

What used to be called 'borderline personality disorder' (BPD) is now slightly more helpfully called 'emotional unstable personality disorder' (EUPD). This highly controversial label is usually applied to women with a history of sexual abuse. In fact, to admit to such a history is often to be instantaneously so labelled. But whereas diagnostic categories can help a skilled therapist to describe back to the child/adult how their experiences have shaped them, labels can instead shut down a therapist's ability to listen respectfully and instead define the other person as if there were nothing more that needs to be said or noticed about them. A distressed person seeking help to manage and understand abuse they have experienced may be further hurt by being told by powerful mental health professionals that there is something fundamentally disordered about who they are, i.e. that it is their personality that was flawed from the outset, rather than that these 'symptoms' are ways in which they have been resourceful and that have allowed them to survive. Even if this use of diagnostic labels is expressed kindly, the affect can feel at best condescending and at worst nasty and pejorative.

> JL was listening to a description by a psychologist of a 'borderline' woman's conversation and actions that appeared healthy. When I commented that the woman seemed fine regarding the situation being described, the speaker explained 'This is typical of borderlines, that they appear absolutely fine one minute but we all know . . .' I wondered what the woman had to do not to have this all-inclusive label.

Diagnoses may be used to alert mental health professionals to a predicted set of relational patterns that they might otherwise not be aware of, including the abnormal intensity of unacknowledged feeling states and the instability of having to dissociate and shift states that might have their origins in the child's response to their abusers' own contradictions and to the denials of those who should have stepped in to comfort and protect them. However, BPD, as a diagnosis, persists in ignoring the roots of these states in trauma while using the term 'disorder' to imply irretrievable damage. A more accurate description would make clear that as opposed to being 'disordered', the individual has learnt to cope with powerfully abusive and lying people.

Being labeled as having 'BPD' is too often taken to mean the individual is difficult and their reactions disproportionate; for example, it implies they are either over-emotional or dissociated, either angry or too compliant, either frightened of being abandoned or manipulatively seeking attachment. But if we reinstate the abuse as the core experience that this person has had to deal with, we can see that their intense state shifts arise as a response to contradictory expectations about what would be considered appropriate behaviour for someone with this history. When one minute you are struggling to survive and the next your reality is being denied, it is inevitable that you develop the capacity to switch from hyperaroused states to numbness and denial. 'I cannot understand how the vast majority of perpetrators of sexual violence walk free in society while people who struggle to survive its after effects are told they have disordered personalities' (Shaw & Proctor, 2004, p. 12).

Labels such as BPD or EUPD locate the damage and dysfunction within the (usually female) survivor's distress, which allows responsible individuals to act as if the problem lies, not in the system that has allowed the abuse to happen, but in the person whose personality is disordered. It is a specific instance of victim blaming. Victim blaming acts to maintain the status quo and distance those who have not been affected, behind the comforting illusion that it could never happen to them or to someone in their family. The increasing acknowledgement of child sexual abuse has not stemmed the flow of ubiquitous sexualised images of children and young people in print and online as if it is easier to maintain the status quo that perpetuates the endemic sexualisation of children and young teenagers and act as if the casualties are to blame. These diagnoses, as Shaw and Proctor (2004) write, far from being objective are constructed around 'concepts and expectations that are fundamentally gendered and which profoundly affect how a patient's behaviour is evaluated and responded to' (pp. 483–490).

Judith Herman's (1981) campaign to include troubled abuse survivors in DSM IV alongside survivors of war, disaster and terror under the diagnosis of post-traumatic stress disorder (PTSD) acted to free them from the insulting implications of hysteria or borderline personality disorder. Bessel van der Kolk (2005) points out that PTSD is not a *disorder* but an *adaptation* and that shifting from a diagnosis that locates the problem in the victim to one that credits people who have been abused with the resilience that enabled them to become survivors, is an important step to take on behalf of victims.

A consensus statement about using personality disorder diagnoses called 'People with complex mental health difficulties who are diagnosed with a personality disorder' (BPS, 2018), made by a number of leading mental health organisations including Mind, the British Psychological Society and the Royal College of General Practitioners, led to this comment from the British Psychological Society's Division of Clinical Psychology's 'Personality Disorder' Reference Group and the Beyond Diagnosis Group:

> The statement shows an encouraging willingness to embrace critiques of the concept of 'personality disorder'. Given that the diagnosis can be experienced as very damaging, service users are entitled to be informed about its limitations and to be offered alternatives such as psychological formulation, rather than have the diagnosis imposed as a fact.
>
> *(BPS, 2018)*

Instead, the Power Threat Meaning Framework (BPS, 2018), summarises and integrates evidence about the role of various kinds of power in people's lives, the kinds of threat that misuse of power poses and the ways people learn to respond to those threats. 'Symptoms' as a medical concept are replaced by 'responses to threat'. CAT is predicated on the strong awareness that people are taught and/or forced to become the way they are. Within CAT theory there is a far more humane approach to BPD/EUPD than other modalities or a purely medical model. But this does not always cut across the attitudes expressed within many exhausted mental health teams. Even within the CAT community, labels may be used habitually to avoid more complex and empathic responses. When that happens, the professional is elided into a conservative, status quo stance in which their professional allegiance and status takes precedence over their humanity. In reciprocal role terms this may be described as 'powerfully professionally defined in relation to gazed upon but unseen'. Often there is also an implicit message of *blaming* in relation to *blamed* that may confirm for the survivor the way that the perpetrator hung responsibility for their actions on to the child. The child also grows up not knowing what exactly they are responsible for, and what they had no influence over. It takes practice and getting it wrong to prevent this from becoming a habitual dilemma of stepping up grandiosely or opting out and blaming others.

For individuals with this history the big risk is that it then provokes an over-shadowing 'diagnosis' as if that history says all that needs to be said about them as an individual, that it explains all their social actions and their sense of themselves including their assumed wish for perfect care. There is no space for individual uniqueness, nor acknowledgement of their multiple subsequent relationships free from abuse and the relational learning achieved through many years lived away from abuse. If they are lucky they will have found themselves in relationships in which they can heal and grow. Unless this assumption that survivors of abuse automatically and always come to act from a dissociated, abusive place in themselves is challenged, the therapeutic journey towards validation and integration is threatened. Validation happens when the therapist can look past labels and hear the real experience of the child and acknowledge the way they coped in the absence of adult protection. Therapists who distance themselves from what is happening in the therapy room and flee to labels will not be able to do this.

Professional changes

Dramatic and significant changes have taken place in political and social attitudes towards survivors of child sexual in the last 50 years, as evidenced by public discourse and legal changes, and these have made it more possible for previously silenced voices to express themselves. National statistics point to a 10% rate in the population for CSA (and a 1% rate for incest), but we have noted that it is rare for people working within mental health professions, and even within ACAT, to own these experiences. Research into attachment implies that the damage sustained by early negative experiences may be mitigated and the cycle of disadvantage interrupted, if the survivor and now caregiver acquires a capacity to fully represent and reflect on mental experience (Fonagy et al., 1995). Professions such as psychology and psychotherapy can provide non-stigmatising opportunities to reflect on both the mental state of others and to enhance one's own capacity for self-reflection. As such, it is likely that people with histories of abuse might be over-, rather than under-represented in the helping professions and the 'wounded healer' literature attests to this. Moreover, we would argue that this should be welcomed explicitly rather than swept under the carpet because it brings an important perspective into our shared work. We have found ourselves wondering whether others have chosen to stay silent because they have concerns that any disclosure would be met with disdain. We would like it to be the case that CSA stops being something mental health professionals 'treat' but do not own, as if they are caught in the dilemma of staying either masked, isolated but safe, keeping true thoughts and feelings inside them for fear of ridicule, aggression, rejection or disappointment, or vulnerable, exposed and likely to be looked down on by colleagues, rejecting others before they can be rejected and abused by them (Maple & Simpson, 1995, cited in Pollock, 2001).

Professionals have a right to their personal privacy and should not be pressured into talking publicly about their private lives or motivations, but it would be a measure of the strength of the CAT community if we moved towards a position of owning that some of our members are survivors of abuse and have 'expertise through experience'. Acknowledging this would have knock-on effects because it would change the way that we talk about people who have been abused in childhood and dissolve the sense of 'us and them', when some of them are indeed seen to be some of us. Moreover, this more respectful stance could be reflected in the way that we offer supervision and in our training. Senior professionals influence junior colleagues when they encounter them as trainees, supervisees or mentors and it would be helpful if they could signal that this is a history that can become a bedrock for insight and resilience, not one that must be hidden from view.

For as long as there is a fear that colleagues would see them as damaged goods, or as likely to re-enact their own difficulties in a professional setting, people will keep these experiences to themselves and our professional community will lose the opportunity to learn from their experiences. If disclosure is framed as a person lacking resilience or robustness and failing to have 'got over it' then openness will not be possible. This is of course a double bind because if disclosure is taboo, we cannot invite colleagues to share times when they have been confronted by client experiences that are close to those they have themselves lived, and this undermines an important structure for safety and reflection.

JL experienced just such a *minimising* in relation to *minimised* relationship when working as a clinical psychologist in a local NHS hospital unit for people with a dual diagnosis of learning disability and mental illness:

> A change in the admissions criteria suddenly resulted in half of the admitted patients being paedophiles. I was expected to work with this client group (new for me) with no supervision or specialist training. I was optimistic at first as I told myself that since what had happened to me was decades ago, and as I was now an experienced professional psychologist, I would be fine. Instead I found myself plunged into powerful relational dilemmas about hating, fearing liking and seeking to be a good psychologist, while coping with my own experiences. I felt just like a child stuck at home again. After nine months I approached the head of psychology, requesting a job change with a brief explanation that this job was homing into my own childhood experiences of sexual abuse. The head refused, pointing out that since she has chosen to stay with her husband who had psychosis, so I should just get on with the job (I think her reasoning was something about soldiering on

no matter what, rather than the positive reports she said she received about my work). She did offer to approach a neighbouring NHS Trust with a request for some sessions of supportive counselling, but that Trust turned me down saying I had an excellent reputation as a good psychologist, so there was no problem. After another nine months, a psychology colleague generously offered to do a unilateral job swap with me as my kind colleague accepted that I found the work disturbing.

Williams (2012) offers support to therapists who believe their credibility would be jeopardised if 'too much came out' about them and/or if they requested any adjustments in their caseload. By mapping the chronically endured pain of a wounded healer, she considers the risks that arise at both ends of this dilemma, in either avoiding being aware of personal resonance with the client's material or of over-identifying with it and joining the client's 'dance' (see Figure 11.2). Williams recommends processing the issues, modeling change, and empathically helping the client to do the same. Being a 'survivor' as opposed to a 'victim' in this context does not have to rest on disavowing the experience of victimisation but of seeing the skills that were involved in coping and harvesting them for your use in later life.

Our professional world is a microcosm and these issues about disclosing CSA reflect much wider issues about the social and political lenses through which survivors are seen. It also, for survivors who are therapists, repeats issues that they

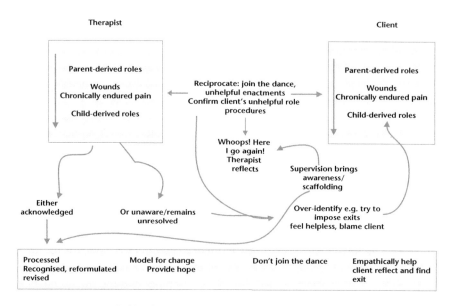

FIGURE 11.2 Wounded healer map.

Source: Reproduced with permission of the author, Barbara Williams.

will have faced in other groups and settings as they decide who to trust with this information and who to stay clear of.

Political and legal changes

We have discussed the personal implications of abuse as well as the political and social influences that have borne down on the stance taken by therapists and we have tried to expose any myths of political neutrality. Fortunately, attitudes have changed since the 1950s and 1960s. The raft of historical abuse cases coming before the courts as we write is evidence of a more accepting attitude but also demonstrates how pervasive these forms of misplaced responsibility and denial have been, especially in those institutions and agencies that have claimed the moral high ground to avoid scrutiny.

In the therapeutic community, Freud's characterisation of revelations by women of childhood sexual abuse as fantasies rather than memories have been largely overturned. While it is acknowledged that this was more acceptable to nineteenth- and twentieth-century society, this was a fundamental error and theoretical fissure and its overthrow was necessary to upend a framework within which children were seen as projecting their fantasies about adult sexuality on to powerful adults in their lives, rather than hearing how powerful adults had projected and acted out *their* infantile fantasies on real children.

The laisser-faire attitude of the 1950s–1980s, jolly and confidently dismissing, was typified by Kinsey et al.'s famous 1953 survey on sex, in which the data on extra-marital and pre-marital sex caused a sensation, whereas the data on incest and sexual abuse was completely ignored. Kinsey reported that a quarter of his 1,075 female respondents had stated that they had been approached sexually during childhood by a man who was at least five years older than them, and that 80% of these victims reported they had been frightened. Kinsey dismissed such fears as laughingly inappropriate.

Thus, the encouraged response by statutory authorities was to view any such disclosures as a 'storm in a teacup' to be contained and downplayed. These attitudes towards children are mirrored in the way that society views the experiences of adult women and men with learning disabilities whose sexual safety is almost routinely ignored or hidden behind a pervasive myth that services are prone to be overprotective when often they leave people open to risk that others would not tolerate. For example, when abuse occurs, they often leave people who have been abused living in the same household as their abuser, or they take no action when powerful individuals exploit the cognitive impairments of a person with learning disabilities, including deficits in their understanding of social situations. Social care professionals often express confusion about when, and whether, safeguards have been put in place to oppress or protect, which undermines their commitment to create safe opportunities for people with learning disabilities to enjoy sexual relationships that are consensual and not coercive.

Real change has been slow to come but from the 1990s onwards, however, there has been sustained media and professional attention on the issues raised by

CSA, especially when it has been perpetrated by individuals who had used their position as celebrities or as powerful players within important institutions such as the church or the BBC to exploit vulnerable young people.

Good honest citizens – abuser/victim

The exposure of these organisations as the nature and extent of systematic abuse has been uncovered has resulted in very real, legal and financial penalties. It has also led to a backlash in that the first response of these organisations was to preserve, protect and loyally defend their institutions from accusations of CSA. The Roman Catholic Church, for example, put in place procedures that bound children who disclosed to silence, while protecting abusive priests from civil sanctions in the criminal justice system. Moreover, these systems for suppressing acknowledgement of abuse have been dismantled at a snail's pace. Anyone whose experiences contradict the image of the institution, whose voice threatens that institution's reputation, respect, profit or smooth governance, automatically became the enemy rather than an innocent victim seeking help or redress. This reframing of the 'real' tragedy as being the damage done to the institution whose reputation is in tatters, as opposed to what was done to the victim continues to be put forward. When victims broadcast their complaints, it is powerful individuals who interpret their mission as serving the institution rather than wronged individuals who use the structural tools at their disposal (such as governance and organisational frameworks) to protect their threatened organisation. These powerful institutions then fail to address the weakness of their safeguards even when these threaten to engulf and derail the projected official purpose of the association: this might be how the response of the BBC to the abuses committed by their 'talent' Jimmy Savile can be understood. JL described how William Mayne took her on a trip to the BBC who employed him, when he showed her around an office that held several other male employees he announced to them, 'This one [this child] is mine'.

It was clear that while he was announcing his 'membership' of a paedophile elite in which the people present were complicit (see, for example, the Dame Janet Smith Review, 2016) in JL's adult view, the lack of response from the institution to such employees at best showed they turned a blind eye and at worst showed they viewed such children as if they were cannon fodder.

However, since the Jimmy Savile inquiry, survivors have had a much higher success rate at getting their voices heard and there have been a series of investigations into how these institutions failed to protect children from sexual abuse. The Independent Inquiry into Child Sexual Abuse is, as we write, examining how institutions have responded to child sexual abuse, and includes the response of law enforcement agencies, in seeking to make meaningful recommendations for change. Confronted by the far greater number of accusations made about institutional condoning and tacit support of CSA than anticipated, Professor Alexis Jay, the Chair, writes:

> There will be no reduction in its [the inquiry's] commitment to exposing the ways in which institutions have failed victims and survivors in the past. Shedding light on wrongdoing which has long been hidden is of paramount importance to so many victims and survivors of abuse . . . this inquiry must deliver on its promise to expose what went wrong in the past and provide a safer future for today's children.
>
> *(IICSA, 2016)*

The inquiry included allegations of cover-ups of child sexual abuse linked to Westminster, Anglican, Jehovah Witnesses and Roman Catholic churches, football clubs, residential schools, children in local authority care, custodial institutions, cadets and other organised networks.

The legal system also contributes to the disempowerment of CSA victims despite helpful changes in the legislative framework and in courtroom procedures. Intermediaries, the use of video link evidence and screens in the courtroom all make the process easier. These are dramatic changes in the judiciary and government in providing avenues for truth telling and holding individuals and organisations to account. The 2005 Sexual Offences Act introduced a prohibition on adults 'in a position of trust' from having any sexual contact with those in their charge. This legal change integrates victim–derived knowledge about the ways in which adults in authority positions use their power to groom and co-opt their victims. Parallel changes were inserted into this act to provide protection to adults with learning disabilities. But despite these developments, these are difficult crimes to prosecute because they usually take place in private/secret and often rest on the jury's perception of the victim's truthfulness, which, as we have seen, is often compromised by the need to lie, both at the time of their abuse and subsequently.

Defence attorneys therefore focus on the credibility of victim/witnesses and while it is of course important that defendants have proper representation and every opportunity to refute charges against them, attempts to discredit vulnerable witnesses may further undermine victims who are struggling to reach a clarity about what happened and whose responsibility it was. Scottish law has a CAT 'middle place' in which a charge can be classified as 'not proven' but in the rest of the UK there are only two verdicts and it is hard for victims when their abuser is found not guilty to know that other adults may still believe them. After the trial when the convicted Mayne went to prison, his defence barrister came up to the prosecution witness JL and told her that he believed everything she had said.

Concluding remarks

Although we had very different experiences, when we discussed our ways of coping we found a common thread that might resonate with other mental health professionals who have difficult lived experiences to contain and manage. We own both damage and resilience. We live fulfilling lives, looking outward, exploring and being open to what is 'out there'. For HB, she initially coped by denial in order to keep her 'normal' intact, acting out in various ways during her teens until it became both important and possible for her to share this experience and bring it in from the cold. For JL, she thought abuse was normal, so what propelled her was to discover something else, something good. Our subsequent lives have been good; we have been lucky in adulthood, have good relationships and have taken up many constructive opportunities. We have both been on a quest to understand how the world works, scientifically and empathically, including putting helpful frameworks around aberrant behaviour. As therapists who are also survivors of sexual assault/abuse in childhood we have tried to translate the intensity of that experience, and its knock-on effects, into our work with patients.

This brings three important ways of working into the foreground:

1. The understanding that dissociation is a necessary coping strategy for children or young people exposed to the disavowed behaviour of adults, whether it is sexual, physical or emotional violence that is at issue, and that a gradual process of bringing this into awareness and of respecting its function is an important route for healing.
2. As we have seen, children who have been abused are required to lie or hide their experiences, so it is important to lessen the stigma of that by locating keeping secrets within the context of key reciprocal roles. We reframe this as evidence of how accurately they have read the willingness of others to hear and how wisely they waited until they found someone they had an inkling could contain their story before sharing it.
3. We try to help survivors use the anger generated by these experiences carefully because they have often come away with polarised states, switching from seeking powerful revenge to feeling isolated and pathetic in the face of others. They demand justice but then cringe at a sexist comment and bringing these two positions on to the same page, as we do in a CAT map, allows survivors to temper both and to translate anger and despair into positive personal and political strategies.

We hope that by unpacking our own experiences and by naming the ways in which society's unstable messages impact on victims, we might help others who find themselves on this road and the therapists who walk with them.

With grateful thanks to three emancipatory psychotherapists: Jane Melton (CAT), David Fender (Gestalt) and Valerie Sinason (Psychodynamic).

Bibliography

Allen, G. & Watson, C. (2017). *UK prison population statistics.* House of Commons Library Briefing paper SN/SG/04334.

Bakhtin, M. M. (1990). Author and hero in aesthetic activity. In V. Lipianov (trans.) & M. Holquist & V. Lipianov (eds), *Art and answerability, early philosophical essays.* Austin, TX: University of Texas Press.

Bentley, H. et al. (2017). *How safe are our children? The most comprehensive overview of child protection in the UK*. London: NSPCC.

British Psychological Society. www.bps.org.uk/news-and-policy/bps-welcomes-new-personality-disorders-consensus-statemen (Accessed 12/01/18).

Crime survey for England and Wales and police recorded crime data. (2018). www.ons.gov.uk/releases/crimeinenglandandwaltesyearendingmarch2018 (Accessed 19/07/18).

Dame Janet Smith Review. (2016). www.bbc.co.uk/bbctrust/dame_janet_smith (Accessed 26/02/16).

Festinger, L. (1957). *A theory of cognitive dissonance*. Evanston, IL: Row & Peterson.

Finkelhor, D. & Araji, S. (1984). Explanations of pedophilia: A four-factor model. *Journal of Sex Research*, 22, 2. https://doi.org/10.1080/00224498609551297.

Fonagy, P. (2008). A genuinely developmental theory of sexual enjoyment and its implications for psychoanalytic technique. *Journal of the American Psychoanalytic Association*, 56(1), 11–36.

Fonagy, P., Steele, M., Steele, H., Leigh, T., Kennedy, R., Mattoon, G. & Target, M. (1995). Attachment, the reflective self, and borderline states. In S. Goldberg, R. Muir & J. Kerr (eds), *Attachment theory: Social, developmental and clinical perspectives*. London: Analytic Press.

Gay, R. (2017). *Hunger: A memoir of (my) body*. London: Little Brown.

Hagan, T. & Smail, D. (1997). Power-mapping II practical application: The example of child sexual abuse. *Journal of Community and Applied Social Psychology*, 7, 269–284.

Hepple, J. (2010). A little bit of Bakhtin: From inside to outside and back again. *Reformulation: Theory and Practice of Cognitive Analytic Therapy*, 35, 17–18.

Herman, J. (1981). *Father–daughter incest*. Cambridge, UK: Harvard University Press.

Hindman, J. & Peters, J. (2001). Polygraph testing leads to better understanding adult and juvenile sex offenders. *Federal Probation*, 65(3), 8–15.

Hirschkop, K. (1999). *Mikhail Bakhtin: An aesthetic for democracy*. Oxford: Oxford University Press.

Independent inquiry into child sexual abuse: Report of the internal review. (2016, December). www.iics.org.uk (Accessed 6/07/17).

Kinsey, A., Pomeroy, W., Martin, C. & Gebhard, P. (1953). *Sexual behaviour in the human female*. Philadelphia, PA, and London: W. B. Saunders.

Lee, J., Jackson, H., Pattison, P. & Ward, T. (2002). Developmental risk factors for sexual offending. *Child Abuse & Neglect*, 26, 73–92.

Miller, A. (1984). *Thou shalt not be aware: Society's betrayal of the child*. New York: Farrar Straus & Giroux.

National Association of People Abused in Childhood. (2017). www.itv.com/news/border/2017-07-24/cumbria-police-to-raise-awareness-of-child-abuse-and-neglect-as-part-of-national-campaign (Accessed 25/07/17).

NSPCC. (2017). It's time. http://tinyurl.com/j9n5gnk (Accessed 04/02/17).

Pollock, P. (2001). *Cognitive analytic therapy for adult survivors of childhood abuse: Approaches to treatment and case management*. Chichester, UK: Wiley.

Radford, L., Corral, S., Bradley, C., Fisher, H., Bassett, C., Howat, N. & Collishaw S. (2011) *Child abuse and neglect in the UK today*. London: NSPCC.

Rhodes, E. (2017). Honest, open, proud. *The Psychologist*, September, 10–11.

Salter, D., McMillian, D., Richards, M., Talbot, T., Hodges, J., Bentovim A., Hastings, R., Stevenson, J. & Skuse, D. (2003). Development of sexually abusive behaviour in sexually victimised males: A longitudinal study. *Lancet*, 361 (9356), 471–476.

Shaw, C. & Proctor, G. (eds) (2004). Women at the margins: A critique of the diagnosis of borderline personality disorder. Special issue on women and borderline personality disorder. *Feminism & Psychology*, 15(4), 483–490.

Simons, D. (2007). Understanding victimization among sexual abusers. In D. Prescott (ed.), *Knowledge & practice: Challenges in the treatment and supervision of sexual abusers*. Oklahoma City: Wood 'N' Barnes.

Summitt, R. (1988). Hidden victims, hidden pain: Society's avoidance of child sexual abuse. In G. E. Wyatt & G. J. Powell (eds), *The lasting effects of child sexual abuse*. Newbury Park, CA: Sage.

van der Kolk, B., Roth, S., Pelcovitz, D., Sunday, S. & Spinazzola, J. (2005). Disorders of extreme stress: The empirical foundation of a complex adaptation to trauma. *Journal of Traumatic Stress*, 18(5), 389–399.

Vygotsky, L. (1978). *Mind in society*. London: Harvard University Press.

Williams, B. (2012). Past hurts and therapeutic talents. *Reformulation: Theory and Practice of Cognitive Analytic Therapy*, 39, 39–42.

12

IMMORALITY, ILLEGALITY AND PATHOLOGY

The sex and gender knots

William Wallace

Introduction

The Western binary view assumes a universal, unchanging and separate biological sex of male and female. This view coincides with the masculine and feminine roles it attaches being distinct and separate from one another, and that heterosexual desires is the 'norm'. It is a view without room for anything in-between, and instead positions the wide variety of diversity not fitting its distinct and separate boxes as sins, crimes and pathology. In doing so it tied itself in knots that it now seeks to loosen, such as around homosexuality. Despite legislation to promote inclusion and remove the label of pathology, homophobic attitudes and behaviours still exist. The trans community are battling similar cultural and pathology knots, struggling for social inclusion. Lev (2004) described the confusion of how the trans community must prove themselves mentally disordered in order to meet the criteria for a diagnosis of gender dysphoria, and therefore be eligible for medical interventions, while also having to prove themselves mentally 'sane' to be granted civil rights. Recent proposed legislation in the UK (Reform of the Gender Recognition Act, 2018) is attempting to untie this particular knot by removing the need for a diagnosis of gender dysphoria in order to access medical interventions. This proposal is in line with research pointing to sex and gender being more of a spectrum than a binary.

This new legislation comes up against the legacy of the binary view internalised within the psyche of all areas of society including mental health professionals and therapists, some of whom may be more accepting and knowledgeable about sex and gender diversity while others still see it as a social 'oddity' or pathology. History shows that legal rights for individuals and acceptance of sex and gender diversity can be restricted or taken away by incoming governments with the power to change policy and influence societal attitudes. Other forms of power include parental influence, encouraging or discouraging gender expression in children wanting to change gender, and the transphobic attitudes of a wider society still tied up in the binary knots. In the modern cash-strapped NHS, those holding limited financial budgets have to prioritise allocation of funds, often resulting in gender issues being relegated in the treatment queue.

The Western binary view is also a product of nineteenth-century European colonialism and imperialism. It suited imperialist and capitalist expansion to have clearly delineated roles for men and women, with women being forced into subordinate roles as bearers of children, ensuring the future labour supply with working-class men supplying wage labour and canon fodder (Mishra, 2018). This rigid binary view was imposed on other cultures where previously recognition of sex and gender diversity along with same sex desires had been accepted, including accommodating a 'third' sex and gender. As intersexed individuals show, there have always been variations in the physical appearance of the human body. Mishra describes the disgust of the British colonialists when they discovered the sexually ambiguous Hindu gods and goddesses and a folk tradition of mutably gendered heroes as well as same-sex eroticism. Historical accounts tell us that there have also been individuals over the centuries whose physical appearance has fitted that expected of male or female but who have felt 'trapped' in the wrong body, an aspect of the self often kept secret to avoid cultural sanctions.

Social control dressed up as science

The increasing visibility of trans individuals today has been described as the latest of several cultural shifts in which people defined by a dominant culture as inferior have redefined themselves (Fraser, 2009). These groups have come together in, for example, the women's movement, the civil rights movement and the gay and lesbian movement, and to paraphrase the words of Plummer (1981) when talking of the latter, 'they all came to realise they were not individually disordered but collectively oppressed' (p. 25). The inclusion and subsequent removal of homosexuality from the DSM highlights the view of Brown (1994, p. 135), who said:

> [T]he decision to call a cluster of behaviours a mental illness is responsive to many factors that have nothing to do with science but a great deal to do with the feelings, experiences and epistemology of those in power and dominance in mental health disciplines.

Sex and gender variance have travelled over the centuries from sins requiring redemption to crimes needing to be punished to pathology needing to be cured. On their travels they moved from an external social problem to a medical one located within the person and therefore to be 'cured'. Cultural views mixed with medical pathologising reinforced the rigid binary view and confirmed anyone stepping outside of it as having a mental illness. This latticework of meaning contributes today to trans individuals having to battle against pathology created by a traditional cultural view of a dichotomy between male/female and the masculine and feminine roles attached to them. Such restrictive views are reminiscent of the 'mind-forged manacles' the poet William Blake describes, which trap individuals (and cultures) into ways of thinking that constrict what we know and what it is possible to know. A broader view sees sex and gender variance being integrated into society as a 'third sex' rather than wilting in the shadow of cultural sanctions and pathology.

Examples of this can be found in some non-Western cultures: the acceptability of same-sex desires between Samoan men and Fa'fafine or other men is seen as rendering the Western concept of homosexuality non-applicable (Dragowski et al., 2011; Vasey & Bartlett, 2007). Lev (2004, p. 59) describes some African tribes in which female husbands can become men by carrying out all the economic duties and receive the privileges of men by paying a dowry for a woman, marrying her and becoming the legal and social father to her children. There are also different views of the appearance of the human body itself. Chiland (2004, p. 61) describes the Hindu view of the 'supreme being' conceptualised as one complete sex containing both male and female sex organs.

Intersexed

In Western society the hermaphrodite body (later described as intersexed) were seen as 'monstrosities' to be hidden away. As intersexed they were operated on to fit them into the dichotomy of either male or female. Lev (2004) describes inter-sex children as being 'psychosocial emergencies' adding that, 'their psychosocial and sexual needs are ignored both socially and clinically (p. 17). Some intersexed children operated on are reported to have spoken of always 'having known' the gender they were raised as was wrong: 20% of these children ultimately rejected their gender assignment (Tamar & Mattis, 2012). These intersex conditions include, androgen insensitivity syndrome, virilising congenital adrenal hyperpla-sia and Klienfelter's syndrome, to name just a few. Changes in societal attitudes toward intersex individuals is evident in how gender reassignment surgeries are now being recognised as causing a great deal of psychological and physical pain to babies born with ambiguous genitalia, described as being, 'to the level of other acts considered torture and cruel' (Tamar & Mattis, 2012). The view that there is a clear and distinct difference between the sexes is questioned in an article by Claire Ainsworth (2015), who states: 'The idea of two sexes is simplistic. Biologists now think there is a wider spectrum than that' (p. 288). The article explored numer-ous studies by biologists and highlights the minefield around what defines sex and asks, 'If the law requires a person is male or female should that sex be signed by anatomy, hormones, cells or chromosomes, and what should be done if they clash?' And ends with the advice that, 'given there is no one biological parameter that takes over every other parameter gender identity seems the most reasonable parameter' (p. 291). The article echoes the view of Bolin (1994) who described it as being 'ironic that the more scientific and complex the determinants of biological sex become the less they can be relied on to indicate gender' (p. 453). Though in a society that sees a clear distinction between male/female and their associated roles anyone stepping outside of the binary view is likely to be seen as either socially deviant or mentally ill.

Knots of the psyche

The root of inequality in society has been seen as 'male centeredness', described by Bem (1993, p. 2) when looking through the three lenses of gender. The third lens of 'biological essentialism' is said to rationalise and legitimise the first two lenses of 'androcentrism' and 'gender polarisation' in which the dominant male discourse is entwined in institutions that reinforce the view of male superiority and female inferiority. This message reflects the view of Ryle (2010) that the political source of reciprocal roles has been enshrined in institutions, justified by religions, embodied in laws and brutally enforced when threatened. This inter-generational internalisation of cultural 'norms' influences our view of the acceptability and unacceptability of sex and gender diversity, and although the current move is toward a more trans-positive and inclusive view, centuries of having viewed sex and gender as a binary has taken its toll on the cultural psyche. Not surprisingly, as such binary views have been reinforced by cultural institutions, including education, employment and the legal system, they have become fixed within the psyche of individuals, including professionals who may work with them. These, often unacknowledged views can surface in unexpected ways revealing themselves and infecting even the most self-aware therapist. In my supervision group when discussing a male who had transitioned to female and wanted to transition back again a female therapist 'joked', 'So, he found being a woman isn't as easy as he had thought it would be'. This simple statement revealed hidden depths and tacit beliefs around her internalised perception of how men view women in society as 'inferior' – a view sometimes internalised by women themselves. The struggle is both with a male-dominated society and the often-unconscious internalisations of its values and assumptions. Despite it being a view none in the group subscribed, or admitted, to, including the therapist who said it, this view could be understood by the other woman and two men in the group without further elaboration. Maybe we were all viewing the situation through Bem' lenses of gender, revealing our hidden assumptions.

Some views are transparent, such as from a consultant psychiatrist in secondary mental health services who in 2015 said he 'had no truck with transsexuals or transgender as it is clearly a mental illness needing specialist services'. This goes against the World Professional Association for Transgender Health (WPATH) that promotes care for the health of transsexual, transgender and gender non-conforming people through the Standards of Care (SOC, Coleman et al., 2012). The overall goal of the SOC is to provide clinical guidance for health professionals to assist gender non-conforming people with safe and effective pathways to achieving lasting personal comfort with their gendered self. Although it is shocking that some highly educated health professionals are so ignorant of the issues, the uninformed and discriminatory views expressed by the consultant psychiatrist referred to above is a reflection of the internalisation of wider cultural views, and highlights the difficulty described by Lev (2004) in severing the link between gender variance and mental illness; it isn't a mental illness. In fact Fraser (2009) points out that many sex and gender variant individuals are perfectly healthy apart from a 'mind body mismatch'. To see those presenting to mental health services with suicidal ideation, self-harm, depression and dissociation, for example, as all resulting solely from an internal gender conflict is dismissive of the part cultural norms and medical pathologising has played in creating the external and internal conflict experienced as mental distress by gender variant individuals from living in a society with narrow views on sex and gender variance and not fitting into them.

Tying sex and gender together in children

Theories that sought to explain variance as pathology did so in relation to cultural norms that do not take account of how those norms defined pathology by constricting sex and gender expression. The impact of cultural attitudes is something the latest edition of the DSM-5 (APA, 2013) points to in its statement that 'the prevalence of mental health problems differs among cultures, those differences may also be related to differences in attitudes toward gender variance in children' (p. 459). It highlights the contemporary Western view of gender variance as being a pathology or socially 'immoral' and not an 'enlightened, civilised or sophisticated way to incorporate it into human society' (Lev, 2004, p. 57). The move toward a more trans-affirming society causes controversy over issues around the age in which the transition process should begin. Currently no irreversible treatments begin before the age of 16, though puberty delaying medication can be given in order to see if the desire to transition persists past puberty. Some also question whether a 'social' transition of gender is even appropriate for children seen as being too young to choose their own bedtime, never mind their gender. A more trans-affirming society is seen by some as being in danger of becoming too 'unconditionally accepting', demonstrated in the concerns of a group of parents based in the UK (Transgender Trend). Their website (www.transgendertrend. com) describes a view that the updated 2017 UK memorandum of understanding around conversion therapies, signed by many therapeutic modalities within the UK, fails to protect children by discouraging exploration of a desire to socially transition. They are sceptical at the current trend to diagnose 'gender nonconforming' children as transgender and 'going along with' the child's 'wish' to make a social transition. Though a social change in children wearing the clothes typical of the opposite sex and gender not only creates divided opinion but also reveals the 'gender schema' Bem (1993) described, we don't need to know the genitals beneath clothes to assign individuals to the male/female dichotomy, it also shows how gender became tangled up with sex to go together in the binary system like peas in a pod.

Historical knots

The view of Kraft-Ebbing on sex and gender variance in the new science of sexology in the 1860s was that many of the paraphilias he categorised, and still in use today in the DSM, such as sadism and masochism, were exaggerations of healthy (dominant) male or (submissive) female behaviour; their perversion was in going against social norms (De Block & Adriaens, 2013). Krafft-Ebbing's view of dominant male/submissive female behaviour shows how tightly the stereotypical knots permeated assumptions of male/female sexuality were, though the anonymity of the Internet today provides opportunity to meet others with similar 'taboo' desires. A search of websites devoted to bondage domination submission and masochism (BDSM) indicates that not only is such behaviour relatively common, but also a considerable number of men enjoy being in a submissive role and a considerable number of women enjoy being in a more dominant role. This perhaps indicates that while adhering to public acceptability and expectations of gender stereotypes socially, private desires operate differently. Historically, wearing trousers was a hard-fought for right for women, which meant going against public acceptability. However, women in trousers are rarely described as 'transvestites', neither are those women who may become sexually aroused wearing male clothes diagnosed as having a transvestite fetish. This 'inequality' is similar to the way lesbian relationships have never been illegal in the UK, unlike male homosexual relationships. Perhaps a patriarchal society that viewed women as second-class citizens did not see those women who indulged in 'immoral' behaviour such as lesbianism (and wearing trousers) as threatening.

Cultural views, internalised shame and statistics

The causes of gender variance have been debated by professionals and the public for many years, and, despite all the research and recent brain investigations, the jury is still out. Meyerowitz (2002) describes something of a 'turf war' in past decades between those adhering to three causal hypotheses: biological, mental illness or the result of 'psychological sex' and later core gender identity. This turf war is evident today between the more trans-affirming views of those who follow the guidance of the SOC contrasted with those of the consultant psychiatrist referred to above, whose view echoes the idea of transsexualism as 'sexual deviants and victims of severe gender role distress' (Billings & Urban, 1982, p. 266) or as 'transvestite homosexuals and schizophrenics with severe sexual conflicts' (Socarades, 1969, p. 1424). While other professionals and the public in general may have less transphobic and dismissive views, even being sympathetic, many people also say they 'simply don't understand it' or just see it as 'odd'. This 'oddity' is internalised by many gender variant people who describe feeling like an 'alien' in their own body and having a 'shameful secret' (Fraser, 2009).

The Gender Identity Research and Education Society (GIRES) is a UK-wide organisation whose purpose is to improve the lives of trans and gender nonconforming people of all ages, including those who are non-binary and non-gender.

In 2012, in partnership with the Scottish Transgender Alliance, the Trans Resource and Empowerment Centre (TREC), Traverse, Sheffield Hallam University and TransBareAll (www.transbareall.co.uk), they conducted research into the mental health and well-being of trans individuals. The shocking results reveal high levels of prejudice and oppression resulting in mental distress: They found that over 90% had been told that trans people were not normal, over 37% had experienced physical threats or intimidation for being trans, 19% had been hit or beaten up for being trans, 53% of the participants had self-harmed at some point and, most shockingly, the majority of participants, 84%, had thought about ending their lives.

Exploring internal knots

As Lev (2004) points out, the pathologising of gender diversity has caused a paucity of therapeutic guidelines to work with trans individuals. The lack includes working with the issues leading some people to present to mental health services, and for whom an exploration of the wider cultural views, along with their own view of masculinity and femininity, may be beneficial in enabling what Hakeem (2012) describes as 'a greater understanding of the meaning they afford to gender as a construct in relation to themselves and society' (p. 19). I found this cultural focus useful in my work with K, a 25-year-old natal born female who was denied a place on a gender reassignment clinic due to depression and suicidal thoughts. She attributed being suicidal to being 'pushed from pillar to post' and not getting the hormones/surgery she wanted that she felt would make things right for her. She described a violent father who was frequently physically and verbally abusive to her mother. K didn't get on with her mother who she described as 'pathetic'. She was in a relationship with a woman and wanted what she described as a 'proper relationship' as she didn't see herself as lesbian, therefore using substitutes for a penis when having sex was not what she wanted. I wondered if her view of herself as male was tangled up with an over identification with her culturally driven view of masculine identity, reinforced by her 'macho' father (idealised), or with a 'dis-identification' with her 'pathetic' (contemptable) mother, as described by Moberly (1983).

It seemed K had no room for both male and female aspects to her and was divided between a strong male who would be taken notice of and a weak female who was ignored. This wasn't the conclusion of a deep analysis as I merely asked for clarification of her statement that she thought that when she was male 'people will take notice of me'. This 'idealised' view of how things would be when transitioned connected to her internalisation of 'pathetic' and ignored female (as she felt now), and powerful, taken notice of male (a post-transition view). To have ignored this might have colluded not with her belief of herself as male but with her view of masculinity as opposed to femininity. Our exploration was helped by discussing the historical and cultural context of sex and gender diversity and how pathologising opinions did not exist in a vacuum but because of the long history of oppressive cultural views that seeped within us all too some extent. Our work together became more around assertion, no matter what the gender.

Increasing the repertoire of sex and gender diversity

The writings of Magnus Hirschfeld contributed to gender variance becoming a recognised phenomenon available for study, discussion and treatment in his work with transsexuals at the turn of the twentieth century. Both Hirschfeld's and Kraft-Ebbing's writings took account of the stories they heard by listening to the 'inverts' and 'Eonists' they saw, but hindsight suggests we might have been further along the road of integrating sex and gender variance into Western society had we listened to the likes of Karl Ulrich, a German lawyer in 1868, who said of himself and others like him, 'We have the soul of a woman in the body of a man' (Meyerowitz, 2002, p. 111). If we move forward almost a century later, their stories are similar to those told to professionals following the possibilities of 'sex change' becoming widely known in the 1950s, as well as those told by others today who report a sense of 'not fitting in' and 'being different' (Fraser, 2009).

Unlike more historically accepting cultures of gender variance, the hidden and silenced desires of Western society in Ulrich's time gravitated to the Molly houses and Bordellos of Europe and North America. A qualified liberation of gender variant desires eventually came with the development of medical expertise and acceptance that it was easier to change the sex of the body to fit that of the mind rather than the other way around. However, it was conditional on meeting strict criteria for a diagnosis of transsexualism, which was seen as a barrier to many accessing medical interventions as it resulted in the criteria being 'wielded over the heads of transsexuals like a club' (Bolin, 1988, p. 51). Part of the criteria was in not only wanting to be rid of natal genitalia but wanting those of the other sex. Whether Ulrich and others in the 1800s would have wanted a 'full' sex change we don't know. In 1950s society there was only one choice, a move from male to female or vice versa, and at a time when stereotypical gender roles were heavily promoted through government sponsored advertising encouraging woman back to the home and out of the war factories, it left no room for shades of grey between male and female. Although 'sex change' operations may have raised questions regarding the morality of surgically treating what was still regarded as a 'mental illness', the transsexual model was well suited to the time, as Denny (1996) observes, as it kept to the male/female dichotomy by not raising questions about the binary view of sex and gender.

As mass media brought more awareness of diversity, gender variant individuals themselves questioned the binary view and challenged the expectations to have a 'complete' change of sex. Some just wanted hormone treatment, or no medical treatment at all to express a gender identity

The paradox Lev (2004) highlights in gender variant individuals having had to prove themselves 'disordered' to receive medical interventions and prove themselves mentally 'sane' to be granted civil rights, was again highlighted with gender diverse individuals driving legislative change by insisting on social inclusion and rebelling against pathology. This reflects the changing ways they have managed their desires in relation to the oppressive views of those in positions of power and influence. From having to hide away in Ulrich's time, and then compliance (resentful or grateful) with diagnostic conditions of transsexuality in the 1950s, to more outright rebellion and an insistence to be included in today's society. Nevertheless, the binary knots have been tightly bound in the psyche of individuals and institutions, so although the label of pathology has been loosened to an extent, major battles for social inclusion are still ahead.

Politics and power

History shows that that such rights cannot be taken for granted and that acceptance and legal recognition of sex and gender diversity can be reversed by those in positions of power and influence with oppressive views, as seen in the current Trump administration's decision to overturn the previous Obama administration's decision to allow transgender individuals in the armed services. President Putin has already initiated repressive legislation against gay rights in Russia, as have fundamentalist religious groups and governments in other parts of the world. Should European governments come to power with similar views as that consultant psychiatrist referred to above, their influence on sex and gender variance may bring today's budding acceptance crashing down again in the face of overt oppression. Political oppression happened not so long ago when the books of Magnus Hirschfeld were burned as he fled the Nazi regime in 1930s Germany. In earlier centuries the traditional Native American tribes who historically honoured same-sex relationships and gender variance, such as the Berdache, were ostracised by many tribes when Western views of Christianity were exported along with Westernisation (colonisation) that taught same-sex desires to be a sin and left no place for gender variance outside of the male/female dichotomy (Nicholson & Fisher, 2014). The resilience of gender variant individuals is shown in the way the Berdache role is being reclaimed and referred to as 'two spirit', which implies a masculine spirit and feminine spirit living side by side. This identity sits on the current sex and gender spectrum along with transsexualism, transgender and intersex in a continually growing range of sex and gender expressions that individuals are using to best describe their own identity and experience. They also struggle with a less politically powerful but nevertheless equally influential form of oppression from family and peers who may exert their own internalised binary views.

Political twists

The trans-affirming views current government legislation is trying to promote around human rights and anti-discrimination laws in areas such as employment, civil rights and education is ironic when they are to be spearheaded by the very cultural institutions that previously reinforced the views of immorality, illegality and pathology. Nowadays, holding such regressive views means being guilty of transphobia, which the government now legislates against. A twist is that now the political elite need to be seen as championing sex and gender diversity through legislation this puts them in the role of liberating, protecting and affirming, rather than the more historic role of oppressing, stigmatising and punishing. In these times of financial constraints on the NHS, a further twist is that by re-externalising sex and gender diversity as something that deviates from social norms (now politically acceptable) and no longer seen as pathology (now politically unacceptable) it not only frees individuals from the need for a medical diagnosis, but also frees the government from the need to fund medical interventions for those who may want them. O'Hartigan (1997) said that, 'provision of health care is dependent upon a need for treatment, and where there is no pathology, there is no need' (p. 46). Should the financial constraints on NHS budgets (as well perhaps some heath professionals' own transphobic views) mean medical treatments take a back seat as it is considered a 'social choice' not a medical necessity? If the public in general questions scarce medical resources being spent on 'cosmetic' procedures, they too can be seen as having the kinds of transphobic views the government legislates against. A final twist is that by putting the onus on institutions, GPs and individuals to have more trans-affirming views, the political elite can absolve themselves of any responsibility their past views of immorality, criminality and pathology had in creating the transphobic attitudes that exist today.

Bibliography

Ainsworth, C. (2015). Sex redefined. *Nature*, 518, 288–291.
American Psychiatric Association (2013). *Diagnostic and statistical manual of mental disorders: DSM-5* (5th ed.). Washington, DC: APA.
Bem, S. L. (1993). *The lenses of gender: Transforming the debate on sexual inequality.* New Haven, CT, and London: Yale University Press.
Billings, D. B. & Urban, T. (1982). The socio-medical construction of transsexualism: An interpretation and critique. *Social problems*, 29(3), 266–282.
Bolin, A. (1988). *In search of Eve: Transsexual rites of passage.* New York: Bergan & Garvey.
Bolin, A. (1994). Transcending and trans gendering: Male to female transsexuals, dichotomy and diversity. In G. Herdt (ed.), *Third sex, third gender: Beyond sexual dimorphism in culture and history.* New York: Zone Books.
Brown, L. (1994). *Subversive dialogues: Theory of feminist therapy.* New York: Basic Books.
Chiland, C. (2004). *Transsexualism illusion and reality.* London: Sage.
Coleman, E., Bockting, W., Botzer, M., Cohen-Kettenis, P., DeCuypere, G., Feldman, J., Fraser, L., Green, J., Knudson, G., Meyer, W. J., Monstrey, S., Adler, R. K., Brown, G. R., Devor, A. H., Ehrbar, R., Ettner, R., Eyler, E., Garofalo, R., Karasic, D. H., Lev, A. I., Mayer, G., Meyer-Bahlburg, H., Hall, B. P., Pfaefflin, F., Rachlin, K., Robinson, B., Schechter, L. S., Tangpricha, V., Trotsenburg, M. van, Vitale, A., Winter, S. Whittle, S., Wylie, K. R. & Zucker, K. (2012). World Professional Association for Transgender Health (WPATH) Standards of care for the health of transsexual, transgender, and gender-nonconforming people (Version 7). *International Journal of Transgenderism*, 13, 165–232.
De Block, A. & Adriaens, P. R. (2013). Pathologising sexual deviance: A history. *Journal of Sex Research*, 50(3–4), 276–298.

Denny, D. (1996). In search of the 'true' transsexual. *Chrysalis: The Journal of Transgressive Gender Identities*, 2(3), 39–44.

Devor, A. H. (2004). Witnessing and mirroring: A fourteen-stage model of transsexual identity formation. *Journal of Gay and Lesbian Psychotherapy*, 8(1–2), 41–46.

Dragowski, E. A., Scharron-del Rio, M. R. & Sandgorsky, A. L. (2011). Childhood identity disorder: Developmental, cultural and diagnostic concerns: Assessment and Diagnosis. *Journal of Counselling and Development*, 89, 360–366.

Fraser, L. (2009). Depth psychotherapy with transgendered people. *Sexual and Relationship Therapy*, 24(2), 126–142.

Hakeem, A. Z. (2012). Advances in psychiatric treatment. *Journal of Continuing Professional Development*, 18, 17–24.

Herdt, G. (1994). Introduction: Third sex, third gender. In G. Herdt (ed.), *Beyond sexual diamorphism in culture and history*. New York: Zone Books.

Hildebrand, T. H. (2014). An integral map of sexual identity. In S. Nicholson & V. D. Fisher (eds), *Integral voices on sex, gender and sexuality*. New York: State University Press.

House of Commons Women and Equality Committee (2016). *Transgender equality*. London: House of Commons.

Lev, A. I. (2004). *Transgender emergence: Therapeutic guidelines for working with gender variant people and their families*. London: Routledge.

Meyerowitz, J. (2002). *How sex changed: A history of transsexuality in the United States*. Harvard: Harvard University Press.

Mishra, P. (2018). The crisis in modern masculinity. *Guardian*, 17 March. www.theguardian.com/books/2018/mar/17/the-crisis-in-modern-masculinity.

Moberly, E. R. (1983) *Psychogenesis: The early development of gender identity*. London: Routledge.

Nicholson & V. D. Fisher (eds) (2014). *Integral voices on sex, gender and sexuality*. New York: New York University Press.

O'Hartigan, M. D. (1997). The GID controversy: Transsexuals need the gender identity disorder diagnosis. *Transgender Tapestry*, 79, 30–46.

Oosterhusi, H. (2012). Sexual modernity in the works of Richard Von Krafft-Ebbing and Albert Moll. *Medical History*, 56(2) 133–155.

Plummer, K. (1981). Building a sociology of homosexuality. In K. Plummer (ed.), *The making of the modern homosexual*. London: Hutchinson.

Reform of the Gender Recognition Act: Government Consultation (2018). https://assets.publishing.service.gov.uk/government/uploads/system/uploads/attachment_data/file/721725/GRA-Consultation-document.pdf.

Ryle, A. (2010). The political sources of reciprocal roles. *Reformulation*, Summer, 6–8.

Ryle, A. & Kerr, I. B. (2002). *Introducing cognitive analytic therapy: Principles and practice*. Chichester, UK: Wiley.

Socarides, C. W. (1969). The desire for sexual transformation: A psychiatric evaluation of transsexualism. *American Journal of Psychiatry*, 125(10), 1419–1425.

Tamar, A. & Mattis, J. D. (2012). *Report to the UN Special Rapporteur on torture: Medical treatment of people with intersex conditions as torture and cruel, inhuman, or degrading treatment or punishment*. http://intersex.shadowreport.org/public/AIC-Testimony-to-the-United-Nations-Special-Rapporteur-on-Torture_December-2012.pdf.

Vasey, P. L. & Bartlett, N. H. (2007). What can the Samoan 'Fa'afafine' teach us about the Western concept of gender identity disorder in childhood? *Perspectives in Biology and Medicine*, 5(4), 481–90.

13

IGNORING IT DOESN'T MAKE IT GO AWAY

Recognising and reformulating gender in CAT

Bethan Davies

Introduction: why think about gender or 'surely we don't need feminism any more?'

Our clients do not choose to see therapists lightly – they are often distressed, disempowered and/or vulnerable, and often come with questions about the reasons for their problems ('Why me?') and sometimes also questions about their identity ('Who am I?'). The privilege of exploring these questions gives us the potential to be either liberatory or oppressive. Where on this spectrum a therapy falls is determined by our ability to recognise and step out of problematic relationship patterns. I argue this ability includes recognising structures of oppression and choosing not to collude with them. Only by discussing these structures and how we can work against them, can we avoid remaining embedded.

Gender is a major area of both actual and perceived difference between the people we see as therapists, between colleagues, and between therapists and their clients. There are significant differences in the way men and women access mental health or other services, and the problems they present with when they do. Some radical feminists argue that patriarchy is the original form of oppression on which all other forms are based, pre-dating other structural differences such as class (e.g. Hartmann, 1997). Radical feminist theory may be criticised on its essentialist stance, for being apolitical, and failing to recognise adequately other oppressive structures such as race. However, the idea of the primacy of patriarchy may be helpfully provocative in understanding and opposing oppression rather than colluding.

Surprisingly and worryingly, a quick search for articles relating to cognitive analytic therapy and gender yields few returns. This chapter aims to contribute to addressing this gap by recognising the history of the relationship between gender and psychotherapy, how CAT can understand gender, and how we can recognise our own gender roles as therapists. I hope this chapter will start a conversation leading us to better practice, hopefully helping us contribute to progressive changes in society, rather than colluding with oppressive practices.

While sexuality and gender are closely linked concepts, there is a risk of seeing these as the same thing, assuming if we know someone's gender identity we know who they are attracted to. For example, if someone comes across as 'feminine', we might assume this indicates they are attracted to men. The important topic of sexuality and desire – a wider issue than just which gender(s) people are attracted to – has also been neglected in CAT literature and warrants exploration.

Standpoint theory (Collins, 1997) derives from black feminism and suggests that experiences of marginalised groups can only be described and explained from the perspectives of people within that group. However, a lot of writings about women and femininity are by male psychotherapists. My standpoint as a clinical psychologist, CAT practitioner and a queer feminist woman, is that I am also a part of a profession whose theory has been dominated by male perspectives. Patriarchy is one of several structural differences in which some groups of people hold power over others and hold the largest share of most resources. I was born as and identify as a woman, but do not identify with, or find politically helpful, binary or essentialist ideas about femininity or womanhood. I can be open and write about these things, because of factors that make me privileged, for example being white, having had access to education and having 'documents' (i.e. proof of identity, nationality and status) and also because of the struggles and sacrifices of women and queer people who came before me.

Formulating the problem

The main title of this chapter could apply to any number of topics. One of CAT's real strengths is its ability to make the implicit (or unconscious/subconscious) explicit, through the process of reformulation and recognition. This brings attention to problems and allows them to be acknowledged, understood and explored in a straightforward way. This provides compassion, hope and validation while also maintaining individual responsibility and recognising our nature as social creatures in a wider culture that can be individualistic and lacking accountability.

The principle of acknowledging problems and their roots can also be applied to political or social situations; recognising that personal difficulties often stem from issues wider than our individual lives. Psychotherapists may attempt to hold a neutral stance (being reflective and traditionally even 'blank canvasses') but this is a risky stance potentially ignoring important issues, not challenging the hegemony and potentially siding with the powerful over the less influential.

CAT describes why 'ignoring it won't make it go away,' using a 'trap', for example:

> Feeling overwhelmed or ashamed, I aim to avoid these difficult feelings. Believing that ignoring the problems causing these feelings will make them go away, I avoid thinking about them or even acknowledging that they exist.

This can seem like it works for a while, but it means that I don't deal with these problems, so they continue to exist and even worsen lead to more difficult feelings.

The book in which this chapter sits is an important step in trying to recognise and find exits from similar traps. Although this chapter focuses on gender, when discussing areas of difference there is a frequent pull to focus on individual privilege, thus ranking individuals or pitting them against each other while potentially forgetting causal harmful societal structures. As therapists, we need to do both; acknowledge individual difference while also recognising those structural issues influencing an individual's difficulties.

These differences include how we are socialised as children, the different traumas and adversities we face, the varied opportunities, resources and freedoms made available to us throughout our lives and the expectations society places on us regarding what is 'normal' for males and females. Despite cultural variations, some gender role differences are relatively stable throughout the world, such as girls being treated as vulnerable and needing protection achieved via limiting their activities, while boys, treated as strong and independent, are encouraged to explore (Global Early Adolescent Study, 2017). As well as within families, these cultural norms are maintained through gender-specific toys, careers advice, how men and women are portrayed in the media, differential wages and by gender-based violence. Not only does this make life harder for females than males, but also makes it difficult for us to behave in ways outside normative gender roles, thus pulling us in to maintain our own and other people's oppression.

In some parts of the world, and at different stages in history, limits on female opportunities and societally sanctioned abuse of girls and women is even more visible, through under-age marriage, female genital mutilation and restriction on independent travel. While we must show solidarity with women struggling against these oppressive practices, those of us living in Western cultures should be wary of seeing our own society as advanced or thinking we have overcome patriarchal practices. We can easily see gender-based oppression and violence, even when expressed differently or more hidden.

Knowing our own history: what got us here

There are some good reasons that modern psychotherapy theory, and psychotherapists themselves, have shied away from focusing on gender. Traditional psychoanalysis focused strongly on gender in its theories; often assuming rigid, normative and binary developmental pathways and assigning generalised and deterministic characteristics to men and women. Gender, sex and sexuality are central in much of Freud's original theory (Freud saw the libido as the main psychic drive).

In Freud's (1933) lecture on femininity he stated:

> Nor will you have escaped worrying over this problem those of you who are men; to those of you are women this will not apply; you are your selves the problem. When you meet a human being, the first distinction you make is male or female.

This bold statement seems inherently misogynistic – though elsewhere in this essay Freud grappled with whether sex/gender and sexuality are binary concepts, or whether a psychological perspective might see masculinity (which might equate with activity) and femininity (passivity) in different measures in different people or at different moments.

Nonetheless, many of the differences that were (and often still are) seen to exist between men and women were viewed as innate, and women were implicitly (and sometimes explicitly) seen as inherently inferior to men. Non-conformity to gender norms or to hetero-normative sexual behaviour was often pathologised, and psychotherapy has been used over the years to try to 'fix' such 'pathologies'. These ways of thinking have not been limited to the world of psychoanalysis – the World Health Organization only declassified homosexuality as a mental disorder in 1992. 'Conversion therapy' as a 'treatment' for homosexuality still exists, with a 2009 study showing that 1 in 6 UK-based psychological therapists had engaged in work attempting to change the sexual orientation of clients (Bartlett et al., 2009). This is a chilling reminder of the ways in which psychotherapists can collude with harmful and oppressive beliefs and practices.

The feminist movement easily challenges sexist psychotherapy theory. Discussing the writings of Freud, Nancy Chodorow (1994), a key feminist psychoanalytic theorist, suggests that Freud seems to equate gender identity with sexuality, as if the identity of a woman is mainly determined by her sexual function. Chodorow goes on to say that what psychoanalytic theory actually explains is how women are seen in the male psyche – even if the therapist is female owing to the dominant discourse being created by men, in a system in which men have more power. Traditional psychoanalytic theory starts from the position that men are the norm and women an aberration from it.

Queering CAT?

Much of modern psychotherapy theory appears to have lost this focus on gender. Is therapy gender neutral, treating everyone equally? With CBT, more of a treatment approach than a developmental theory, this is perhaps understandable. Is this lack in CAT literature also understandable, as CAT, a flexible approach not bound by diagnoses, can work with what each individual brings? Post-modern approaches challenge the binary, essentialist assumptions of traditional therapy approaches and see gender as a more fluid concept, which rather than being limited to a biologically determined sex is culturally constructed – while also intersecting with a range of other factors influencing our identities and privilege. And in line with the recognition in the introductory chapter regarding cross-fertilisation, conversations and debates with our colleagues in the Pink Therapy community (see http://pinktherapy.mobi) may help as we move forward with this issue.

As a model that focuses on social development CAT surely needs to be able to unpick these social constructs, understanding them in our models of personality development. We should understand better the systems of oppression that contribute to mental health difficulties. By failing to attempt to understand thoroughly the socio-political influences on our mental health, modern psychotherapy theory risks finding itself at the opposite extreme to traditional psychoanalytic approaches.

We are left then, in CAT terms, with a dilemma around gender. That is, either assuming prescriptive and binary differences between the genders, or else ignoring altogether the differences that sex and gender make to the people we become and the kinds of problems we are faced with. For all dilemmas, this is a false choice, which our task is to recognise then find our way out of.

Being explicit . . . turning blank canvasses into maps

Explicit differences between men and woman are seen in mental health statistics. The figures show women are more likely to use community-based mental health services, more likely to attempt suicide and more likely to be diagnosed with 'borderline personality disorder', while men are more likely to be admitted to mental health wards, be caught up in the criminal justice system, to complete suicide and to be diagnosed with 'antisocial' and 'narcissistic personality disorders' (DOH, 2008).

What causes these differences? How the CAT community positions itself on this question is important to find an exit from the dilemma of either assuming or ignoring differences. The exit is a place where we recognise and comprehend how differences exist, but these are generalised and represent trends and averages not applicable to everyone. The exit will acknowledge a vast range of difference in people's experience of their gender, through cultural (macro) differences and individual (micro) differences in gender identity and other areas of unique life experience.

Ryle and Kerr (2002, p. 157) state that

> [c]ertain procedural patterns remain tied to gender stereotypes [which] are still instilled and sustained by cultural and economic pressures. They are also to some degree rooted in . . . complex evolutionary predispositions . . . In our culture, patterns of placation and submissive denial are much more commonly found in women . . . while the avoidance of emotional expression and denial of emotional need remains a largely male characteristic.

The 'male' and 'female' procedures described above are reflected in the Psychotherapy File (see the Appendix), which states these as dilemmas:

- As a woman, either I have to do what others want or I stand up for my rights and get rejected.
- As a man, either I can't have any feelings, or I am an emotional mess.

While not ignoring gender, this runs the risk of returning to normative assumptions, not allowing for individual differences and alienating people who may not fit with traditional gender norms. This may cause problems for people who find that they tick the 'wrong' box, which does not match their gender, and for those who are non-binary, transgender or intersex. At this early assessment stage in therapy, care should be taken to use this tool in a curious and non-judgemental way to avoid seriously hindering forming a therapeutic alliance. There are numerous ways in which gender can be part of someone's story and influence the ways they have learned to cope and the strategies they use to survive.

In CAT, we start to map out reciprocal roles and associated procedures early on in therapy. It may be helpful to note whether someone's roles seem to be related to patterns typically seen in people of their gender, and to acknowledge the social and cultural factors that influenced their development. This can be done explicitly:

- 'Do you think that being expected to be the one to care for others was related to you being a girl?'
- 'Do you think that your parents expected you to be tough because you were a boy?'

Being explicit, for me, means letting go of the 'blank canvass' and showing we have noticed inequalities exist and our clients' roles and procedures relate to distal as well as more immediate factors. It is not just that men and women are different, but throughout history men have taken positions of power over women and had greater levels of autonomy and opportunity in many areas. This is not to blame individual men, nor to deny the difficult positions, pressures and traumas that society also subjects men to.

How validating is it to let clients know we notice these issues? There are moments in therapy when it is possible to state this directly, or when it is helpful to state more specific facts about the effects of patriarchy, e.g. 'We do still live in a world where the caring role more often falls to women'. We can acknowledge how society can push people into particular ways of relating to themselves or others. However, the influence of gender on reciprocal roles and their associated procedures may be less direct, for example the boy who is dismissed or bullied for not liking football, or the girl who is neglected because their parents really wanted a little boy. Looking out for these in someone's account, reflected in the reformulation letter is a good way of showing our awareness of their significance.

This leads to exploring significant roles that are harder for people to identify with; for women this may be rageful, abusive parts of themselves, and for men parts that are vulnerable and afraid. This may be harder owing to the shame associated with these roles, which do not fit with our normative assumptions about gender.

This is linked to Howell's (2005) idea that early traumatic experiences can lead to dissociation and disavowing of parts of our personality. The parts we cut off differ due to our experiences and the expectations that are placed on us, and gender in turn influences these things significantly. Girls more often experience sexual and interfamilial abuse than boys, and the effects of this seem to match stereotyped female traits such as dependence and passivity. Other effects of this might be enraged or violent states, however as these are discouraged in women and girls, who are expected to be other-oriented, they are likely to be repressed. These kinds of states may present themselves in some of our female clients but may come with feelings of shame or they may be disowned or partially dissociated.

Boys tend to be more often exposed to physical abuse outside the home. This, along with an expectation that they do not show feelings other than anger, particularly feelings associated with vulnerability, leads to boys disavowing states seen as more 'feminine' and becoming hyper-masculine leading to the denial of vulnerability and thus difficulties in processing loss. Shame is related to being a victim – a role that society usually gives to women. Theories of trauma and dissociation link with the types of problems – particularly those labelled as 'personality disorders' – that men and women tend to present with to services (Davies, 2015). While the kinds of difficulties described as 'personality disorders' do cause clients problems, a big part of this is related to societal expectations and perceptions, influenced by gender. Gender influences the process of diagnosis, as well as the development of diagnostic criteria. These issues are discussed in more detail in Chapter 11.

Taking part in the 'dance'

Clients' relationship patterns and procedures will present in therapy and at times we get involved with or enact these roles. In CAT this is called 'joining the dance', which is unavoidable and potentially helpful briefly to join clients in providing insight and material to work with, as long as we can notice that it is happening and step out of it to a position of reflection.

Perhaps the dancing analogy is particularly helpful in a discussion around gender – for traditionally in Western culture dancing is often a partner exercise with male and female roles. It is no coincidence that men lead, and women follow, or that women have more complex steps to learn. For example, I have been told by one client that they hadn't expected me to be competent when they first met me, owing to being a 'young lass' but I have also been described as being like a longed-for, attentive, caring daughter by another. Age is a factor here of course, as well as other aspects about one's appearance. In the latter example, the idealised projection helped with engagement, but in order for therapy to be helpful the 'mother–daughter' dance had to be spoken about and my client had to realise that I wasn't going to be there for her in an ongoing caring role – and in doing so, I believe her sense of autonomy and confidence soared. I know the steps of the 'attentive daughter' dance (and also the potential to refuse), which made it particularly important for me to hold on to therapeutic boundaries in this instance.

So we need to think about how our gender affects us as therapists. A caring, other-orientated role is more often expected of women than men, so it is no surprise that there are a higher proportion of female than male therapists. There is evidence to show that there is no difference in outcomes for male or female therapists – though clients do tend to report better alliances with female therapists (Jones & Zoppel, 1982), which could perhaps be related to this expectation. We should be able to think more about choice of therapists with our understanding of CAT and gender in mind – something I have written about previously (Davies, 2015).

As a female in the caring profession, am I colluding with an unjust society by going along with a role that is expected of me? I wonder whether there is a further dilemma here: 'either unquestioningly assume an expected role, or else refuse it altogether'. Perhaps it is possible for us to all play to our strengths, while also looking for times when our procedures are unhelpful or extreme. An example of this is times when I feel the pull to over-responsibility or rescuing. Inversely, there are also times when I have felt unkindly about clients who I have felt have been pulling me into meeting their needs and I did not want to listen to them. There is the potential to swing between those two positions of over-responsibility and pushing away, and it is important to find a middle ground in which we can support and empower our clients, whatever their gender, while allowing them their own autonomy and responsibility.

It is well known that it is easier to see people as either 'victims' or 'perpetrators' in connection with gender with women as victims (think damsel in distress) and that women are more often seen in certain parts of mental health services, including psychotherapy services. Men are seen more as perpetrators, presenting with anger issues, violent crimes and are more often seen in the criminal justice system or involuntary mental health services. If we are to help people integrate and find different ways of relating to themselves and others, we need to see the whole person. CAT's use of reciprocal roles can really help with that – especially if clients are able to see their potential to take on both parts of their reciprocal roles. For me, this is a way out of the dilemma about my own gender roles, as I don't have to endlessly care and empathise but nor do I have to blame and push away or cut myself off emotionally.

Case examples

I will now use two composite case examples to illustrate the complexity of gender issues, how they can arise in therapy and how the theory discussed so far might be relevant. The first example uses a formulation to think about split states, considering the corners that women tend to be pushed into and how this may influence the development of these states. It also shows how a client's exploration of their gender identity can be a core part of therapy. The second example continues this theme in relation to male identity.

Helena, a student in her twenties, moved to the UK from Greece with her family as a child. She always struggled to feel like she fitted in, and recalled a challenging family background. Helena's mother worked long hours and her father was away a lot, so her parents struggled to meet Helena's needs. Helena was left to look after younger siblings, or otherwise left to her own devices a lot of the time, which left her vulnerable to being sexually abused by a neighbour as a young child. Helena came to therapy struggling with her identity and moods that were

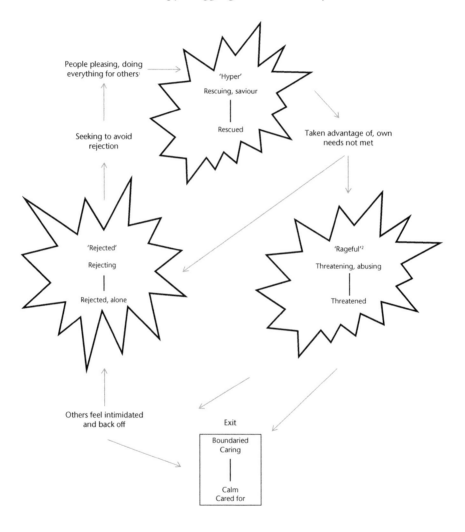

[1] Procedure that, in very general terms, is familiar to and expected of women– in line with the 'as a woman' part of the psychotherapy file

[2] The consequences of anger, and the feelings of shame associated with it, may be different for women than for men, as it is less expected of them. The rageful state for Helena was associated with a male voice – perhaps related to a denial of angry feelings which are not expected of women.

FIGURE 13.1 How Helen was pushed from one stage to another.

extreme and changeable. She identified three key states: one of feeling incredibly rejected and lonely, one of being 'hyper' and feeling like she could save the world, and another that was rageful and in which she could be quite aggressive towards others. In her rageful state, Helena would hear a voice with a male identity, which would call her insulting names and also encourage her to be aggressive to others. A key procedure linking these states was one of people pleasing: Helena did this to avoid rejection but ended up burning herself out in a frantic rescuing state and would end up angry and resentful. Helena had questions about her gender, saying that at times she felt quite male, and also felt unsure about her sexuality. She had a relationship with a much older man in which I sometimes felt she was vulnerable, and she was also attracted to women. Her attendance was erratic and Helena at times approached me with some suspicion but at others seemed to defer to me and describe me in idealised terms.

A non-judgemental space to explore the issues she was facing, but with firm interpersonal boundaries, seemed really important in helping Helena to explore her identity, including her gender identity and sexuality. We spent time mapping out the different states and the procedures that maintained them (see Figure 13.1) and recognising that the 'people pleasing' trap that women are so often pushed into was contributing to the difficulties. I also learnt about aspects of Helena's culture that contributed to these patterns through what was expected of her – as well as the challenges of growing up as someone who was not born in the UK.

Phil, a man in his fifties, was initially referred for post-traumatic stress disorder (PTSD) although his presentation included low mood and anxiety with interpersonal difficulties. Phil came from a working-class background, growing up with a critical and self-absorbed mother. She criticised him for not doing well enough at school where he was also bullied. Phil referred to himself as a child as a 'sissy' and strongly questioned his masculinity. However, he also told a story about a heroic act in his thirties, in which he protected someone from an attack, and at assessment he spoke vaguely about intrusive memories and nightmares around this. He would often tell 'macho' and even misogynistic stories, but also about how difficult life was and his struggle in relating to others and facing the world.

We used a 'narcissistic-' type reformulation (see Nehmad, 1997) to understand Phil's difficulties, and for him the 'split egg' diagram seemed to make a lot of sense. This formulation is shown in Figure 13.2. He was able to recognise that his storytelling and 'bigging himself up' could take him to a place where he felt admired, but this could lead to him being critical of others and to being disconnected. He also identified with a place in which he felt like a failure, which often triggered memories of his mother telling him he was no good as a child and he would tend to use language describing himself as effeminate when talking about this.

Phil seemed to have learnt that as a man, he should be strong and brave and not show his feelings – to do anything else was weak and made him a 'sissy', something to be avoided at all costs. He had learnt to deal with difficult feelings

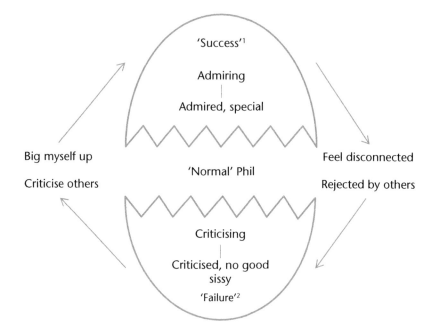

'State that seems to be associated with a way of being that can be quite 'macho' and cut off from difficult feelings–perhaps expected of men if they are to 'succeed'

²In this state, Phil tended to use derogatory feminine terms indescribing himself, as if struggling and experiencing difficult feelings was associated with a challenge to his masculinity

FIGURE 13.2 Searching for the middle ground.

by competing or by telling tales of times he had been brave or successful. Therapy involved questioning this and trying to sit with some of the more vulnerable feelings that Phil had cut off from, and we worked towards finding some middle ground between being a 'success' or a 'failure' – with an aim to find out what it meant to be 'normal Phil'.

The way forward: getting our house in order

Thinking about gender explicitly can help us avoid the trap and dilemmas I have described. Our therapeutic responsibility involves a number of levels: self-reflection, in direct work with clients, with wider services and developing theories and practices. First, we consider the influence of gender, now and in the past, on our own personal and professional development; then we ask this question of our clients. This requires understanding gender diversity. Chess Denman (2004) suggests that, 'successful psychotherapy with transgendered, transvestite or intersexed clients needs to be conducted from a position that is well informed . . . and benignly disposed towards the patient' (p. 249). Remaining curious and non-judgemental may start with, when appropriate, checking out which pronoun (he, she or they) clients prefer (for further discussion on working with gender variant clients see Chapter 12).

At work gender may be discussed in an unhelpful way or when staff collude with unhelpful problem procedures. When a client was discussed who was going out a lot socialising and drinking and leaving her young children in the care of her husband, I realised that if a man presented with these behaviours this would probably not cause the staff team concern. On another occasion a team were discussing a transgender client, and repeatedly using the wrong gender pronoun. This produces an issue about how to respond.

Conclusion

Like other forms of prejudice, sexism is a structural issue that exists all around us. It is embedded in our society, and in us, as we have all grown up in a system that expects different things from men and women, presents them with different types of adversity and offers them different opportunities.

Dealing with sexism, as with all forms of structural prejudice or oppression, is like brushing your teeth – an analogy used by Smooth (2011) to describe racism. It's not enough to do it once and then forget about it, or assume you are a 'clean person' so you do not need to do it. Sexism is there all the time, all around us and within us and needs regular attention. It is our responsibility as therapists to not ignore it, but to formulate it and look towards revision.

The people who come to see us are often disempowered and sometimes struggling with aspects of identity. Gender is a key part of our identity and something that we should be supporting clients to explore in an open-minded, empathic way, holding in mind the wider context in which people's problems have developed.

References

Bartlett, A., Smith, G. & King, M. (2009). The response of mental health professionals to clients seeking help to change or redirect same-sex sexual orientation. *BMC Psychiatry*, 9, 11.

Chodorow, N. (1994). *Femininities masculinities sexualities: Freud and beyond*. London: Free Association Books.

Collins, P. H. (1997). Defining black feminist thought. In L. Nicholson (ed.), *The second wave: A reader in feminist theory*. London: Routledge.

Davies, B. (2015). The gender dilemma: Can CAT find the middle ground between EITHER prescriptive norms and assumptions, OR ignorance of the differences that sex and gender make to the people we become and the kinds of problems we are faced with? *Reformulation, Journal of the Association for Cognitive Analytic Therapy*, Summer, 10–11.

Denman, C. (2004). *Sexuality: A biopsychosocial approach*. New York: Palgrave Macmillan.

Department of Health. (2008). *The gender and access to health services study*. www.sfh-tr. nhs.uk/attachments/article/41/The%20gender%20and%20access%20to%20health%20 services%20study.pdf (Accessed 04/01/14).

Freud, Sigmund (1933). Femininity. *New introductory lectures on psychoanalysis: Lecture III*. www.psychology.sunysb.edu/ewaters/345/2007_freud/femininity.pdf (Accessed 05/01/14).

Global Early Adolescent Study. (2017). Press release: Special supplement of the *Journal of Adolescent Health*. www.geastudy.org/blog/2017/9/20-jah-press-release (Accessed 25/09/17).

Hartmann, H. (1997). The unhappy marriage of Marxism and feminism: Towards a more progressive union. In L. Nicholson (ed.), *The second wave: A reader in feminist theory*. London: Routledge.

Howell, E. F. (2005). *The dissociative mind*. Hove, UK: Routledge.

Jones, E. E. & Zoppell, C. L. (1982). Impact of client and therapist gender on psychotherapy process and outcome. *Journal of Consulting and Clinical Psychology*, 50(2), 259–272.

Nehmad, A. (1997). CAT and narcissism: The missing chapter. *Reformulation, ACAT News*, Winter. www.acat.me.uk/reformulation.php?issue_id=36&article_id=373 (Accessed 21/03/18).

Ryle, A. & Kerr, I. B. (2002). *Introducing cognitive analytic therapy: Principles and practice*. Chichester, UK: Wiley.

Smooth, J. (2011). How I stopped worrying and learnt to love discussing race. TEDx talk, 16 November, text adaptation. www.illdoctrine.com/2011/11/my_tedx_talk_how_i_stopped_wor.html (Accessed 08/09/17).

14

WHY HATE MATTERS

An introduction to René Girard's theories of mimesis and the scapegoat mechanism and their relevance to CAT theory and practice

Matthew Tinker

Hate matters. Even a cursory glance at the news reveals a world that is seemingly riven with conflict and rivalry. At an international level there is war in Syria, Afghanistan, Iraq and Darfur as well as a deeply troubling escalation in hostility between the United States and North Korea. We have also witnessed in the last few decades the emergence and rise of global terrorism. Nationally it is reported that hate crime has rapidly increased since the 2016 referendum to leave the European Union. Professionally we often encounter conflict in the lives of our patients, while on a more personal level it seems we must inevitably face the pain of acrimony and division within our relationships, and within our own hearts.

There is today among therapists an increasing recognition of the need for us to develop the capacity for compassion and empathy. Compassion-focused therapy, for example, explains our human propensity for violence by emphasising that our 'tricky' brains, although endowing us with the capacity for love and kindness, have evolved to leave us vulnerable to hatred and 'in-group–out-group' behaviour.

In cognitive analytic therapy we approach hatred and violence from a relational perspective. Nobody exists in complete isolation, we are all inter-connected. We draw attention to the internalisation of early maladaptive reciprocal roles and their continuing enactment within the patient's web of relationships. We might also believe that these formative reciprocal roles make us susceptible to acting violently or cruelly. As helpful as this approach is, I believe that it is inadequate.

In this chapter I therefore suggest an introduction to the work of René Girard (1923–2015). Girard, a French literary critic, anthropologist and academic, who lived and worked in America for most of his life, has had an enormous influence in a variety of fields, especially philosophy, anthropology, psychology, theology and politics. He developed a theory that human desire is 'mimetic'. The word mimetic comes from the Greek word mimesis, which means to imitate. Girard's theory of mimetic desire is broad ranging but basically suggests that we desire things because we admire as models other people who desire them. He asserts that human culture developed and survived by institutionalising the violence that grows out of mimetic desire. This leads us to scapegoat, and in turn to sacralise our scapegoats because they provide us with a mechanism for temporary release from the tension and conflict generated by interpersonal rivalries. Here I will discuss the relevance of some elements of Girard's work to CAT, in particular its political implications.

Mimetic desire

The most central and important insight that Girard can give us is about the nature of human desire – something that CAT has little to say about. Girard makes a distinction between our 'appetites', such as the need for food and shelter to survive, and our desires, where objects possess a symbolic value such as the desire for admiration, a new iPhone or a promotion at work. Girard believes that we do not generate our own desires – instead we imitate the desires of others. Our desires might be conceptualised as social, mimetic, contagious and often outside our conscious awareness rather than individual, self-generated and based on our personal choice or preference. This is a radically different way of thinking about our desires when contrasted with a more familiar predominantly individualist paradigm.

Girard developed this insight through his analysis of the works of novelists such as Dostoyevsky and Cervantes. He found that these novelists displayed in their works an almost instinctive understanding of the mimetic nature of desire. Whereas Bahktin sees Dostoyevsky's *The Brothers Karamazov* as a 'dialogic' novel of different voices, Girard sees it as a classic novel of mimetic desires with most of the main characters as love rivals. In Girard's reading of the novel *Don Quixote*, the central character, having read many romantic novels about chivalry, seeks to emulate them and adopts the name Don Quixote. In desiring to revive chivalry he imitates the desire of his fictional romantic hero, the knight Amadis de Gaule.

Girard brings our attention to the fact that the protagonist desired to become a famous knight only because he liked to read books about knights. This also illustrates another subtle aspect of Girard's theory: that we imitate the desires of others because we desire to be like the person or persons we are imitating.

In our everyday life, an example of mimetic desire is to be found in the expression 'keeping up with the Joneses'. Marketing departments and sales representatives seem to have a good understanding of the mimetic nature of human desire: why else would they use celebrities and models to sell their products? They understand that it is not the product that attracts us but the famous celebrity or attractive model and our desire to be just like them.

Research by neuroscientists demonstrates that we humans are naturally inclined to value what we perceive others valuing. For example, participants in one study watched a video of two identical objects. On screens they watched an anonymous person select one of the two identical objects. The participants were then asked to rate how much they liked the objects and it was found that the objects that had been selected by the anonymous person were seen as more desirable.

Now for Girard what is important is that this is often an unconscious process. Girard terms the person or group with whom one is in a 'mimetic relationship' as the 'model'. Our models *mediate* our experience of reality to us. This is why Girard sometimes refers to mimetic desire as triangular desire and why he describes human beings as 'interdividuals': he is pointing out that we are beings who are run by and constituted by these mimetic relationships.

Girard is profoundly critical of 'individualist' accounts of what it means to be human – for Girard human beings are thoroughly interdependent beings – which is a source of both creativity and vulnerability. Drawing on Girard, theologian James Alison (2007) describes what we think of as 'the self' as being formed by the 'social other': the complex web of culture, relationships and mimetic desires that preceded it.

Mimetic desire and science

There has been some critique of the 'unscientific' nature of Girard's theories and while it might be tempting to say that we can find ample evidence of the mimetic nature of human desire simply by signing in to our Facebook accounts, we can point to a growing body of evidence that seems to be arriving at some intriguing conclusions about human imitation that correlate well with mimetic theory.

In his overview of the history of scientific and philosophical perspectives of human imitation, Garrels (2011) observes that imitation was long understood to be important. However, he suggests that during the modern era imitation was largely sidelined and ignored, in part owing to the Enlightenment's emphasis on the autonomy of the individual self. But he notes that more recently there has been a great resurgence of interest in the importance and role of imitation in the fields of neuroscience, social psychology and developmental psychology.

The discovery of mirror neurons strongly suggests that imitation is a foundational part of what it means to be human and that it is linked to our ability to empathise (Gallese, 2009; Iacoboni, 2009). The more traditional or 'cognitivist' theory (very closely associated with Theory of Mind but somewhat wider in its scope) suggests that objectively, like scientists, we make and revise inferences about the mental states of other people based on evidence that we gather from observing behaviour. This is contrasted with Simulation Theory, which instead suggests a more immediate and subjective kind of cognitive empathy: 'What would I feel or do?' There is growing evidence that mirror neurons are involved in enabling us to automatically and largely unconsciously anticipate and simulate the actions and intentions of the person we are interacting with.

The classic accounts of infant development as articulated by Freud and Skinner, although differing in some respects, tend to conceptualise the newborn baby as initially almost autistically cut off, a kind of blank slate, only to be gradually socialised over time. In stark contrast to this, more contemporary accounts recognise the importance of imitation; for example Reddy (2008) states that there are almost a hundred studies that demonstrate neonatal imitation in humans. Meltzoff (2011) believes that there is clear evidence that infants not only imitate the actions of others, but by following the gaze of others are able to understand their intentions and so also imitate their desires.

Mimetic desire leads to rivalry

I remember observing my 6-year-old daughter playing on a swing in a park. Eventually, her interest waning, she jumped off to find something else to do. But as she began walking away from the swing another girl of about her age began to approach, her gaze fixed on the swing and clearly desiring to play on it. You can probably guess what happened: as soon as she noticed the other girl's intent my daughter abruptly jumped straight back on it.

This illustrates another aspect of mimetic desire: how it leads to rivalry and how mimetic desire tends to escalate and reinforce itself.

Girard would see in this an example of a 'model' becoming a 'model-rival'. The two girls are unconsciously imitating each other – they desire to play on the swing because they see the desire the other has for it, the value the other ascribes to it. The girl's desire for the swing increases as they both imitate the desire of one another and so at this point there is the prospect of conflict.

Girard makes an important distinction between what he terms 'external mediation' and 'internal mediation'. Internal and external mediation will influence the degree and nature of the rivalry that results from mimetic desire. The mimetic rivalry between my daughter and the girl of about her own age is an example of internal mediation. Internal mediation is when the subject and model are close, when their worlds or social spheres interpenetrate to some degree. With internal mediation there is the increasing possibility of conflict or violence. External mediation is when the 'distance' between the subject and model is greater. So, for example, if it had been me rather than my daughter on the swing it would be an example of 'external mediation'. Here there is little chance of rivalry or real conflict. The girl and I inhabit largely separate worlds and although the girl might still imitate my desire for the swing we would not be genuine rivals. Other examples of external mediation might be when the model is a famous actor, or character in a book. Here the model is likely to remain just a model. But when the model is a sibling, colleague, neighbour or partner there is more likely to be internal mediation and the prospect of the model becoming a model-rival. Of course, a relationship of external mediation can also develop into one of internal mediation, such as when a gifted pupil becomes the equal of her tutor, leading to intense rivalry, or at a more extreme level the phenomenon of fans stalking their idols.

Rivalry leads to scapegoating

So far, we have seen how human desire is mimetic and although this is in many ways beneficial, it also leaves us vulnerable to conflict and violence. Our inherent tendency to imitate one another means that when our desires inevitably coalesce on the same object there is the possibility of what Girard termed a mimetic crisis: the possibility of collective violence and acts of revenge that perpetuate an escalating cycle of hostility to a degree that in very early human communities – with an absence of the mediating influence of the observation and enforcement of rules – might have threatened their very survival. But at some point, very early on in human history we learned a way to avoid mass undifferentiated conflict: we learned to scapegoat.

Girard contends that it was during an escalation of contagious violence that the desires of multiple protagonists to harm one another coalesced or converged on to a single victim. Girard's hypothesis is that this person was likely lynched or expelled with a seemingly miraculous result: the primitive human community suddenly experienced a sense of peace and solidarity.

Scapegoating can operate at different levels. The persecution of Jews in Nazi Germany and the Genocide against the Tutsi in Rwanda are both appalling examples of scapegoating on a national and international scale. But it also occurs in small groups or organisations, for example when a person becomes a scapegoat in a place of work, or at an individual level when our scapegoating of a spouse or family member becomes a way of us feeling better about ourselves.

Girard even suggests that what we know as civilisation has been built upon such a foundation of scapegoating: he believes it is how human beings have learned to manage the inevitable conflict and rivalry that arises from mimetic desire, functioning a bit like a 'pressure cooker' releasing steam.

Girard's Christian faith (which can be described as a kind of Catholic humanism) influenced his work on mimetic theory, leading him to making contributions to Christian theology – he interpreted the crucifixion of Jesus as being responsible for exposing the scapegoat mechanism to the world. Girard believed that in modern times we have become more aware of and concerned for the victims of scapegoating. Although this presents the possibility of conversion from the whole mechanism it has also deprived us of its cathartic power, which derives from it being an unconscious process. The paradoxical result of all this is that we live in a world where we are ever more vulnerable to the effects of mimetic rivalry.

Films such as *The Hunger Games* (2013) and *The Purge* (2013) offer us modern meditations on scapegoating that have much in common with Girard's ideas. Both also illustrate how historically the ritualisation and institutionalisation of violence and scapegoating provided a way of managing mimetic desire and keeping polarised and unequal societies from falling apart. Both these films, in their own ways, articulate a vision of the moral and political consequences of human culture being built upon a foundation of institutionalised violence.

Mimetic theory in clinical practice

It seems to me that there is already plenty of common ground shared by mimetic theory and CAT. An obvious example of this would be that the CAT model is informed by theories that tend to emphasise the importance of imitation and reciprocation in early infant development (Ryle, 1997; Ryle & Kerr, 2002). CAT's use of the Vygotskian concept of internalisation clearly resonates well with mimetic theory.

A particular area of interest might be the potential for mimetic theory to inform the concept of reciprocal roles. Although CAT would not claim that reciprocal roles are 'set in stone', both in theory and practice it has tended to emphasise the importance of the early acquisition of a core repertoire of such roles that are relatively stable over time. While not necessarily abandoning this position, mimetic theory allows for a much more immediate, fluid and unconscious dimension to be added to the acquisition and enactment of reciprocal roles. This is reflected in our society's use of social media that creates a 'hyper-mimetic' environment to the extent that the little understood phenomena of 'social contagion' is being linked to suicide (Kravetz, 2017). Mimetic theory also suggests that reciprocal roles could be horizontal as well as vertical. A horizontal reciprocal role could describe the relationship between two people who are pursuing the same desires. Perhaps the nature of the reciprocal role might indicate the nature of the mimetic relationship: for example whether it is that of a model (a kind of 'positive mimesis'), model-rival (the model now seen as rival, but can also sometimes have positive aspects – an obvious example being in competitive sport), or model-obstacle (the model is now conceptualised as an obstacle that blocks that acquisition of the object).

How our early experiences, temperament and indeed the internalisation of early reciprocal roles mediate our susceptibility to the influence of mimetic desire is as yet unclear. Experiments in social psychology have repeatedly demonstrated how susceptible we are to the influence of others and how very easy it is to create environments that effortlessly seem to facilitate prejudice against out-groups. Intriguingly, a recent study testing the automaticity of emotional contagion concluded that so called 'negative' emotions – specifically anger – seem to be more contagious than 'positive' emotions.

It seems to me that there is an opportunity for mimetic theory to richly complement CAT's use of dialogism, particularly its appropriation of Bakhtinian ideas around the concept of 'internalised voices'. The use of therapy as a means of identifying these voices has obvious parallels with Girard's concern with becoming aware of the extent to which we are 'run' by mimetic desire.

The concept of mimetic rivalry might also re-introduce the importance of the role of envy and unconscious imitation in our work with patients. It might in effect add a kind of third pole to the reciprocal role that identified an 'object' of desire associated with it – either physical or metaphysical. In particular mimetic rivalry gives CAT a way of conceptualising envy that sits well with its use of 'internalisation' and mimetic theories' understanding of how relationships can shift so that our models (whether parent, partner or boss) can become 'model-rivals' or even 'model-obstacles' and can be of immense clinical usefulness.

In my own practice I have found that mimetic theory can help to shed light on instances of conflict and animosity in my patients' relationships and that it is often the case that the development of a mimetic rivalry can be traced. An example of this being a patient who as an adolescent was a talented athlete, who adored and 'idolised' his war veteran father, only to feel crushed and angry at his father's increasingly dismissive attitude towards him and his father's eventual refusal to sign the papers that would have allowed him to join the very same regiment his father had served in.

A criticism of mimetic theory that has been made is that it appears to be somewhat fatalistic and that it paints a picture of human beings as being like puppets, robbed of all free will and personal responsibility. But this doesn't necessarily have to be the case. Instead it might help CAT to pay more attention to some of the unconscious processes that often shape our behaviour. Mimetic theory would simply have it that we are unaware of the extent to which we depend on 'the other' for our own sense of identity – an idea that surely resonates with CAT – and that this leaves us subject to a kind of illusion that we are autonomous individuals, the authors of our own desires – which paradoxically leaves us ever more vulnerable to mimetic rivalry and scapegoating.

Politics, mimetic theory and scapegoating

Individual therapy issues cannot be divorced from the family nor from the wider social and political sphere. Put bluntly, being poor and deprived impacts on a person's mental health. Significantly too the interest in the book *Spirit Level* is very apt for mimetic desire: perceived relative deprivation compared with colleagues or neighbours is as relevant as deprivation in real terms (Wilkinson & Pickett, 2010). At the same time, we can often witness that the individual psyche serves as a microcosm of a wider world.

The concept of mimetic escalation could help CAT to account for the sometimes rapid escalation in the intensity of the enactment of reciprocal roles where abuse, aggression and hatred are present, whether that is within the context of an individual therapy session or international politics. The mirroring of angry or attacking behaviour and emotions often leads to an angry and attacking response, which is again mirrored in an ever-escalating cycle. Girard talks of people becoming like 'doubles' or 'enemy twins' in which they become more and more indistinguishable from one another in their responses. Such escalations are readily observable in political discourse, perhaps a recent illustration of this is the increasingly insulting and derisive language used by President Trump and Kim Jong Un to describe each other – clearly these are rivals who are fascinated by one another. Linked to this is Girard's insight that mimetic desire for an 'object' increases in proportion to the resistance it meets with in acquiring it – thus the harder President Trump tries to prevent Kim Jong Un from acquiring nuclear weapons the more valuable they may appear to North Korea.

Whereas Girard contends that mass scapegoating usually occurs when there is a crisis in society and a building up of mimetic rivalry, citing various historical examples such as the persecution of Jews during episodes of the plague in Europe, psychiatrist Jean-Michel Oughourlian (2012) draws our attention to the important

role that scapegoating often plays in politics, seeing the identification and designa-
tion of scapegoats as being at the heart of political life. Contemporary examples of
this are not hard to find, whether it be the Rohinga in Myyanmar, LGBTQ people
in Russia or 'Western decadence' in Saudi Arabia.

In the UK immigrants have been blamed by some for shortages in housing
and other social problems and, like the Rohinga in Myyanmar and the LGBTQ
community in Russia, their position on the margins of society (Girard would use
the term 'marginal outsider') seems to leave them particularly vulnerable to being
scapegoated. The fact that in the UK immigrants are blamed by 'some' rather than
'all' highlights that in modern times scapegoating has become an increasingly ineffective way of dispelling interpersonal rivalries and uniting the community. Why
is this so? Girard would contend that we are no longer so naïve when it comes to
scapegoating, we can often see it for what it is, at least in its cruder manifestations.
While there have been many in the media who have repeatedly employed 'parasitic
metaphors' to label immigrants as 'scroungers' – the most virulently racist examples
found in the so called 'blogosphere' – there have also been many who have decried
this and called attention to the fact that immigrants are being scapegoated.

Building on this, Oughourlian (2012), sees in contemporary society another factor at play: the constant torrent of digital and media information and imagery that
we absorb on a daily basis. He posits that this has both positive and negative consequences. Positively, he believes that it is increasingly less likely that nations, politicians
and indeed people will become completely 'fixated' upon one another – simply put,
we are too aware of the wider world – there are too many pulls on our attention.
Perhaps an example of this is how '24-hour news' cycle dictates that a story or event
that initially saturates the media and our consciousness will give way to the next 'big
story' or the next scapegoat, within a matter of hours or days. Although I sympathise
with Oughourlian's contention I do also wonder whether it is in part contradicted
by the impact that 'confirmation bias' has on our media consumption. Confirmation
bias posits that in our digital age we simply gorge on the media that confirms what
we already believe while paying much less attention to media that challenges our
views: in this scenario there would be an *increased* potential for mimetic escalation
and scapegoating.

Girard believed that in our modern society, with its increased awareness of
scapegoating and its concern for victims, scapegoating has tended to become ever
subtler. It seems to me that politicians of all political persuasions are at times guilty
of scapegoating. A recent book about the Trump presidency (Levitsky & Ziblatt,
2018) described one of the worrying 'signs' of a slide towards authoritarianism as
the denial of the legitimacy of opponents. In the political and media spheres in the
UK it seems there has been an increasing legitimisation of a kind of self-righteous
anger: an 'outrage economy' as Rafael Behr (2017) has memorably described it.

To have a scapegoat is always largely to be unaware of it because we are always
able to find a valid reason to condemn some person or group. Girard exposes a
fairly common modern permutation of scapegoating as our tendency to scapegoat
those who scapegoat. Scapegoating is regarded as repugnant and so it gives us the

perfect cover for our own scapegoating. Does the CAT community have its scape-goats? CAT's founder Anthony Ryle was a lifelong socialist and CAT continues to embrace communitarian values but are we in danger of scapegoating people who do not hold progressive or left-wing political opinions? Is it possible to be a politically conservative CAT therapist, for example, or one who is conventionally religious? I remember attending a psychotherapy training session about spiritual-ity where the speaker began by pressing her hands together and giving the rather beautiful Hindu valediction 'Namaste' – meaning I bow to the divine in you. As a thought experiment I would ask you to visualise the reaction had she instead made the sign of the cross or recited the Lord's Prayer.

It might also be interesting to think about CAT's relationship with cognitive behavioural therapy (CBT) through the lens of mimetic theory. Girard reminds us that the more we unconsciously imitate our model, the more like them we become, and the more important it will seem to us to assert our uniqueness and individuality over and against them – James Alison (2013) calls this the 'narcissism of small differences'.

René Girard invites us to become aware that we are all, to some extent, driven by mimetic desire and rivalry and that the result of this is a world riven with conflict and violence. He invites each of us to step away from reciprocal cycles of animosity and hatred. This does not mean passivity in the face of injustice. Proponents of non-violent resistance (see for example Wink, 2003) such as Martin Luther King and Gandhi, teach us that there is a world of difference between an anger that compels us to stand up to bigotry and oppression and the hatred that dehumanises and degrades the other.

Conclusion

Girard believed that human mimetic desire, although in many ways responsible for much that is good, also leaves us vulnerable. His contention is that mimetic desire almost inevitably leads to rivalry and that the way that communities have learned to deal with mimetic rivalry is by scapegoating.

Scapegoating is something that many of our patients are all too familiar with. We work with people who have, often without their realising it, been scapegoated by their partners, families or their communities. It is important that we are able to make some sense of these experiences and a mimetic understanding of desire and rivalry is a very helpful way of doing this. I also believe that Girard's theories can not only help CAT therapists to think about the role of rivalry and envy in both our patient's and our own relationships but can also enrich and broaden our conceptualisation of reciprocal roles.

Much like Gilbert's (2014) compassion-focused therapy, Girard suggests that we have a propensity towards violence and rivalry and some may find this assertion troublesome. But I believe that the insights he offers can help CAT therapists take seriously both the interpersonal and the political realities of rivalry and violence in a way that is thoroughly relational and intersubjective.

Bibliography

Alison, J. (2013). *Jesus the forgiving victim: Listening for the unheard voice* (1st ed.). Glenview, IL: Doers.

Antonello, P. (2015). *How we became human: Mimetic theory and the science of evolutionary origins.* East Lansing, MI: Michigan State University Press.

Bailie, G. (1995). *Violence unveiled.* New York: Crossroad Publishing.

Bakhtin, M. M. (1984). *Problems of Dostoevsky's poetics.* Minneapolis, MN: University of Minnesota Press.

Behr, R. (2017). You can log off, sure. But you can't stop the outrage economy. www. theguardian.com/commentisfree/2017/dec/27/log-off-stop-outrage-economy-media-dark-side (Accessed 20/01/18).

DeMonaco, James (Dir.) (2013). *The purge* [Film]. United States: Platinum Dunes, Blumhouse Productions, Why Not Productions.

Gallese, V. (2009). The two sides of mimesis: Girards mimetic theory, embodied simulation and social identification. In S. R. Garrels (ed.), *Mimesis and science* (pp. 87–108). East Lansing, MI: Michigan State University Press,

Garrels, S. R. (2011). *Mimesis and science: Empirical research on imitation and the mimetic theory of culture and religion.* East Lansing, MI: Michigan State University Press.

Gilbert, P. (2014). The origins and nature of compassion focused therapy. *British Journal of Clinical Psychology*, 53, 6–41.

Girard, R. (1986). *The Scapegoat.* Paris: John Hopkins University Press.

Girard, R. (1996a). Desire and the unity of novelistic conclusions. In J. G. Williams (ed.), *The Girard reader* (pp. 45–61). New York: Crossroad Publishing.

Girard, R. (1996b). Python and his two wives: An exemplary scapegoat myth. In J. G. Williams (ed.), *The Girard reader* (pp. 118–141). New York: Crossroad Publishing.

Girard, R. (1996c). Sacrifice as sacral violence and substitution. In J. G. Williams (ed.), *The Girard reader* (pp. 69–93). New York: Crossroads Publishing.

Girard, R. (1996d). The surrogate victim. In J. G. Williams (ed.), *The Girard reader* (pp. 20–29). New York: Crossroad Publishing.

Girard, R. (1996e). Triangular desire. In J. G. Williams (ed.), *The Girard reader* (pp. 33–44). New York: Crossroad Publishing.

Girard, R. (2001). *I see Satan fall like lightning.* Herefordshire, UK: Gracewing.

Girard, R. (2016). *Things hidden since the foundation of the world.* London: Bloomsbury Academic.

Hardin, M. (2015). Sacrifice, myth and gospel. In M. Hardin (ed.), *Reading the Bible with René Girard* (pp. 42–56). Lancaster, UK: JDL Press.

Iacoboni, M. (2009). *Mirroring people: The science of empathy and how we connect with others.* New York: Picador.

Kelly, J. R., Iannone, N. E. & McCarty, M. K. (2016). Emotional contagion of anger is automatic: An evolutionary explanation. *British Journal of Social Psychology*, 55, 182–191.

Konner, M. (2011). Sacred violence, mimetic rivalry, and war. In S. R. Garrels (ed.), *Mimesis and science* (pp. 155–174). East Lansing, MI: Michigan State University Press.

Kravetz, L. D. (2017). *Strange contagion: Inside the surprising science of infectious behaviors and viral emotions and what they tell us about ourselves.* New York: Harper Wave.

Lebreton, M., Kawa, S., Forgeot d'Arc, B., Daunizeau, J. & Pessiglione, M. (2012). Your goal is mine: Unraveling mimetic desires in the human brain. *Journal of Neuroscience: The Official Journal of the Society for Neuroscience*, 32(21), 7146–7157.

Leiman, M. (2004). Dialogical sequence analysis. In H. J. M. Hermans & G. Dimaggio (eds), *The dialogical self in psychotherapy* (pp. 255–269). Hove, UK: Brunner-Routledge.

Levitsky, S. & Ziblatt, D. (2018). *How democracies die*. New York: Crown.

Meltzoff, A. N. (2011). Out of the mouths of babes: Imitation, gaze, and intentions in infant research – the 'like me' framework. In S. Garrels (ed.), *Mimesis and science* (pp. 55–74). East Lansing, MI: Michigan State University Press.

Musolff, A. (2015). Dehumanizing metaphors in UK immigrant in press and online media. *Journal of Language Aggression and Conflict*, 3(1), 41–56.

Oughourlian, J.-M. (2012). *Psychopolitics*. East Lansing, MI: Michigan State University Press.

Oughourlian, J.-M. (2016). *The mimetic brain*. East Lansing, MI: Michigan State University Press.

Palaver, W. (2013). *René Girard's mimetic theory*. East Lansing, MI: Michigan State University Press.

Pollard, R. (2008). *Dialogue and desire: Mikhail Bakhtin and the linguistic turn in psychotherapy* (1st ed.). London: Karnac.

Reddy, V. (2008). *How infants know minds* (1st ed.). Cambridge, MA, and London: Harvard University Press.

Richardson, F. C. & Manglos, N. D. (2013). Reciprocity and rivalry: A critical introduction to mimetic scapegoat theory. *Pastoral Psychology*, 62, 423–436.

Ross, Gary (Dir.) (2013). *The hunger games* [Film]. United States: Color Force.

Ryle, A. (1997). *Cognitive analytic therapy and borderline personality disorder*. Chichester, UK: Wiley.

Ryle, A. & Kerr, I. B. (2002). *Introducing cognitive analytic therapy: Principles and practice* (1st ed.). Chichester, UK: Wiley.

Ryle, T. (2010). The political sources of reciprocal role procedures. *Reformulation*, Summer, 6–7.

Sharman, J. & Jones, I. (2017). *Independent*. www.independent.co.uk/news/uk/home-news/brexit-vote-hate-crime-rise-100-per-cent-england-wales-police-figures-new-racism-eu-a7580516.html (Accessed 30/09/17).

Vygotsky, L. S. (1978). Internalization of higher psychological function. In *Mind in Society* (pp. 53–57). Cambridge, MA: Harvard University Press

White, H. (1978). Ethnological 'lie' and mythical 'truth'. *Diacritics*, 8, 2–9.

Wilkinson, R. & Pickett, K. (2010). *The spirit level: Why greater equality makes societies stronger*. New York: Bloomsbury.

Wink, W. (2003). *Jesus and non-violence: A third way*. Minneapolis, MN: Fortress Press.

15

OWNING PRIVILEGE AND ACKNOWLEDGING RACISM

Hilary Brown

Running throughout this book is the conviction that people are shaped by their experiences, by the intense and survival-driven interactions as infants and pervasive social positioning that shapes our adult lives, driven by economic relations, structural inequality and cultural (dis)avowal. This chapter explores these dynamics in relation to race, considering how racial sameness and difference impacts on the therapeutic alliance and our interactions as patients, therapists and colleagues.

Psychotherapy is predominantly a white middle-class profession and although diversity is a stated aim of our professional bodies, it continues to elude us. When people from black and minority ethnic (BAME) communities seek therapy they often enter an asymmetric conversation with someone white and, given what is known about these encounters, the norm is to skirt around these issues. Msebele and Brown (2011) characterised this as 'polite evasion', as if the best strategy was to 'not see' race rather than to proactively grapple with its impact, 'out there' and 'in here'. Not noticing race means not noticing racism; experienced as if colluding, rather than challenging, or validating, the sense of injustice that people often bring into therapy.

The British Psychological Society (BPS, 2018, p. 1) recently endorsed trauma-informed practice in relation to people with personality disorders, emphasising 'the importance of talking about the difficulties experienced by people, especially young people, in ways that do not position them as the problem'. This should embrace people who come to therapy worn down by racism; both the dripping tap, pervasive kind of racism and the easily recognised impacts of a single terrifying incident. Many people from BAME backgrounds have had cumulative experiences of being with white people that felt constricted and scrutinising.

All therapies tend to work with difficulties that are *inter*-personal, but CAT is well placed to insist on this focus given that enculturation is at the heart of our understanding of the self. Reciprocal roles that exist in the outside world are internalised as the building blocks of our inner selves so that our internal world reflects, as well as acts on, our interactions back in the external world. Poverty and disadvantage are not meted out evenly but black and Asian people,[1] both in the UK and the US, are significantly more likely to face barriers that operate as actual traps and snags, not internalised processes that could be dismantled from the inside.

I want to start by positioning myself because this is not a chapter that can be written in a disembodied voice, I can only write about race from the lived experience of my generation – as a white woman who has lived in the UK during the latter half of the twentieth, and the first decades of the twenty-first century. This is the relatively privileged and narrow vantage point from which, however critically, I view the world

Traditionally, a chapter on race would be about the 'others', those groups labelled as 'disadvantaged', marginalised or unfairly treated; it would not focus on white people and their taken-for-granted ethnicity. This focus on groups who *differ* rather than on those who claim to be the universal reference point from which others diverge, conforms to age-old academic practices of studying the poor rather than the rich, the disadvantaged rather than the privileged and the helped instead of the helpers. It is time to turn this on its head so that we can own privilege and understand its operation.

Race and class

Racism has been expressed in very different terms across my lifetime. When I was growing up it was a very visible source of conflict and distress but more recently it seemed as if progress toward the goal of integration was a done deal, only to find that once again solidarity has melted away with 'austerity' pitching communities against each other (Malik, 2018). Sometimes it has seemed as if issues of race were really only issues of class but as Barack Obama said in his 2008 memoir, black communities do not only struggle with the harsh realities of poverty and marginalisation but are often the focus of 'a very particular experience of hate' (Obama, 2008, p. 195). Public discourse is being shaped by the perception that any visible gain on the part of people from minority ethnic groups is detrimental to the white community, contributing to resentment and distrust on both sides.

Economic oppression interacts with but cannot be taken as synonymous, with racial oppression: the fracture lines overlay and overlap. Problems in the white community are not usually put down to being 'white' but to being working class or left behind, when problems for black young people are seen as rooted in their ethnicity despite the complicating factors of poverty and migration cited by Malik (2018, p. 2). In the context of education, he argues against conflating race and class to avoid a situation in which 'whites are seen as divided by class, non-whites as belonging to classless communities. It's a perspective that ignores social divisions within minority groups while also racialising class distinctions' (p. 2). Gender and sexuality also create complex 'intersections' of identity and experience that militate against simplistic assumptions of a singular white or a singular black experience but despite these complexities, race remains a visible and durable dividing line.

Naming race and racism in therapy

White people often think that race is not an issue for them, or not something to be brought up in conversation or in therapy. But, working honestly in relation to racism requires a white therapist to own the unearned power and benefits of the doubt that flow from 'whiteness', even where a person may feel hard done by as an individual, because the evidence is clear that *at a group level* the left behind of BAME groups are faring worse. Engaging with these issues is uncomfortable and challenging despite the fact that, as Sliwa (2017, p. 1) remarks,

> The privilege of pondering the ramifications of race and racism, when it is convenient, is vastly different from the experience of walking around in the shoes of someone who can't, for a second, forget about their skin color when it becomes inconvenient.

To be white means to choose whether or when we engage with race, when for anyone from a BAME group, as Celeste Ng asserts, 'your existence is politicised for you, whether you like it or not' (Laity, 2017, p. 1). Ryde (2009) suggests instead developing 'white awareness' as a way of being mindful of race across the helping professions and of bringing it into the centre of the therapeutic alliance in a way that is neither implicitly racist nor colour-blind and 'power-evasive' but what Frankenberg (1993) termed 'race cognisant'. The same alert and validating position can be sought in relation to other forms of 'difference' – class, gender, disability and sexual orientation – and learning the confidence to have conversations that go against the grain of not seeing, seems an essential part of the therapist's task and training.

By inference, to be black in our profession requires another kind of robustness that allows one to stay centred when on the receiving end of undermining interactions and the tenacity to assertively seek support from supervisors and colleagues without allowing them to deflect the discussion away from race or to interpret difficulties that are located in racism as personal or professional issues. As supervisors or colleagues, there are dilemmas about when, whether and how we open up these conversations because acting neutrally and failing to name race as a site of anxiety or conflict, leaves the person carrying alone what should be a shared commitment, silencing their thinking about unjust realities and failing to canvas alternatives to the strategy so eloquently summoned up by Langston Hughes (1926) in the phrase 'pain swallowed in a smile'.

Becoming more mindful of whiteness

DiAngelo (2011, p. 54), writing about race in the United States, describes white people as living in a 'social environment that protects and insulates them from race-based stress . . . [that] . . . builds white expectations for racial comfort while at the same time lowering the ability to tolerate racial stress, leading to . . .White Fragility'.

She describes how white people develop strategies to defend this zone of racial 'comfort', for example in discussions where race is made an issue, white people deny that racism is prevalent, or they segue into discussions of gender or class, or they may take challenge so personally that they inadvertently silence people of colour who are trying to bring difficult issues into the open.

CAT provides models for understanding the ways in which people are positioned, and position themselves both as individuals and as representatives of different ethnic groups. Black communities continue to labour under huge material disadvantages, exacerbated by forced migration and daily experiences of systemic racial prejudice and as a result they are unsurprisingly over-represented among those with severe and enduring mental health problems. White therapists who are not able to notice or effectively speak about the impact of this racial disadvantage cannot hope to be effective or to validate the experiences that have brought their patients to therapy. But opening up these issues holds a mirror up to their own privileged positions and asks uncomfortable questions about those elements of a person's competence, personality and confidence that have been shaped out of their privileged position.

One response to challenge is to switch roles, pushing an unjustly treated person's claims or legitimate complaints aside and muscling in on the victim position, as Karpf (2017, p. 2) commented in the context of recent sexual harassment claims, 'in a weird transposition, the status of victim seems to have become desirable. As a way of holding onto power, the powerful are claiming victimhood themselves'. This is what happens when white people deny that racism exists, when they refute attempts to hold them to account as witch hunts or when they characterise initiatives designed to redress inequalities through positive discrimination as being unfair to them: 'To the privileged, equality is oppression. Such people see all action to address inequality in zero-sum terms; any gain by previously less powerful groups inevitably means a loss for those who have been more powerful in the past' (Karpf, 2017, p. 2).

DiAngelo (2011) described a mandatory racial awareness course in which members of the group expressed resentment when the issue of discrimination was raised even though the participants were an all white group of employees in a particular company that gave grounds for wondering whether there had been a recruitment bias. Others point to positive discrimination initiatives that are designed to encourage diversity and misconstrue them as black people having been given unfair advantage.

These ways of thinking provide the context for feelings of resentment and entitlement that are present in the work we do with patients from all classes and racial backgrounds. Even when working as a white therapist with a white patient, issues of race are not absent and may manifest as procedures for managing painful feelings that work by colluding against racial 'others'.

Individual and group identities

As we have seen throughout this book, CAT not only draws on specific bodies of knowledge that help us to understand how the outside world comes to be represented in our internal dialogues, but also on a wider body of 'social constructionist' theory that explores how reciprocal roles operate at a societal level, between groups and communities, as well as within them. Sometimes the borders between these identities are porous and a person can nominate those they wish to own, but others, including race and gender, rest on more visible differences that cannot be sidestepped, so a person is seen to be affiliated with a group whether or not they want to stand with, or represent, their co-affiliates.

Theoreticians of race and colonisation refer to this capacity to move in and out of group identities at will as a dominant group that goes 'unmarked' in relation to a group that has been 'othered' by 'marked' members. When described in public spaces, a person is far more likely to be identified as black even when this is not salient than to be described as white even when it is. A similar process works for women who are seen as the 'second' sex, that is, the atypical sex, the one that deviates (de Beauvoir, 1949). Yankah (2017, p. 1) explained racism to his young black son saying, 'Some people hate others because they are different . . . to be met with the response but I am not different'. Maya Angelou (1985, p. 97), in the second volume of her autobiography, *Gather Together in My Name*, recounts returning to her home in rural Arkansas from a more racially liberal California and being reprimanded by her grandmother for acting in an 'uppity'/assertive way in the local department store. Her grandmother told her that her behaviour might trigger the local Klu Klux Klan (KKK) to attack their community in retaliation. She could not be free to act as an individual, taking her own risks, when her individual behaviour was going to be policed as if it were a transgression by the whole community. In a context of racial oppression or enmity, it falls to the elders of the whole community to contain and sanction any behaviours that could not be tolerated by the dominant white group, adding layers of stress and distress to the tasks of parenting.

Ta-Nehisi Coates (2015, p. 71), in an extended letter to his son, warns him to be careful because of this indivisibility from his community, saying,

> You are a black boy, and you must be responsible for your body in a way that other boys cannot know. Indeed, you must be responsible for the worst actions of other black bodies, which, somehow, will always be assigned to you. And you must be responsible for the bodies of the powerful – the policeman who cracks you with a nightstick will quickly find his excuse in your furtive movements.

Conversely, DiAngelo (2011, p. 59) refers to whiteness as

> an unracialized identity or location, which functions as a kind of blindness; an inability to think about Whiteness as an identity or as a 'state' of being that would or could have an impact on one's life. In this position, Whiteness is not recognized or named by white people, and a universal reference point is assumed. *White people are just people.*

> *[My emphasis]*

So when faced with conflict around race, white people may experience themselves as 'fragile' when they are subsumed back into their group as may happen when a patient specifically asks to see a black counselor, or 'assumes' that a white therapist shares racist views or holds their position in the hierarchy of an organisation as a result of privilege rather than hard work.

When white people are suddenly reminded that they belong to this wider group and that from the perspective of a person of colour, that group is potentially hostile, they cross into an unfamiliar space. As therapists we may lack the agility to move between being seen as an individual and a skilled helper at one moment and as a representative of an oppressive group at another.

The resurgence of more overtly racist themes in political life has led black people to question whether, when push comes to shove, they can rely on individual white people at all, however liberal they say they are. Suspicion may lead individual white therapists to advertise their political correctness, 'virtue signalling' to the point of overplaying their hands. Yankah (2017, p. 1) writes about the importance of trust as a bedrock of personal friendship and comments on how white people, 'relying on everyday decency as a shield, are befuddled at the chill that now separates them from black people in their offices and social circles'. He writes, in an article questioning whether 'my children [can] be friends with white people' that 'even a child's joy is not immune to this ominous political period'. And nor of course is the therapeutic alliance immune to these shifts in political discourse.

Reciprocal roles are at the heart of 'racism'

Whiteness scholars cited in DiAngelo (2011, p. 56) define racism as the economic and cultural practices, both overt and covert, that *systematise and perpetuate* the unequal distribution of resource and privilege between white people and people from BAME groups so that white people are the heirs to structural privilege, even when they don't want to be and even if they feel themselves to be oppressed and economically disadvantaged within their own communities. The reciprocal roles that characterise racism, including superiority and contempt, anger and defeatedness, may be complementary but they are one-way:

> Racism is not fluid in the U.S.; it does not flow back and forth, one day benefiting whites and another day (or even era) benefiting people of color. The direction of power between whites and people of color is historic, traditional, normalized, and deeply embedded in the fabric of U.S. society.
>
> *(DiAngelo, 2011, p. 56)*

Understanding that there is no such thing as 'reverse racism' allows us to see the resurgence of resentment that white working people are expressing in relation to globalisation and economic downturn, as a function of class rather than of race, but to see how racism provides a phoney explanation. An angry white identity can 'seem to align their [white working-class people's] interests with those of the rich and dominant, offering them a false sense of social status and a safe set of scapegoats for their grievances' (Morrison, cited in Haas, 2017, p. 1). The yearning to turn the clocks back to a more 'secure' age in both UK and US working-class culture (Vance, 2016) was to a time when white people could always feel secure in looking down on black people and now feel entitled to seek the restoration of this situation in response to economic threat and dispossession; they may bring these beliefs, attitudes and targets into therapy with them and therapists will have to find a way of responding without collusion.

It is difficult to challenge seams of racism once they have been legitimised by public officials, political leaders and social media. There can be no doubt that racial lines have been redrawn in recent elections and referenda in order to divide and rule, creating sleights of hand that divert attention from complex social problems requiring collective and long-term solutions. Examples of this might include the Stephen Lawrence case and subsequent Macpherson report in 1999, or the detailed review of the death of David 'Rocky' Bennett in 2004. These were regarded as breakthrough reports at the time because they framed problems in the criminal justice system and mental health services respectively as *institutional* racism and not simply as failed casework. Conversely the elevation of one black person to the presidency or the royal family, while hugely important symbolically, seems to herald a new tolerance but it has proved to be illusory and is easily reversed, often without disturbing these dynamics.

Movements of large numbers of refugees fleeing wars and destitution have challenged erstwhile homogenous communities, exacerbating tensions and creating the illusion of there not being enough to go around. But while these displaced individuals float ashore in makeshift boats to reach a supposedly safe haven, rich people deposit their surplus assets on offshore islands, sucking out the resources that would make true humanitarian aid possible.

Facts and figures

Facts and figures act as a brake on white people, including those in the helping professions, who might otherwise be tempted to downplay racial privilege. Given this knee-jerk reaction to deny or deflect, it is important that our services, and our profession, is informed and actively engaged in monitoring equality of access to training, methods of supporting people from BAME backgrounds in their professional journeys and assuring the quality and relevance of curricula. Research should identify and take ethnicity fully into account when developing models for understanding mental distress but also when evaluating intervention.

Monitoring the effects of hidden discrimination is also a critical function of government and of professional bodies, including our own. The government's Racial Disparity Audit in 2017, for example, shows that black and Asian families in the UK are more likely to be poor and that their poverty is more likely to be long-standing when compared to white families. Research shows that 1 in 4 children in Asian families live in persistent poverty, 1 in 5 children in black families and 1 in 10 children in white families, and that 1 in 25 people from a white British background are unemployed as opposed to 1 in 10 adults from a BAME background. Pakistani and Bangladeshi workers have the lowest hourly pay rate when compared with other groups. Black men are 3.5 times more likely to be arrested than white men and are then more likely to be held in custody. Average first-time custodial sentences are 18 months for white British people, 24 months for black people and 25 months for Asian people.

Dyer (2017), in discussing these findings, points to the over-representation of black people 'wherever there is exclusion or detention in this society' (p. 1) and argues that the notion of the black person as 'big, black and dangerous' still holds sway in institutional service settings. She speaks to racial disadvantage not only as a cause of heightened risk in relation to mental illness, but as a source of unequal treatment *within* mental health services. Moving from rural to urban environments and migration have been pinpointed as critical triggers in journeys that result in mental distress and these affect black communities disproportionately. Black women have a raised incidence of anxiety and depression while black men have a tenfold risk of being diagnosed with a psychotic disorder when compared with their white peers. A recent US study by Singhal et al. (2016) suggests that discrimination even creeps into areas of practice that would seem, on the surface, to present few grounds for bias including the routine prescription of pain relief in emergency departments.

The same audit reveals that black people are under-represented at senior levels of management in health and social care professions even though most individual managers in the health and social care sector would be at pains to emphasise the inclusive nature of their organisations and their sensitivity to treating people who use their services in equal and culturally appropriate ways. Independent audits also shows that black people are *less* likely to be receiving treatment and that even where they have been able to access talking therapies, these do not necessarily meet their needs because as Dyer (2017) comments, 'How can we have the same outcomes when we're not having the same experiences' (pp. 2–3). She argues that success cannot be assumed until black people find they can access services earlier in the trajectory of their mental illness, until black communities are better served by mental health services and until fewer black people die in custody (p. 3). Therapists need to be properly informed about these differential experiences and the ways in which they lead to mental distress, delay appropriate recognition of need and distort the ways in which services are commissioned and delivered.

Bringing awareness of racism into the consulting room

The challenge, as a white therapist, is to be both authentic and supportive of BAME colleagues and patients but that is not an aspiration that is easily achieved. This leaves awkward questions to do what Yankah describes as 'the reaching out, the moderating, the accommodating' (2017, p. 4): 'Does our professional training provide sufficient opportunities for challenge and dialogue?' 'How can we learn these skills without risking offence if it goes wrong?' 'Does the responsibility for making these conversations happen rest disproportionately on the shoulders of colleagues from black and minority ethnic backgrounds?' Are those of us who are white, willing to share what Yankah (2017) calls 'the risks required by strength and decency?' (p. 5).

One way of becoming more alert to internalised as well as external racism is to construct a reflective timeline of one's own journey and/or a journal of day-to-day experiences describing how race is brought into acknowledgement, what this elicits and how it was handled by the parties involved. Reading about the experiences of black people and/or about individuals and movements that challenge the status quo can also be included and provide reflective tools. The purpose of this is not to judge or blame, or to parade 'political correctness' by 'virtue signaling' but to think and to learn.

The opening paragraphs of my Personal Race Awareness Journal (PRAJ) reads like this:

> Growing up in the 1950s and 1960s, much of my experience reflects current understandings of racial dynamics – of denial, of white detachment and 'fragility' (Di Angelo, 2011). Although as a teenager I was interested in, and energised by, the American civil rights movement and an embryonic supporter of the anti-apartheid movement, I could not see the racial dynamics closer to home. I attended a girls' school in the inner city of Bristol but, until I was in my last year, our school was entirely white; the word segregated would not have been out of place but it wasn't ever used. The filtering that had been done to create this island in the inner city had been via the much disputed 11 plus examination, based as it was on notions of IQ as a 'culture free' and valid sorting mechanism. We were led to believe we operated in a fair meritocracy.
>
> Our school was described as a 'good' school, as if the absence of people from other cultures added to, rather than detracted from, our educational experience. As DiAngelo (2011) asserts:
>
>> The quality of white space being in large part measured via the absence of people of color (and blacks in particular) is a profound message indeed, one that is deeply internalised and reinforced daily through normalised discourses about good schools and neighborhoods. This dynamic of gain rather than loss via racial segregation may be the most profound aspect of white racial socialisation of all. Yet, while discourses about what makes a space good are tacitly understood as racially coded, this coding is explicitly denied.
>
> Moreover, 'my' school had been endowed by a slave owner, whose name has since become synonymous with the shadow side of Bristol's mercantile history that was founded in, and flourished on, the back of the slave trade and its offshoots in sugar and tobacco. The origins of his money and its

journey down the generations, capitalising various institutions within the city, was like a river watering a fertile plain, and was celebrated uncritically. Each year we marched to the city's cathedral to commemorate this founding father wearing, for obscure reasons, a bronze chrysanthemum, despite the obvious disconnect between the school's aspirations and its original endowment. I have dined out on the absurdity of this annual outing for many years. As psychotherapists we decry an unexamined life, and we need also to decry unexamined and unaccountable flows of wealth.

Nevertheless, while denouncing racism as an idealistic teenager, I was nonetheless beginning a journey as a white person, awakened through feminism to assert my entitlement to be treated as an equal to white men, while ignorant of the extent to which I had already benefitted, and would continue to benefit, from the unequal distribution of wealth and social capital that accrues to me as a white person. My sense of self was also shaped by gender and class and these intersecting identities were more conscious and seemed more salient but behind them all, as presaged by my education, the film of white privilege ran quietly in the background. Moreover of course this film also flickers through my inner life leaving images that I would prefer to rub out, but that add a sepia wash to the way I think and feel.

This process of reading and journaling led me to see how the ideology of meritocracy, which was explicitly espoused within my family and throughout my education and that remains deeply ingrained in public discourse, served as a justification for the unfair and unequal outcomes that might otherwise have been held up as evidence of class and race-based privilege.

Reaching for difficult but authentic connections

Our patients do not come to therapy to be on the receiving end of a polemic or of a confession, but they do deserve to meet with therapists who are informed about the ways in which racism operates in society and its institutions, including its mental health services. They also need to have confidence that their therapist will have thought carefully about these issues for themselves, reflecting on how they learned about race as a site of discrimination and on how they have engaged with the issues in their own lives, relationships and communities. Curiosity about the reverberations of racialised public discourse and political hostility, for them and for their communities and how racial difference is represented in a person's inner world and relationships, including the therapeutic relationship, may help both therapist and patient to open up painful areas of silence.

The process of denigrating 'others' is so ubiquitous that we will be working with some people whose spirits have been broken by it; we have to invite our patients to speak of the deep and corrosive hurts of racism and work with them respectfully when they trust us by doing so. Without clear signals that racism can and should be part of the therapeutic conversation, our patients may otherwise 'read' silence as the price of help and our BAME colleagues, on encountering reticence, mistake it for indifference.

Note

1 Definitions of race are contentious given that there are no clear biological boundaries, only political and social ones. For a detailed discussion of these issues and of what is meant by the term racism see Msebele and Brown (2011).

Bibliography

Angelou, M. (1985). *Gather together in my name*. London: Penguin Random House.

Blofeld, J. (2004). Independent inquiry into the death of David (Rocky) Bennett. https://prezi.com/7khgeuwqwsff/the-david-bennett-inquiry (Accessed 15/01/18).

British Psychological Society. (2018). BPS welcomes new personality disorders consensus statement. *BPS News*. www.bps.org.uk/news-and-policy/bps-welcomes-new-personality-disorders-consensus-statement (Accessed 27/03/18).

Cabinet Office. (2017). Race disparity audit: Summary of the findings. www.ethnicity-facts-figures.service.gov.uk (Accessed 27/03/18).

Coates, T-N. (2015). *Between the world and me*. New York: Spiegel & Grau.

de Beauvoir, S. (1949). *The second sex*. London: Penguin Random House.

DiAngelo, R. (2011). White fragility international. *Journal of Critical Pedagogy*, 3(3) 54–70.

Dyer, J. (2017). Talking about race and mental health is everyone's business. *Guardian*, 8 November. www.theguardian.com/society/2017/nov/08/jacqui-dyer-race-mental-health-act-black-people-detentions-inequality (Accessed 15/01/18).

Frankenberg, R. (1993). *The social construction of whiteness: White women, race matters*. London: Routledge.

Haas, L. (2017). *The origin of others* by Toni Morrison – review: The language of race and racism. *Guardian*, 18 October.

Karpf, A. (2017). How best to silence the powerless? Play the victim. *Guardian*, 4 December.

Laity, P. (2017). It's a novel about race and class and poverty: Review of Celeste Ng's novel, *Little fires everywhere*. *Guardian*, 4 November.

Langston Hughes, J. M. (1926). www.brainyquote.com/quotes/langston_hughes_752809 (Accessed 15/01/18).

Macpherson, W. (1999). The Stephen Lawrence inquiry. www.gov.uk/government/uploads/system/uploads/attachment_data/file/277111/4262.pdf (Accessed 15/01/18).

Malik, K. (2018). In British education, the central issue is class, not ethnicity. Guardian, 7 January. www.theguardian.com/commentisfree/2018/jan/07/british-education-failure-white-working-class (Accessed 17/01/18).

Msebele, N. & Brown, H. (2011). Racism in the consulting room: myth or reality? *Psychoanalytic Review*, 98(4), 451–492.

Obama, B. (2008). *Dreams of my father*. London: Cannongate.

Ryde, J. (2009). *Being white in the helping professions: Developing effective intercultural awareness*. London: Jessica Kingsley Publishers.

Singhal, A. Tien, Y. & Hsia, R. (2016). Prescriptions at emergency department visits for conditions commonly associated with prescription drug abuse. *PLOS*, August 8. https://doi.org/10.1371/journal.pone.0159224.

Sliwa, M. (2017). Understanding the relationship between poverty and white privilege. https://goodmenproject.com/featured-content/understanding-relationship-poverty-white-privilege-wcz (Accessed 15/01/18).

Vance, J. D. (2016). *Hillbilly elegy*. London: William Collins.

Yankah, E. (2017). Can my children be friends with white people? *New York Times*, 11 November. www.nytimes.com/2017/11/11/opinion/sunday/interracial-friendship-donald-trump.html (Accessed 11/12/17).

16

HOW TO RELATE

The Italian dilemma – trust and cooperation make the world go around, but do we trust and can we cooperate?

Cristina Fiorani and Marisa Poggioli

Introduction

In this chapter we discuss the relational 'dance' we are invited to join or reject in Italy. We write as practising clinical psychologists and CAT therapists and also as Italians with our differing experiences of growing up, working and living in Italy. We draw on CAT concepts about human development to think about Italian societal reciprocal roles and their effects on the way patients and staff in the Italian public health system relate. We will also reflect on our own experiences as Italian citizens, one of us growing up in northern Italy and the other in both Italy and the UK, attempting to link the personal with the political in our discussion about the Italian family and the Italian state and the relationship of both to the Catholic Church.

We interviewed 30 Italian people from different parts of Italy and diverse social backgrounds including a small number of patients from the north. We know this small sample does not represent the whole of Italy: as we hope to show, 'Italy' is an idea it is impossible to generalise about!

Fundamental to CAT, as we are social beings born into relationship with others, the interpersonal within a particular time and context comes first and is reflected in our inner lives or subjective experience – the ways in which we relate to ourselves. CAT theory and practice are informed by the Bakhtinian understanding that language, human relationships and consciousness are dialogic (Leiman, 1995): consciousness as a process develops and operates at the interface between self and others and higher orders such as culture. The 'self' is formed and maintained through relating and communicating with others, and through the internalisation of shared meanings. The self is a process continuously transformed through the experience of differing patterns of relating or 'dances', between self and other. This occurs throughout the lifespan within the context of a culture and a period of history. We think we speak and act in the world always in relation to a visible or invisible other. We are always in dialogue with someone or something, real or imaginary. The range of dialogues and relationships we encounter throughout the lifespan is either constrained or opened by the families and societies we are born into and live in.

We are also in a life-long dialogue or relationship with culture. Tylor (1871, cited in Helman 1984) stated that culture is 'that complex whole which includes knowledge, belief, art, morals, law, custom and any other capabilities and habits acquired by man as a member of society' (p. 3). Another way of thinking about culture is as a set of guidelines that individuals inherit as members of a particular society; culture tells us how to behave, how to view the world, how to experience it emotionally, how to relate to others (Helman, 1984).

Our belief is that cultures and individuals are shaped by their habitat, by the history of the people and the events taking place around them and their shared cultural myths. Just as a child who has been subjected to a hostile caretaker tends to continue to practice strategies that were necessary for survival even if these are no longer useful, so groups and societies continue to use strategies that were once useful for survival but that now compromise societies' capacity for successfully living together for the common good.

A brief introduction to Italy, Italian history and culture from a cognitive analytic perspective

Prior to the nineteenth century when the Italian peninsula and Sicily underwent a process of unification under Garibaldi, the area now known as Italia or Italy had been fragmented since the Roman Empire, its history centuries of battles, domination and invasions. However political 'unification' did not lead to cultural or even economic unification. Even today some regions are independent economically. Notably Alto Adige and Val D'Aosta both in the north have their own German and French identities, and do not see themselves as Italian. Trentino alto Adige is an autonomous region in the eastern part of northern Italy with a special statute, where German is the official language. The Valle D'Aosta located in the northwest is another autonomous region with a special statute, a strong French cultural influence and French as the official language.

Geography and climate have a strong influence on Italian history and politics: The Apennines divide west from east, with vast cultural differences between north and south. Government by many foreigner invaders has given a different flavour to different regions. To name a few, Greeks settlers established themselves in Sicily and in other parts of the southern mainland. In Calabria, the name of the Calabrian Mafia 'Ndrangheta' is thought to be of Greek origin. In Sicily, there were also Arab and Berber influences, which also touched parts of Puglia. There was also a century of Norman rule, the Spanish also ruled there and there are still Albanian communities in Sicily to this day. The Albanian language has been preserved in the towns populated by these immigrants who were escaping the expansion of the

Ottoman Empire in the fifteenth century. The language they speak to this day bears the marks of fifteenth-century grammar and diction. The north of Italy was invaded by people of Germanic stock, the Goths and the Lombards who changed the ethnic stock of northern Italy and there was Austrian rule in the eighteenth century. Italians are an ethnically varied people. The region where we live used to be ruled by Maria Luigia of Austria who was Napoleon's second wife, as we illustrate in Figure 16.1.

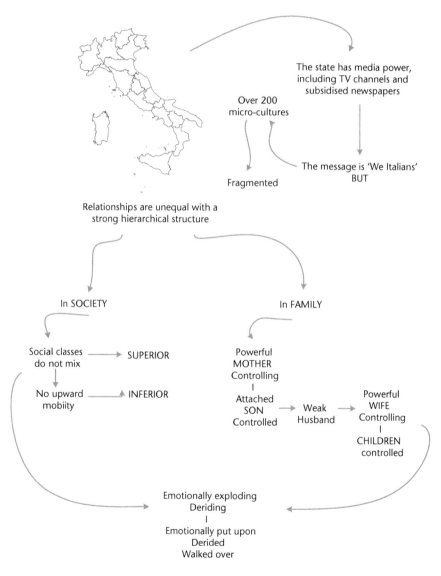

FIGURE 16.1 Family and socio-political culture.

What is true of Bologna is unlikely to be true of Sicily but also what is true in a small village may not be true of village 30 kilometres away. It is as if Italy is made up of up to 200 little countries, each with their own fictions and identities and local dialect (Hooper, 2016). However the regional dialects are in the process of dying out as many younger Italians move to the cities. This emptying out of the rural areas and the expansion of the cities is a relatively recent phenomenon, which is changing the way some Italians feel and think about themselves. Italian state-run television has both influenced the way people speak and contributed to the increasing assumption of a national rather than a regional identity.

The relational 'dance' we are invited to join in Italy has been choreographed by this history of trauma, fragmentation and domination by foreign powers. There were undoubtedly powerful collective emotional responses to the loss of land, language, culture and spiritual traditions. There has always been a high degree of inequality in the distribution of wealth and power in Italy and it is primarily to the family that people turn to for support, and identity. The primacy of the family has become Italy's trap or 'snag'. A 'snag' in CAT terminology is when our attempts to change some aspect of our lives are thwarted by those around us, usually our families, and as adults that can become an unconscious form of self-sabotage. Trauma, loss and inequality can create psychological injuries that are held collectively as well as personally; the effects transmitted over generations. For many Italians the family is their primary source of social belonging, but it can also be a deeply conservative institution that makes change for many individuals hazardous if not impossible.

The commedia dell'arte

A constant throughout Italian culture for centuries has been the 'commedia dell'arte', a form of satirical comedy theatre with grotesque, farcical characters. In the past it was often performed by travelling theatre troupes, with actors empowered through improvisation with the audience, while being entertained with some familiar scenes, often not knowing what was coming next. The tradition dates back to the fourteenth century as a response to and a need to rebel against authority and those in power. It is borne out of tragedy, desperation, a response to moral and physical violence as well as from hunger and hardship and the struggle for survival. Bakhtin (1984) saw the carnival tradition of parody and irreverence to authority as a vital counterbalance to totalising authoritarian discourses: 'Laughter purifies from dogmatism, from the intolerant and the petrified; it liberates from fanaticism and pedantry, from fear and intimidation, from didacticism' (p. 123). Not surprisingly the church opposed the subversive 'commedia dell'arte' as it risked destabilising conservative societal values upheld by the church authorities. The enduring popularity of this art form in Italy has perhaps been due to centuries of invasion, domination by foreign powers, authoritarian rule as well as the power of the Roman Catholic Church. It is a tradition continued in the work of the Nobel prize-winning playwright, Dario Fo, who combined political critique with carnivalesque comedy and satire. Figures 16.2, 16.3 and 16.4 illustrate how common

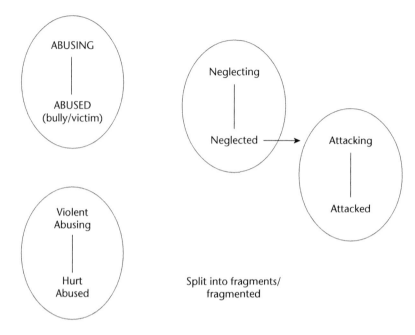

FIGURE 16.2 Frequent family relational patterns.

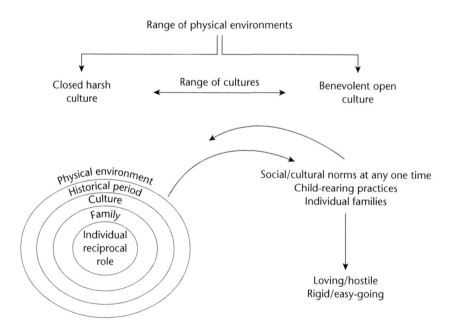

FIGURE 16.3 Physical and cultural context.

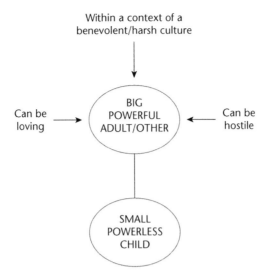

FIGURE 16.4 What Italians learn to expect.

familial reciprocal roles in Italy develop from its physical and cultural environment and what people learn to expect.

We now explain who we are and the influences that shaped us, our reasons for becoming psychologists and writing this chapter. From discussion with our 30 interviewees, we describe reciprocal roles found in the health care system in a small Italian town in Italy and we describe, link and map how the Italian culture has shaped the politics of a mental health service.

Cristina's story

I was born in 1959 in a provincial town in the north of Italy. As I grew up I was distantly aware of the echoes of Milan and the political infighting that went on there. Milan was only 70 kilometres away, but we were worlds apart, we were the ones on 'the other side of the river Po'.

In the 1960s and 1970s my family aspired to the lifestyle of the 'Borghesia' (bourgeoisie), thus, I attended the Liceo Scientifico and helped out in the parish. Like any good, young middle-class girl in the north of Italy I volunteered, aiding the poor and earthquake victims. As a young woman, the 1960s, with the student protests, rebellion and demands for civil rights were behind us, but the influence of that decade lingered so that I was idealistic and loved the singers who sang about the great social themes; they spoke of a way where values could change the world. I dreamt of Bob Dylan, of challenging the system, of De Andre, an important Genovese singer whose songs spoke of people on the margins of society, of rebels and prostitutes. His songs were also poetry, quoted in school books and in literature:

he challenged dominant bourgeois conventions and the reality of Italian society. He sang, 'Nothing comes from gold, but flowers are born out of compost'. I remember distant echoes of 'the years of lead', a name given to the period from 1970 to 1980 when an extreme political dialectic between left and right took hold, causing terrorism and violence. The name 'the lead years' comes from a 1981 film by the German director Margarethe von Trotta, who portrays an analogous experience in Germany describing the wider context of terrorism. In the 1970s we were also frightened by the threat of nuclear war between the United States and the Soviet Union as well as terrorism; it seemed as if we were one step away from an apocalypse.

Fondly, in the midst of this I remember peaceful Sundays riding a bicycle, a sign of austerity due to the 'oil crisis' of 1973 after the 'Yom Kippur' Israeli Arab war. So even though we lived with fears of war and terrorism, there were also hopes for a cleaner and less polluted world with no petrol fumes.

There was a lot of love in my family and my parents valued honesty and freedom. My experiences made me want to understand our society and its effect on people and I wanted to contribute towards social improvement. In 1978 (the same year Aldo Moro the prime minister was abducted and murdered by the 'Red Brigades'), Franco Basaglia, a radical psychiatrist influenced by social psychiatry, was instrumental in legislation, known as the 'Basaglia Law', which forever closed our mental hospitals. Basaglia maintained that traditional psychiatry upheld a biological model of organic disease, neglecting the social origins of mental distress. His social focus on the origins of distress meant he became involved in politics, trying to create a better society. However, he was widely criticised for not planning the next step and what happened after the closure. When the state delegated responsibility for care provision to regions, many different solutions were implemented in an idiosyncratic way. There were no national guidelines and although some regions forged ahead and created adequate structures, unfortunately many did not. One result was the establishment of the psychiatric services where I now work.

My work seemed like a vocation, a mission. Notions of money and career seemed unimportant both for myself and my colleagues. This united us and kept us in contact with the people who used our services. We developed service models geared for change. We believed that it was possible to make the world a better place; that we could help improve the quality of life for our clients and enable people to have better relationships. We thought that this formula would be a winning card, better than medication. Our egalitarian model would increase people's happiness. To this day I continue to believe that change for the better is possible.

However, gradually an increasing indifference to or even tolerance of corruption showed in various sections of Italian society. Several Italian politicians are involved in corrupt practices with the tacit acceptance of the political parties themselves; a complex system evolved between politicians, private firms, public entities and at times, the mafia.

Our experience of reciprocal roles in the state-run mental health system emerges from our position as clinicians with ethical responsibilities but little power, contrasting with managers who are more independent, earn a lot more money but are too often unaccountable. Within the clinical parts of the service there is a hierarchical system, which defines very precisely the competences, position, responsibilities, salary and the decisional power of any individual clinician independent of one's level of training.

However, in the Italian state-run health system, as in any Italian public sector job, it is extremely difficult to be sacked. There are no financial or personal rewards for being a conscientious clinician with good outcomes, which promotes variable levels of personal motivation and clinical standards. Team meetings are usually concerned with line management and organisational issues, unbothered by clinical effectiveness or variable outcomes between different clinicians. Supervision of clinical work is arranged privately, if the clinician is so motivated, often with no formal requirement to do so.

For clinicians, as there is no support or encouragement to achieve high standards of clinical practice, we are left with a choice of either do the minimum possible, knowing that we will at least get paid for it, or work hard and do one's best but feel neither recognised nor rewarded (see Figure 16.5).

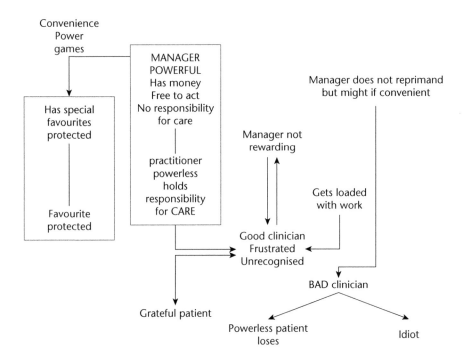

FIGURE 16.5 Typical manager–staff working alliance.

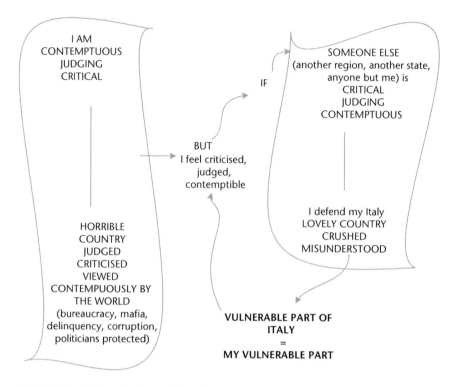

FIGURE 16.6   Cristina's relationship to Italy.

Marisa's story

I was born in London in 1950 and travelled with my family to Brazil when I was 3 years old, where I lived until age 8. I then lived in London and Italy for two years but my family settled in London when I was 10, where I grew up, left home, had an education and worked. I stayed in London until I was 44 years old, when I moved to Italy. I have, however, continued to return to the UK to work periodically, so that for the past 23 years I have had a foot firmly in two countries. Sometimes I have felt split and fragmented, sometimes integrated: two countries, two identities, two very different ways of relating to other people and to the state (Figure 16.7).

From an early age I appreciated that there were different realities, that different cultures make one a different person, which I experienced at a visceral and emotional level, only in later life finding the ways to express it all in words. I always knew I could contribute a different point of view but did not always see the advantages when I wanted so much to belong to the group. Now I accept being different and value it. In Italy, I am the same but also a different Marisa than I am in the UK because of the way people respond to me and I respond back in return and of course, because of my expectations of how they will respond.

London seemed to me the cultural centre of the world. Even though my father had an English education he was very much an Italian when it came to his daughter leaving home. I, however, wanted to get out there and live my life and escape my father's control and my mother's depression; thinking myself way above the unhappy repressions of my parents' marriage. I knew without doubt that I was equal to men; I was a woman born in the era of feminism.

I was 17 in the 'Summer of Love' – we would save the planet and there would be love, not war, I even wore the badge. I went on CND marches and listened to Beatles songs, I dreamed of going to San Francisco wearing flowers in my hair. I lived in the post-war world where it was easy to get a job and I promptly did so at the age of 18. I paid my own rent for a bedsit in Notting Hill (in those days a working-class area of London), it was my castle.

I 'knew' science ruled over religion, having long ago stopped listening to the nuns. I believed that there would be a triumph of 'truth' and that humanity would live in peace, tranquility and equilibrium with the other creatures we share this planet with. When the Americans landed on the moon I was in Paris on my way to India. Like many of my generation I read Camus, Tolkien, Tolstoy, Dostoevsky, Herman Hesse, Simone de Beauvoir and Jean Genet because I felt the nuns would have greatly disapproved. Interestingly, most of the authors I read were men.

By the age of 27 I had a mortgage. I returned to education at the age of 32. Mine was a generation that was fortunate enough to have free university and a maintenance grant. I became a psychologist believing my profession would be about truth and unearthing the causes of distress. I thought that I would enable people to solve their problems and live a better life. 'Know thyself' and 'to thine own self be true' was the key, I thought, to creating a better world, understanding the causes of violence and distress and breaking the cycle so that people could live in peace.

In the UK, I now find myself as if back in a world that I remember being positioned at university as 'the past'. A past where individuals were blamed for problems outside their own control and even more so for their reaction to them. Some half-forgotten lectures on World War I remain salient: In the UK, the entrenched class system determined how a soldier's experience of 'shell shock' would be treated and responded to. Common soldiers or working-class men were diagnosed with 'hysteria' and often prosecuted for malingering whereas officers (made up of men from the upper middle classes), were diagnosed with 'neurasthenia' and given leave from active service. Shell-shocked individuals (mostly of the working class) were also thought to have been degenerates.

It is as if the thinking behind the *Beveridge Report* that led to the 'welfare state' and the NHS has gone into reverse. As young adults we believed that the NHS provision of free medical treatment to all was both necessary and right and psychology would do the same for our mental health.

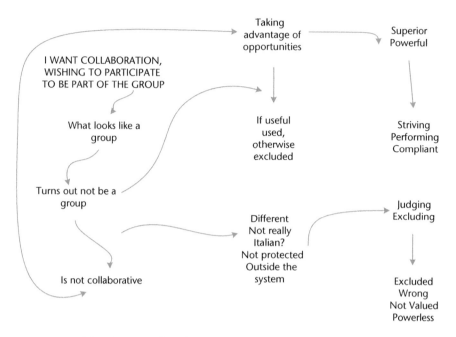

FIGURE 16.7 Marisa's sense of a culturally dual self.

As Josephine Ahmadi refers to in Chapter 6 of this volume, Joanna Moncrieff (2009), a cogent critic of biological psychiatry, warns of the dangers of adopting a disease-centred model in which the individual's problems are divorced from their social context, more than 40 years after Basalgia did the same in Italy. It seems as if people with mental health 'issues' are treated as 'Children of a Lesser God'. That they might be poor, traumatised, neglected and have few opportunities in life is no longer considered. Nor is the fact that such disadvantages might be accumulated over a lifetime or generations. Joanna Ryan (2017) writes that 'the hard-won achievements of the welfare state are being cut back and fragmented. The people are increasingly blamed for their condition, and increasingly we blame patients [for being] unmotivated if they do not find a solution to their problems' (p. 7). As Ryan points out, class bias permeates treatment offered to the majority of NHS patients as CBT that focuses on people's 'diagnosis' rather than their subjective experience of mental distress, their life histories and society's inequalities. CBT makes it easier to forget how interconnected we all are by making us all uniquely responsible for our own lives.

> [H]uman beings seem to be invested with a developed capacity to mould their bodily experiences to the norms of their cultures, they learn the scripts about what kind of things should be happening to them as they fall ill and about the things they should do to feel better, and then they literally embody them.
>
> *(Davies, 2013, p. 238)*

CAT, on the other hand, makes it explicit that we are shaped by our interpersonal and social environment, we are all interrelated; it offers a respectful whole-person, trans-diagnostic approach.

The most important ideal that remained with me to this day is that it is still possible to have a state that is for the benefit of all and that we can find solutions for a happier world, although I am sad when humans behave rapaciously, greedily using all the planet has to offer without respect for other species, or for our own tomorrow.

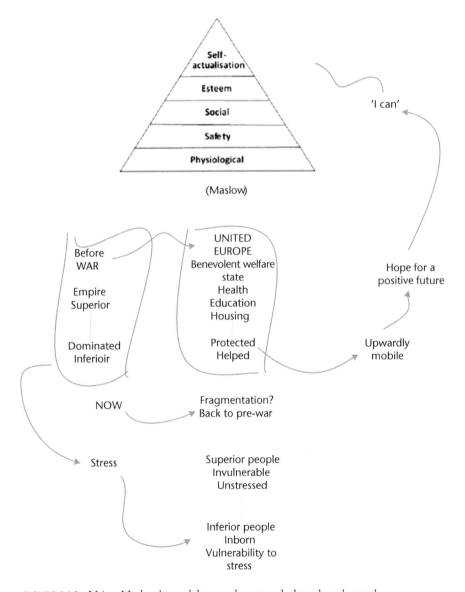

FIGURE 16.8 Using Maslow's model to see how psychology has changed.

I also notice the attack on free speech, how Voltaire's 'I might not agree with what you say but I will none the less defend your right to say it' has been replaced by 'what you say is insulting and offensive and I will attack you for it'.

Because I have lived and still do live in two counties, I have usually worked as a locum, which has brought its own difficulties when working in different paradigms, but working transdiagnostically has also set me free (Figure 16.8).

The Italian family

The concept of 'amoral families' is often used to describe the strong attachment Italians have to the idea of family, which in practice means overprotective maternal and nearly absent paternal roles. Giovanni Levi (2017) describes how in predominately Protestant countries power emanates directly from God, whereas Catholicism states that because humans are sinners, God had no role in human-devised institutions. 'Free will' meant that we could create whatever government we wanted but all would be imperfect, requiring the Church to mediate between humans and God and lead humans to salvation.

Levi (2017) argues that Italians are cut off from their past and their history; that although today Italy appears to be a secular nation where religion seems to be no longer particularly important, centuries of cohabitation between the State and the Church have created a weakened political system with a proliferation of feeble and disrespected rules and laws. In the UK we have common law and we can do whatever we like unless it is expressly forbidden; in Italy, as in the rest of Europe, there is civil law. A citizen can only do something if it is something the law expressly permits. In practice this means that in the UK many people observe the few community rules, whereas in Italy many make every effort to break a plethora of conflicting rules as in Italy unregulated is paramount to illegal. The State, like the Church, has become an institution that everyone has the right and 'almost a duty' to defraud.

This is a major unresolved Italian problem. Levi describes a kind of anarchism, evolved with suspicion of public institutions and a contractual idea of religion veering between sin and forgiveness, 'between the pardoner and the pardoned' and the weakness of the sinner. I have noticed that this also applies to the relationship Italians have with the tax man, as mapped out in Figure 16.9.

An image of Italy has taken shape, a country that is simultaneously anarchic and unable to take collective decisions or complete projects. It is a nation that combines individual initiative with bureaucratic paralysis, corruption and infighting. Levi (2017) describes its lost interest in its own culture and the beauty that tourists flock to see, because it seeks a type of modernism devoid of culture, cut off from the past and with no vision of a future. Individual Italians try to live a good life, adapting and accepting corrupt dysfunctionality as normal. Mistrust is reinforced when people learn early in life from their families and immediate communities that they cannot rely on the state, which does not meet their needs, is not there equally for all and some have more 'rights' than others. The term 'Campanilismo 'describes

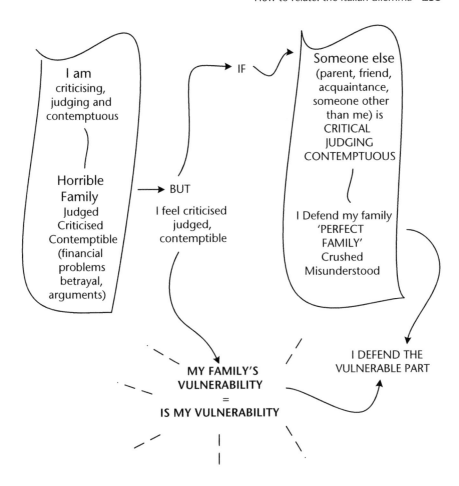

FIGURE 16.9 The Italian family.

how Italians relate to people from their village as an extended family but tend not to trust those beyond its borders.

Recent research suggests that our brains may develop differently depending on whether the person is reared in a culture based on trust or mistrust. Experiments on the persistence of social trust between people in a 'trust game' described by Sigman (2015, p. 95) seemed to show that,

> when players made confident, cooperative and altruistic decisions in the trust game the regions of the brain that codify dopaminergic circuits of pleasure are activated. In other words, our brains react similarly when exposed to something pleasurable (sex-chocolate-money) as when displaying solidarity.

Wilkinson and Picket (2009) write that higher levels of trust are found when there is equality between people: 'It is inequality that effects trust and not the other way round' (p. 53). Ulsner shows that 'people who trust are optimists with a strong sense of control over their lives' and 'trust cannot thrive in an unequal world' (Uslaner, 2002, cited in Wilkinson & Pickett, 2009, p. 53).

> The emotional makeup which prepares you to live in a society in which you have to fend for yourself, watch your back and fight for every bit you can get is very different from what is needed if you grow up in a society in which (to take the opposite extreme) you depend on empathy, reciprocity, and co-operation, and in which your security depends on maintaining good relationships with others.
>
> *(Wilkinson & Pickett, 2009, p. 205)*

Levi (2017) speaks as though everyone in Italy mistrusts everyone outside their own family. I do think, however, that it is possible to meet like-minded individuals in Italy, that there can be trust between people outside the family. However, I have found it hard and rare to find people to collaborate with. That is partly why the collaboration between Cristina and myself has been so valuable. Corruption, like trust, is reciprocal, as you cannot be corrupt all by yourself.

Ryle (1997) describes the association between gross neglect and abuse in childhood and often the resulting poor capacity for self-reflection, trust and cooperation in adult life. He describes self-damaging patterns of behaviour that are maintained even though they no longer serve to meet a person's needs. We have argued that in Italy habits picked up as a response to constant domination by foreign powers has had a similar effect on the fabric of Italian society. Hooper (2016) writes that it is remarkable that any nation should retain as part of its national anthem 'a verse that is so candid about its own humiliations; let alone one that declares that "we are not a people because we are divided"' (p. 29).

> Noi fummo da secoli
> Calpesti derisi
> Perche 'non siam popolo
> Perche' siam divisi
>
> [We were for centuries
> Downtrodden derided
> Because we are not a people
> Because we are divided]

In CAT, Ryle gave us the tools to look at ourselves within the context of a society. He created not just a therapy but also a theory about human development. We have used CAT language and concepts to describe the complex link between the social, the cultural and the inner subjectivity of the individual; the 'intra', how people relate to themselves and the 'inter', how people relate to others. CAT gives us the tools to think about the reciprocal roles imbedded in the cultural shared myths and stories in a society within a historical context. Writing this chapter has enabled us to think about Italy, to try to better understand the society we live in that is also part of us, so that we do not fall into the trap of criticising and devaluing out history and culture but rather trying to understand by standing back, describing what we see and what we have experienced and find possible ways forward.

Bibliography

Bakhtin, M. (1984). *Rabelais and his world*. H. Iswolsky (trans.). Bloomington, IN: Indiana University Press.

Barzini, L. (1968). *The Italians*. London: Penguin Books.

Beard, H. (2007). *An introductory workshop in cognitive analytic therapy*. Lecture, St Thomas Hospital, 23 November.

Cobb, R. & Davila, J. (2008). Internal working models and change. In J. H. Obegi & E. Berant (eds), *Clinical applications of adult attachment*. New York: Guilford.

Davies, J. (2013). *Cracked: Why psychiatry is doing more harm than good*. London: Icon Books.

Diamond, J. (2005). *Guns germs and steel*. London: Vintage.

Duggan C. (2008). *The force of destiny: A history of Italy since 1796*. London: Houghton Mifflin Harcourt.

Dunn, M. (2009). A cognitive analytic formulation. In P. Sturmey (ed.), *Clinical case formulation: Varieties of approaches*. Chichester, UK: Wiley.

Foot, J. (2010). *Italy's divided memory*. London: Palgrave Macmillan.

Harari, Y. (2017). *Homo Deus: A brief history of tomorrow*. London: Harvill Secker.

Helman, C. (1984). *Culture health and illness: An introduction for health professionals*. Oxford: Butterworth Heinemann.

Hooper, J. T. (2016). *The Italians*. London: Penguin.

Jeffries, S. (2017). A relational map of politics, the media and the public: Cognitive analytic therapy and contextual reformulation. *Clinical Psychology Forum*, May p. 293.

Leiman, M. (1995). Early development. In A. Ryle (ed.), *Cognitive analytic therapy developments in theory and practice*. Chichester, UK: Wiley.

Levi, G. (2017). Italy: Catholicism, power, democracy and the failure of the past. In Peter Furtado (ed.), *Histories of nations*. London: Thames & Hudson.

Luigi, B. (1997). *'Gli italiani' virtù e vizi di un popolo*. Venice: BUR Saggi.

Marco, G. (2010). *Storie d'Italia degli anni ottanta*. Marsilio: Mondadori Universita.

Mariano, S. (2015). *The secret life of the mind: How our brain thinks, feels and decides*. Glasgow: William Collins.

Moncrief, J. (2009). *The myth of the chemical cure: A critique of psychiatric drug treatment*. London: Palgrave Macmillan.

Moss, G. (2000). Shell shock as a social disease. *Journal of Contemporary History*, 35(1), 101–108.

Pollard, R., Hepple, J. & Elia, I. (2005). A dialogue about the dialogical approach in psychotherapy. *Reformulation: Journal of the Association of Cognitive Analytic Therapy*, Autumn, 18–24.

Putman, R., Leonardi, R. & Nonetti, R. (1993). *Making democracy work: Civic traditions in modern Italy*. Princeton, NJ: Princeton University Press.

Ryan, J. (2017). *Class and psychoanalysis: Landscapes of inequality*. Abingdon, UK: Routledge.

Ryle, A. (1997). *Cognitive analytic therapy and borderline personality disorder, the model and the method*. Chichester, UK: Wiley.

Ryle, A. & Kerr, I. (2002). *Introducing cognitive analytic therapy: Principles and practice*. Chichester, UK: Wiley.

Sigman, M. (2015). *The secret life of the mind: How the brain thinks feels and decides*. London: William Collins.

Variousfakis, Y. (2017). *Talking to my daughter about the economy: A brief history of capitalism*. London: Penguin Random House.

Warburten, N. (2011). *A little history of philosophy*. New Haven, CT: Yale University Press.

Wilkinson, R. & Pickett, K. (2009). *The spirit level: Why equality is better for everyone*. London: Penguin Books.

Winnicot, D. (1997). Further thoughts on babies as persons. In *The child, the family and the outside world*. Reading, MA: Addison-Wesley.

17

A SOCIAL JUSTICE FRAMEWORK FOR TRAINING IN COGNITIVE ANALYTIC THERAPY

Inequalities, power and politics in psychotherapy

Anne Benson

Introduction

Our health is influenced and determined by far more than our genetic makeup (Buck & Maguire, 2015). Poverty increases the risk of mental ill health and can be both a cause and consequence of mental health difficulties (Elliott, 2016). Socio-economic conditions also help to explain systematic inequalities in health between different groups, whether defined by class, gender, age, income, intellect or ethnicity (McManus et al., 2016). The most marked inequalities are frequently found at the intersection between these different characteristics.

Conceptually, issues of difference and diversity are crucially important because our relationships with difference and diversity, both individually and societally, generate and sustain inequalities. Fundamentally these inequalities are in relation to power. How these relationships operate and are governed both historically and currently is a matter of politics. If we are to address the harmful inequalities in our society then we cannot ignore power or politics.

Poverty, trauma, isolation, stigmatisation and prejudice produce environments that are extremely harmful to the mental health of individuals, families, communities and society. The interplay of factors that generate and sustain such environments is complex. These include the historical and current legacies of competing world economic forces and ideologies, the structures that govern decision-making, the distribution of wealth and policy development at both local and national levels, as well as the intrapersonal, interpersonal and intergroup dynamics of prejudice, desire, competition and envy. These factors influence and define who holds power and authority and how it is exercised and are, by their very nature, political.

It is not the purpose of this chapter to explore this complexity in all its depth, however it does contend that these issues are of considerable significance for psychotherapists and are inadequately addressed in many current psychotherapy training programmes (Lowe, 2014). The first part of the chapter offers an argument for the importance and potential significance of embedding explorations of inequality, power and politics in psychotherapy training. It then goes on to offer some thoughts as to why they are currently inadequately addressed. Finally, some ideas to redress the balance are proposed.

Why should inequalities and politics be part of psychotherapy training?

The purpose of psychotherapy is to help people make sense of their lives, to help them bring about changes to improve their mental well-being and in many instances the well-being of those around them. The focus is frequently on the individual. However, we know that the causes of mental distress do not originate solely with individual subjective experience and as feminists have long recognised, subjective experience is inseparable from political realities.

As identified in the introduction, there is an intricate interplay between issues of inequality, poverty, difference and mental health. If we are to be effective psychotherapists and promote the mental well-being of individuals and communities, we must engage with and not avoid these issues. Such engagement and understanding has the potential to bring many benefits. At the level of interaction between individual therapist and client it is important that we hold these issues in mind and be open to notice and explore how these factors play out in the process of therapy; the different roads each may have travelled to reach the therapy room and the impact of these. As a therapist, understanding oneself and one's clients within their own social and political context can help ensure that therapists are aware of individual and institutional biases and the potential impact of these. Non-recognition, avoidance or denial results in the maintenance of the status quo and therefore a perpetuation of inequalities. Such in-depth exploration is likely to increase therapists' ability to work effectively with people from a range of demographic and socio-economic backgrounds.

At a wider level, some knowledge and understanding of how inequalities develop, are maintained or redressed leaves psychotherapists individually and collectively better positioned to influence for positive change. It is possible to influence in many ways, for example in the recruitment of people on to training programmes, in the design of training programmes, considering issues of access to psychotherapy, developing networks with other resources in the community, becoming involved with professional or other political bodies to lobby and influence policy, being active on social media, supporting other groups or campaigns that share a common cause to address inequalities and improve mental well-being.

The professional bodies that govern psychotherapy training recognise the importance of such issues. The United Kingdom Council for Psychotherapy (UKCP) requires that all training should operate within an equality and diversity framework. They stipulate that this should include:

- a broad understanding of some of the key systemic hurdles affecting those, but not exclusively those, covered by the Equality Act 2010;
- contemporary and significant discriminatory discourses throughout training raising awareness of conscious and unconscious bias;
- equipping students and trainees to work with clients across the diversity spectrum;
- equipping students and trainees to engage with their own fear and prejudices and those of their clients re difference;
- arrangements to ensure that the students and trainees can identify and manage appropriately their personal involvement in and contribution to the processes of the psychotherapies that they practice.

(UKCP, 2012)

Significantly these requirements focus primarily on difference and diversity and less on the connection between these and the inequalities and exercise of power in our society.

The current situation

Despite these professional imperatives and the potential for increasing individual and societal well-being; conversations, teachings and explorations of inequalities and politics are limited in many psychotherapy training programmes. Lowe (2014) argued that 'when it comes to debating, considering matters across the boundaries of race, class culture, not academically but in a more personal way that our profession demands, we freeze up and become defensive' (p. xviii). He suggests that a vicious circle develops; the more we avoid talking about these things the more difficult they become to talk about and the avoidance and denial continues. This is expressed diagrammatically as a reciprocal role procedure in Figure 17.1.

I agree that there is little discussion about how issues of difference, power or politics affect us personally in psychotherapy training. I am not convinced we do it very well academically either. Gender and sexuality may get mentioned in relation to erotic transference issues. Differences in race or ethnicity between a client and therapist may get named as something theoretically relevant. However, socio-political understandings of how class, gender or cultural power imbalances function in society and their contribution to determining mental ill health are rarely explored. The inequities experienced by people with learning disabilities and the dynamics arising within the therapeutic relationship when working with learning disabled clients are usually absent from generic training. People training in the field of learning disability are required to gain experience working with those of average intelligence, however the requirement is not reciprocated. Working with people with learning disabilities thus becomes a specialist field, further restricting access to therapy for people with learning disabilities.

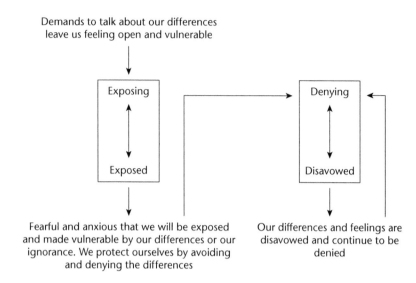

Demands to talk about our differences
leave us feeling open and vulnerable

Exposing

Exposed

Denying

Disavowed

Fearful and anxious that we will be exposed
and made vulnerable by our differences or our
ignorance. We protect ourselves by avoiding
and denying the differences

Our differences and feelings are
disavowed and continue to be
denied

FIGURE 17.1 When uniformity rules.

Diversity is frequently addressed in a tokenistic manner; often covered in a single lecture or possibly a module, sometimes as a choice between, for example, a session on gender and sexuality or one on race. Usually differences are addressed as unitary identities with the inevitable competition for space and hierarchies of oppression. Such approaches often serve to generate paralysis, dissatisfaction, division and disengagement with any thinking or learning. Such attitudes potentially originate from a number of sources, e.g. as a defence against the painful reality of our own prejudices, or an apolitical stance that views encounters as events between individuals without any account of societal power dynamics or historical context. Finally, I think they may be expressions of anger, hurt or shame emerging from personal experiences of being marginalised or excluded because of something that is less immediately visible than skin colour or gender, such as class, poverty or intellectual capability. These sources of inequality in our society rarely even get a token session in the curriculum.

Single-identity politics have been a source of strength, solidarity and change over many years for many people (e.g. women's movements, gay rights movements, anti-racist movements). Part of the power and influence of such movements was the recognition that what was previously seen as personal or individual was in fact social and systemic (Crenshaw, 1991).

However, it is frequently at the intersection between class, gender, race, intellectual ability or sexuality that the impacts of mental ill health are most acutely experienced. Given this, the teaching of single identity issues of difference in single sessions is an inappropriate approach to learning about inequalities as a psychotherapist. Teaching and learning within a social justice framework may provide a useful way forward and could provide an overarching frame for the whole training curriculum. This approach views people, organisations and communities in a socio-political context and explores privilege and marginalisation through the intra-personal to the global lens (Chung & Bemak, 2012). Such an approach enables the exploration of interdependencies, and points of tension and synergy at the intersections of identities. The possibilities offered by a social justice framework are explored later in this chapter.

Politics, class and poverty are rarely addressed at all, particularly at any societal or systemic level. Power may get a little airplay through an exploration of the power relationship between therapist and client. However, the socio-economic differences (or sometimes similarities) and associated power dynamics between the two are rarely spoken about or worked with. The structures of power in society, how they developed, were sustained and the implications of this are rarely taught. An American professor of family therapy recalls in his own training a professor remarking to him, 'My job is to teach you the rudiments of family therapy. Your job is to learn them. Race and these other social issues that you continue to raise have no significance whatsoever' (Hardy, 2015).

Why is it missing?

So why is there at best lip service paid and at worst absence or contemptuous dismissal of this important aspect of psychotherapy theory and practice? Many writers on the subject point to the demographic makeup of those in the psychotherapy profession. We are a predominantly able-bodied, middle-class, white, female (although men are disproportionately represented in senior positions), cisgender, heterosexual profession (Davies & Barker, 2015; Thomas & Samuels, 2015).

Such characteristics place psychotherapists in the more powerful pole in most binary power relations: White–Black, able bodied–disabled, middle class–working class, wealthy–poor. People in more powerful positions are more likely to deny the existence of power differentials. Heterosexual people rarely get accused of shoving their sexuality down people's throats despite the almost ubiquitous representation of heterosexuality throughout our society. Inequalities around class, although evidenced repeatedly in research, remain largely unspoken and unacknowledged in many of our public services including their difference and diversity training. While in many liberal circles it is not ok to make racist, sexist or homophobic remarks, to have a joke at the expense of the working class is fair game (Jones, 2012). Recently Jon Snow (2017) spoke about this divide when considering the position of journalists and the Grenfell Tower tragedy.

> I felt on the wrong side of the terrible divide that exists in present-day society. We can accuse the political classes for their failures. But we are guilty of them ourselves. We are too far removed from those who lived their lives in Grenfell.

He may equally have been talking about many psychotherapists. There is plenty of evidence that people on one side of the binary polarities are over represented in boardrooms, government, senior management positions in public and private sector organisations, the media, the judiciary and so on. Despite overwhelming evidence, many deny the truth of these inequities or argue they are coincidental or irrelevant.

Such denials and assertions serve to maintain the status quo, support and shore up the existing power relations of our society. Thus, one argument to be offered as to why inequalities, power and politics do not get discussed in psychotherapy training is that if they were this would ultimately threaten the privileges enjoyed by many psychotherapists.

The argument here is that people who benefit from a system, especially at the expense of others, will deny the existence of such a system. The structures and functions of our society have been built up over many generations. They are in our laws, our economic practices, our judicial, education and health systems. It becomes difficult for us to recognise them and for many it behoves us to support them, we gain from and are privileged by them. Such systemic processes have been named as institutionalised racism or sexism (again class is missing) and more recently unconscious bias.

It could be argued that psychotherapy itself by placing the burden of distress on the individual to be addressed through individual psychotherapy is one of the structures and processes developed by our society to ensure that the prevailing order of things is not disrupted. Such a focus alleviates the need to address wider societal inequities. Mirroring this individual focus, identifying and addressing our own biases, prejudices, triggers for distress, patterns of projective identification, authority relations and personal histories are often seen as properly belonging to the private space of our personal therapy or supervision. The opportunities for learning through working with these issues in the group setting of a training programme are rarely grasped. This could in part be because trainers did not experience it as part of their training and feel deskilled and vulnerable when attempting to incorporate these issues into training.

Facilitating discussion, thinking and learning about these topics is extremely challenging. It requires the capacity to work with enormous complexity and unbearable feelings of rage, despair, humiliation, destructiveness, entitlement, shame and guilt, one's sense of self and identity. These feelings can all be aroused at an intra-personal level including inter-generational legacies and artefacts and become increasingly complex when explored within a group context of a training programme where interpersonal and group dynamics also come into play.

Many programmes attempt to avoid this pain and complexity by adopting a rather superficial approach that frequently fails. For example, one-off sessions to comply with accreditation requirements, sessions where people are left feeling preached at, basic instructions about the dos and don'ts of working with diverse clients or teaching about different cultures, which often leads to cultural stereotyping (Lowe, 2014).

In addition the individual and collective anxiety raised in and by such sessions militate against learning, rather evoking flight, fight or freeze responses including silence and withdrawal, attack or splitting into 'goodies' and 'baddies'. The experiences identified by Lowe (2014) may be familiar to many of us:

- fear of saying what you think for fear of being criticised or labelled;
- being politically correct to gain approval;
- being silent for fear of getting it wrong or causing offence;
- becoming part of or witnessing angry exchanges where people are battling between 'right' and 'wrong';
- feeling guilt or shame about self or others;
- avoiding such events because of all the above.

Across the range of training programmes, all pay some attention to the understanding of self as person and therapist. Such self-understanding must include knowing our capacity to use others to our benefit e.g. to use others to cope with our own primitive anxieties, or for power money or glory. Our ability to unconsciously tell lies – not least to ourselves – is a difficulty in facing all aspects of ourselves, including our hateful destructive aspects (Lowe, 2014).

Ways forward

Having outlined some of the challenges and difficulties above, in this section we offer some ideas about how issues of inequalities, power and politics can be addressed in psychotherapy training programmes. These are explored at the conceptual level of principles rather than specific details about particular activities.

Working within a social justice framework

The importance of difference and inequality within psychotherapy extend beyond the need to understand each person as an individual, to political issues relating to the cultural and historical contexts of individuals and groups within society. These include power relations, understandings of 'normal' and 'abnormal' and the origins of psychological difficulties that may bring a person to psychotherapy, together with their ability to access such an intervention.

CAT, as a model, explicitly incorporates socio-cultural understandings in its core theoretical framework. This places it in a potentially fruitful position to teach and explore socio-cultural and political issues within its training. However, Brown (2010) suggested that while CAT has the theoretical potential to address issues of social inequality, the full scope of this is unrealised. The interventions used do not currently fulfil their potential to either reduce the negative or increase the positive psychological and political forces that would help address social inequalities. Ryle (2010), concurred and argued that despite our awareness of the socially constructed nature of the self we continue to provide reformulations and remain focused mainly on role relationships derived from parents and families and fail to 'explore adequately the historical antecedents of these or the influence of their current social realities' (Ryle, 2010, p. 7).

Locating training programmes within a social justice framework would help redress this. Social justice can be defined as the condition in which 'society gives individuals and groups fair treatment and an equal share of benefits, resources and opportunities' (Chung & Bemak, 2012, p. 27). A social justice-informed approach sees people's problems as rooted in socio-political factors including oppression (Hoover & Morrow, 2016). Ratts et al. (2016) have developed a framework for Multicultural and Social Justice Competencies for Counsellors (MSJCC). In an adaptation of their work here 'therapist' has replaced 'counsellor'. The competencies are framed within the axes shown in Figure 17.2.

Looking at the positions of privilege and marginalisation for both therapist and client enables an exploration of the intersection of identities and the dynamics of power, privilege and oppression present within the relationship. Being explicit about this also allows for discussion of inequalities regardless of the makeup of the group. If a group considers itself to be homogenous it is not unusual for such a group to think that difference, diversity and the exercise of power do not apply to them. A model such as this forces a group to face and work with an identity of privilege and what that means.

Within each quadrant there are competencies in relation to:

- therapist self-awareness;
- client worldview;
- therapy relationship;
- therapy and advocacy interventions.

The intention is to develop attitudes and beliefs, knowledge, skills and action in each of these domains.

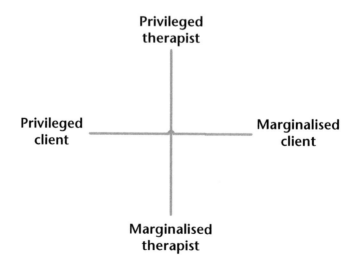

FIGURE 17.2 Where are therapists and clients on this grid?

In the fourth domain of therapy and advocacy interventions, six levels of intervention are identified:

1. Intrapersonal
2. Interpersonal
3. Institutional
4. Community
5. Public policy
6. International and global affairs.

Designing training programmes within a framework such as this enables issues of inequalities and politics to be openly on the agenda throughout. Many current psychotherapy training programmes are not explicit about notions of privilege and marginalisation for both therapist and client. This can potentially leave marginalised trainees feeling further marginalised and privileged trainees unaware or denying of their privilege. Both groups miss developing competencies to work with and address issues of inequality and power at the intersection of identities. Consequently, clients miss benefiting from these competencies. Equally, few programmes explore or expect competency development in interventions beyond levels 1 and 2 above. Given that currently most therapy trainees fall into the privileged group, the identity of therapist is in itself a privileged one, developing therapists with competencies in intervening at levels 3–6 has the potential to make a powerful contribution to our society.

Increase diversity of people accessing training programmes

The fact that psychotherapists are drawn from a relatively small and privileged section of society is reported and seen as problematic repeatedly. Samuels (Thomas & Samuels, 2015) argued that 'entry to our trainings is for the elite and the elect' (p. 6) and considers the question of access to training as a political one. He berates psychotherapists for not being honest about the money-making industry of many psychotherapy trainings and argues that the institutions around training are 'preserving their own safety and feathering their own nests'. This refers back to the argument made earlier that those who benefit from a system are unlikely to change it.

Having a broader range of people entering training programmes creates multiple possibilities. There are more perspectives to hear about and learn from. The possibility of developing psycho-political literacy (Prilleltensky & Fox, 2007) is immediately enriched. The single black or lesbian or working-class person in the cohort does not have to represent that entire group or identity; nor receive *all* of the unconscious projections likely to be forthcoming. Role models will be created so that increasingly potential psychotherapists will see 'people like me' in the profession.

CAT has great potential for attracting a wider range of people into training. Having a core profession is one of the entry requirements for CAT practitioner training. There are many doctors, nurses and social workers from black and minority ethnicity (BME) backgrounds, and arguably a higher number of people from working-class backgrounds in nursing and social work than some of the other professions. However, cuts in the NHS have significantly reduced training budgets; this restricts access to training programmes for people less able to fund themselves. It becomes even more important that CAT programme directors, and indeed all programme directors, actively explore ways of reaching into these diverse communities when marketing programmes and recruiting trainees. This requires some imagination, creativity and a commitment to the principles of social justice, finding out where different people meet, what forms of media are popular among different groups, who and what might influence people from different groups to come into training. Marketing strategies including materials should be scrutinised for unconscious bias. Similarly, recruitment processes should be examined to ensure that they do not consciously or unconsciously discriminate in favour or against certain groups. Programme structures themselves, e.g. length, timing and location of modules can also contribute to restricting access for some groups. Undertaking equality impact assessments as a core part of all these marketing and recruitment processes can be a helpful way to increase diversity within cohorts and militate against unconscious bias.

Finally, we need to think as creatively as possible about the cost of training. We need to ensure that all possibilities for reciprocal arrangements around placements, personal therapy and supervision are fully exploited; that opportunities for bursaries and secondments are explored and created within a social justice framework. Crowd funding and ethical sponsorships and collaborations with business, industry, higher education institutions, faith groups, community interest companies, social enterprises may produce fruitful sources of funding. Developing people within a framework that focuses beyond the personal and interpersonal to the institutional and societal is likely to increase creative capacity to exploit a range of approaches to marketing, recruitment and securing finance.

Creating the space to learn

Creating cohorts with some black members and where you think one or two people may be gay or working class is insufficient. Conscious effort is required to create a culture where it is possible to counter implicit prevailing norms, otherwise people will be required to disavow aspects of themselves, to assimilate, 'pass' or fit in. Or if individuals choose not to follow the norms or conformity proves impossible, they then risk being seen as troublemakers or having a chip on their shoulders. Can we seek to create a culture within training programmes where the histories, power relations, projections and feelings experienced, evoked and enacted through the diversity represented within cohorts may be fully explored? This opens the possibility to more genuinely and fruitfully examine and understand these issues and their implications for us as psychotherapists and more widely for society.

Using experiential learning methods can contribute powerfully to creating such cultures. Heron (1989) described experiential learning as learning through direct encounter; it involves a 'process of being there, face to face with the person [or self] at the event in the experience' (p. 13). The process of direct encounter in the 'here and now' provides opportunities for us to face the unconscious lies we are all skilled at creating. It can help get beneath the rational rhetoric we tell ourselves to protect the version we have of our selves e.g. that we are not racist, homophobic, full of rage or shame, competitive, desirous, envious or destructive and so on. These are some of the powerful and painful feelings likely to be evoked by explorations and experiences of injustice, inequity and power imbalances. This includes the feelings evoked by the seldom spoken to experience of working with someone you know is not as clever as you are. The feelings evoked when working with someone with a learning disability for both the therapist and client are rarely explored and worked with.

If purely evoked, then this maelstrom of feelings will impede rather than enhance our ability to learn. Our flight, fight or freeze responses will be triggered as we feel threatened and our responses will be attacking or defensive – common experiences in response to diversity training. We therefore need to think carefully about the design of activities intended to enable exploration and learning.

Bollas (1992) was interested in unconscious thinking as a means to increase self-knowledge and creativity. He argued that a facilitated space is required to enable unconscious thinking where a dialectic between the conscious and the unconscious can be established – he sees this as a waking/dreaming space where one can be lost in thought. Beck (2002) identified six characteristics of conscious thinking that are relevant to Bollas' notion of the dialectic between conscious and unconscious thinking:

1. It begins with stopping practical involvement with the world and becoming in touch with ourselves.
2. It involves turning away from reality as directly perceived and turning towards the mind including memories, opinions, hypotheses.
3. It is like a conversation between different parts of the mind.
4. It can be logical objective or subjective.
5. It is always in relation to the thoughts of others – parents, friends, teachers, society.
6. It is always connected to the concept of truth, however, as there are different types of thinking there are different kinds of truth.

We can work to create such spaces in training programmes.

Lowe (2014) and others established 'Thinking Space' at the Tavistock Clinic 'to develop the capacity of staff and trainees to think about racism and other forms of hatred towards difference in ourselves and others' (p. 11). In establishing such space, he drew on Bion's (1962) distinction between 'knowing' and 'knowing about'. Knowing about being frequently used as a defence against knowing something in a deeper and emotionally connected way. In designing a space intended to stimulate curiosity and foster learning and 'knowing' he identified a number of values and methods critical to achieving this aim and these principles can inform our curriculum design.

VALUES

Thinking space events should be as safe as possible, which means all participants should be treated respectfully, and that the ordinary rules that operate at learning events should apply:

- To not promote a particular view, but to foster openness to different perspectives and encourage discussion and debate.
- To not assume there is one correct answer or the 'truth' but to consider that there may be many truths.
- That it is ok to explore and to make mistakes as part of the learning process.

Methods

- To create a relaxed and informal atmosphere.
- To encourage participants to co-operate with and challenge each other in order to learn and develop.
- To encourage and support the group and the individual to expand capacity to accept, tolerate and work with anxiety, conflict and ambivalence.
- To allow and support participants to take responsibility to work things out for themselves.
- To regard the pain and frustration, difficulties and imperfections of trying to know as a critical, valuable and normal part of the process of getting to know and learning.
- To encourage participants to have a receptive mind and consider new ways of looking at things.
- To tolerate strong feelings or 'emotional storms' for long enough so that they can be thought about and given meaning.
- To attend to thoughts and feelings at the margins.
- To face the truth of one's experience and share ones genuine reflections.
- To try to achieve a balanced outlook.

(Lowe, 2014, p. 28)

Group relations methodologies developed by the Tavistock Institute (Rice, 1965) are powerful ways of exploring the dynamics that occur within and between groups. These groups study their own behaviour within and across groups as they develop in the 'here and now', providing excellent opportunities to 'know', explore and learn about how the dynamics associated with inequalities operate and the roles we individually and collectively take up to create, sustain or change such dynamics. Several psychotherapy training programmes include attendance at a group relations conference and others draw on some of the methods, for example a small or large study group. However, many programmes miss the opportunities for learning presented by the cohort itself, i.e. part of the curriculum that focuses on the here and now experience of being in that cohort.

Being political as a psychotherapist

Finally, some thoughts about being political. It is not possible not to be political. Everything we do is political in that it is either serving to maintain, increase or change existing power relations. The issue is that many of us do this unawares, this is just how things are, 'normal', getting on with life, politics is for politicians. As psychotherapists we sit among the privileged in our society. Over the years I have run many sessions for NHS staff on developing political skills. I often begin with a free association to the words 'politics' or 'political'. Words such as sly, two faced, untrustworthy, dishonest, self-serving, ruthless, manipulative, grandiose, narcissistic, out of touch, ambitious, fickle, dirty, irrelevant, waste of time, not the real work, nothing to do with me, gets in the way, all quickly come to mind. I have never done this exercise with a group of psychotherapists, but I expect it might be similar. If this is what people associate with being political then a call to be political is likely to meet with resistance. If we are to incorporate a true exploration of inequalities, how they operate and influence the mental well-being of individuals and society, we should also talk explicitly about being political. These might include why it is important, what it means, why it is resisted and raising awareness or the huge scope and range of 'political actions' from daily conversations to national or international policy development and many in between.

Once you begin to view the world through the perspective of power relations, who is making decisions about what, who or what is included or excluded, spoken or unspoken, seen or unseen, heard or silenced, privileged or marginalised, then it is difficult not to see every aspect of life as political. The next questions then concern how we individually and collectively choose to use our own power and work politically as psychotherapists to make a difference.

References

Beck, J. (2002). Lost in thought: The receptive unconscious. In J. Scalia (ed.), *The vitality of objects: Exploring the work of Christopher Bollas*. London: Continuum.

Bion, W. (1962). *Learning from experience*. London: Karnac Books.

Bollas, C. (1992). *Being a character: Psychoanalysis and self-experience*. London: Routledge.

Brown, R. (2010). Situating social inequality and collective action in cognitive analytic therapy. *Reformulation*, 35, 28–34.

Buck, D. & Maguire, D. (2015). *Inequalities in life expectancy*: London: King's Fund.

Chung, R. & Bemak, F. (2012). *Social justice counseling: The next steps beyond multiculturalism.* Thousand Oaks, CA: Sage.

Crenshaw, K. (1991). Mapping at the margins: Intersectionality, identity politics, and violence against women of color. *Stanford Law Review*, 43, 1241–1299.

Davies, D. & Barker, M. (2015). How gender- and sexually diverse-friendly is your therapy training? *The Psychotherapist*, 61, 8–10.

Elliott, I. (2016). *Poverty and mental health: A review to inform the Joseph Rowntree Foundation's anti poverty strategy.* London: Mental Health Foundation.

Hardy, K. (2015). The attack on diversity. *Psychotherapy Networker*, March/April, 39.

Heron, J. (1989). *The facilitator's handbook.* London: Kogan Page.

Hoover, S. & Morrow, S. (2016). A qualitative study of feminist multicultural trainees' social justice development. *Journal of Counseling & Development*, 94, 306–318.

Jones, O. (2012). *Chavs: The demonization of the working class.* London: Verso Books.

Lowe, E. (2014). *Thinking space: Promoting thinking about race, culture and diversity in psychotherapy and beyond.* London: Karnac Books.

McManus, S., Bebbington, P., Jenkinsm R. & Brugha, T. (eds) (2016). *Mental health and wellbeing in England: Adult psychiatric morbidity survey 2014.* Leeds: NHS Digital.

Prilleltensky, I. & Fox, D. (2007). Psychopolitical literacy for wellness and justice. *Journal of Community Psychology*, 35, 793–805.

Ratts, M., Singh, A. A., Nassar-McMillan, S., Kent Butler, S. & McCullough, J. R. (2016). Multicultural and social justice counseling competencies. *Journal of Multicultural Counseling and Development*, 44(1), 28–48.

Rice, A. K. (1965). *Learning for leadership: Interpersonal and intergroup relations.* London: Tavistock.

Ryle, A. (2010). The political sources of reciprocal role procedures. *Reformulation: Journal of the Association of Cognitive Analytic Therapists*, 3, 6–7.

Snow, J. (2017). www.theguardian.com/media/2017/aug/23/jon-snow-grenfell-mactaggart-media-diversity.

Thomas, V. & Samuels, A. (2015). Let's change training standards, says Professor Andrew Samuels, former UKCP chair. *The Psychotherapist*, 61, 6–8.

UKCP (2012). *Standards of education and training.* London: UKCP.

APPENDIX

Psycho-social checklist

The social and political circumstances of our lives can have as much, if not more, influence on how we feel as our own individual histories and experiences. It can sometimes help us make sense of how we feel if we understand and recognise the effects of social and political forces in our own lives.

Please tick the boxes that you feel apply to you:

Aspects of myself or my life that I feel unhappy about, disadvantaged by or in which I feel 'different' from other people:

	Applies strongly	*Applies*	*Does not apply*	*Comments*
1. Mental health issues				
2. Ethnicity				
3. Class (e.g., money/status/job)				
4. Housing problems or homelessness				
5. Education				
6. Religion or culture				
7. Being female/being male				
8. Sexual orientation				
9. Physical disabilities/Ill heath				
10. Marital/family situations				
11. Age				
12. The law				
13. Nationality/refugee status				
14. Politics				
Other – please specify				

'The Psychotherapy File: An Aid to Understanding Ourselves Better' and other CAT tools are printed in full in the following:

Pollock, P. (2001). *Cognitive analytic therapy for adult survivors of childhood abuse*. Chichester, UK: Wiley, pp. 270–281.

Pollock, P., Stowell-Smith, K. & Gopfert, M. (2006). *Cognitive analytic therapy for offenders*. London: Routledge, pp. 331–390.

Ryle, A. (1993). *Cognitive analytic therapy: Active participation in change*. Chichester, UK: Wiley, pp. 243–248.

Ryle, A. (1997). *Cognitive analytic therapy and borderline personality disorder*. Chichester, UK: Wiley, pp. 164–171.

Ryle, A. & Kerr, I. (2002). *Introducing cognitive analytic therapy*. Chichester, UK: Wiley pp. 232–240.

Adapted psychotherapy files:

Jenaway, A. (2017). An alternative Psychotherapy File reformulation. *Journal of the Association of Cognitive Analytic Therapy*, 49 (Winter) pp. 48–55.

Three further adapted versions of the Psychotherapy File are printed in full in:

Lloyd, J. & Clayton, P. (eds) (2014). *Cognitive analytic therapy for people with intellectual disabilities and their carers*. London: Jessica Kingsley Publishers, Appendices 1–3, pp. 237–269.

INDEX

Note: Illustrations are denoted by *italics*.

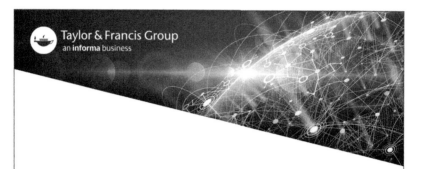